— Exeter Remembers The War —

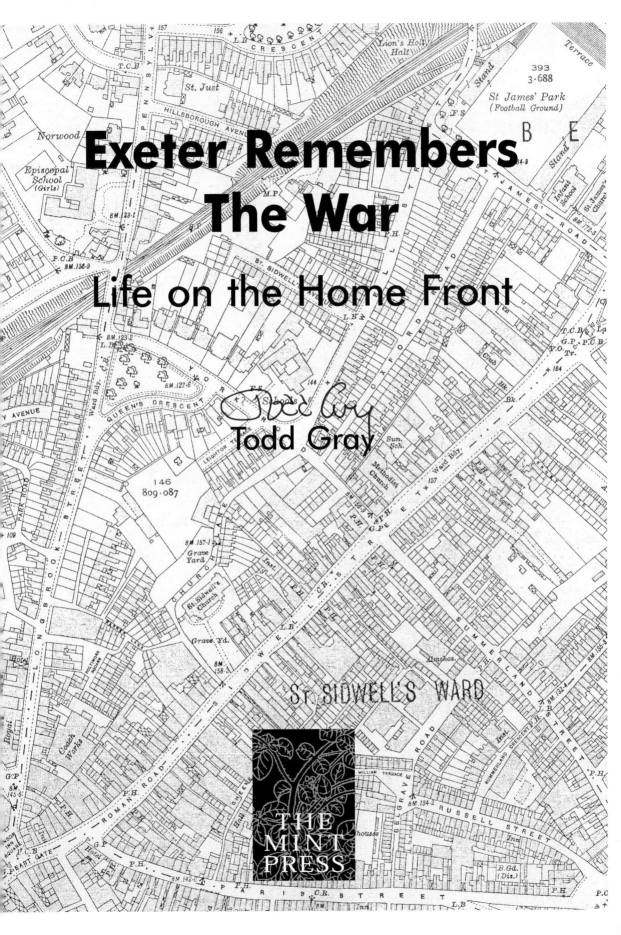

Exeter Remembers The War

Life on the Home Front

Todd Gray

THE MINT PRESS

For

Miss Elizabeth Maycock

First published in Great Britain by
The Mint Press, 2005

© Todd Gray, 2005

The right of Todd Gray to be identified as editor of this work has
been asserted by him in accordance with the Copyright, Designs &
Patents Act 1988.

ISBN 1-903356-41-5

Cataloguing in Publication Data
CIP record for this title is available from the British Library

The Mint Press
18 The Mint
Exeter, Devon
England EX4 3BL

Designed and typeset in Futura Book 11/15 by
Mike Dobson, Quince Typesetting

Cover design by Delphine Jones

Distributed by Stevensbooks
18 The Mint, Exeter, Devon, UK EX4 3BL
tel.: 01392 459760
www.stevensbooks.co.uk

Printed and bound in Great Britain
by Short Run Press Ltd, Exeter

C O N T E N T S

– PART TWO: DESTRUCTION –

ACKNOWLEDGEMENTS

This book has been written only with the help of many others. Firstly, I would like to thank the more than two hundred people who have contributed memories. I have been privileged to be asked into many homes and share the lives of the interviewees. Without their generosity the book would never have happened. Each of them is credited in the text except for those who wished to be anonymous.

Original letters and written copies of the interviews will be deposited at the Devon Record Office and have not been given separate references within this book. I am grateful to the Trustees of the Imperial War Museum and to the individual copyright holders for access to the manuscripts held by the Museum and for permission to publish extracts from them. Some other accounts are by permission of the BBC. *WW2 People's War* is an archive of wartime recollections gathered by the BBC. The stories were contributed by members of the public and the views expressed are theirs and the copyright remains with them. Text from these stories may not be reproduced. Other accounts which have already been published are identified as such within the text. While every effort has been made to secure permission, it has in a few cases proved impossible to trace the author or the executor. I apologise for any apparent negligence and the publisher invites correspondence.

Many others helped identify people to interview or assisted with the book in other ways. Among them I would like to thank Tom Arkell, Jonas Bender, Paul Cleeve, David Cornforth, Caroline Cornish, Lady Violet de Vere, Father John Deeny, Monsignor Canon Harry Doyle, Elizabeth Franceschini, Clare Greener, Colin Hadley, Councillor Jean Hadley, Nell Jarvis, Andy Jones, Delphine Jones, Professor Robert

Leaper, Bob Letcher, Jenny Lloyd, Councillor Barry MacNamara, Ian Maxted, Margery Rowe, Peter Oakford, Elizabeth Parkinson, Graham Parnell, Jan Parnell, Stuart Raymond, Dr Tim Rees, Gill Selley, Councillor Hazel Slack, Keith Stevens, Iris Sutton, Jean Taskis, Peter Wale, Gillian Westell, Father Michael Wheaton, Mary Whitton and Geoff Worrall. I am grateful to all those who have allowed publication of illustrations including a number of private individuals, Group Archive Aviva plc and the *Express & Echo*. Copyright of images rests, where appropriate, with those who have supplied them.

I would also like to thank Linda Rowland, Shanne Lane and the rest of the team of Red Coat Guides who generously gave their time in recording memories during the autumn of 2004. I am grateful to them all. I would also like to thank Rachel Foss of Brynmor Jones Library at the University of Hull and the staff of the archive department of the Imperial War Museum for their help. I am particularly grateful to Jacky Hodgson of Special Collections in Sheffield University Library for her advice and assistance.

Finally, I would also like to thank Dr Mike Dobson for design and typesetting and Delphine Jones for the cover.

INTRODUCTION

This is a book of the personal experiences of nearly two hundred people who were in Exeter during the second world war. It is a follow-up to *Exeter In The 1940s* which explained the course of the war mostly from official sources. In contrast, this book tells the story of wartime Exeter through another source, the experiences of some of the people who lived through it.

All of the accounts are memories, although a small portion were recorded almost immediately after the events. Nearly all are from men and women interviewed during the last year or who sent in their own written accounts. Other oral histories were collected by Geoff Worrall, Ian Maxted and Jenny Lloyd and these interviews were made as far back as the 1970s.

There is a great range in the types of individuals. Many were born and bred in Exeter but a great number have come from other places. There is a good mix of men and women and there is a wide range of ages: the oldest person interviewed is 103 and the youngest is in her early 60s. The majority of the interviewees in 2005 were children during the war and not surprisingly they have different viewpoints from those who were then adults. For example, Tony Hoskin was only a young boy when he came to Exeter to visit his grandmother. He overheard a conversation in High Street about Bedford Circus and went to investigate; his search did not reveal one lion, tiger or clown. This is unlikely to be the memory of many older people. It is unfortunate that in the past more interviews were not made with those who were adults in the war, particularly those with memories of the First World War. The perspectives of those who fought in the trenches, or who were widowed, would be very different from the number of former boys who enjoyed the war because it provided excitement. The relatively few number of former adults now available limits the variety of experiences although considerable efforts have been made to find as many as possible with longer memories. In 2005 someone who was 18 at the start of the war is 84 today. Another difficulty is that some older people have less detailed memories. This is, it has to be said, not always the case. One woman of 101 is, in particular, far more adept at remembering the past than many who were in school during the war.

There is another limitation in these accounts: there has been a very real need to be discreet. Some experiences involve other individuals who are still alive or their families and friends are. The subject matter has had to be treated sensitively. For instance, in matters regarding wartime romances there is reluctance on the behalf of some inter-viewees to be candid if it is thought that individuals could be identified. Therefore some of the accounts have been attributed anonymously and individuals' names have not always been supplied.

This book also includes some accounts by people written much nearer the time: these original letters and diaries are from the collections of the Imperial War Museum and the Devon Record Office. They were made by men and women attempting to explain what was then hap-pening around them. There is no official account of the war years: the council did not publish a book at the time or since. There were plans to do so but these were thwarted by the individuals concerned. Only one official wrote his memories: James Whiteside, City Information Officer, recorded his experiences at the request of the former mayor. He explained to the City Librarian on 25 June 1970 'a fortnight ago I called at the City Record Office attracted by the notice above the door. I had a pleasant talk with the lady in charge in the course of which she told me that the records *had very little about the blitz of 1942*.

As an incident of my retirement I have been going through the many many personal papers that I had accumulated at the Court House. I enclose a copy of what I describe as *my personal story* and two copies of the Emergency Information Service that were broadcast from loud-speaker vans in the days immediately following 4th May 1942 – as is mentioned in *the story*.

The story came to be written in response to a suggestion made by Mr Roland Glave Saunders, who was Mayor of Exeter during the war. He had an idea (and 28 years later we may think it a good one) that he and all the executive officers, Town Clerk, City Surveyor, Medical Officer of Health . . . and the rest, should each put into writing the story of how the air-raid upon Exeter hit him, in his home life as well as in his operational activity. It was the Mayor's intention to have the whole bound together for deposit in the City Archives.

I produced the story of which the enclosed in a carbon copy. I handed the top copy to the Mayor. About a month later I asked him how the thing was going. He replied that mine was the only contribution: he indicated that he was so hurt at the poor response that he had not even produced his own version.'

Oddly, Mr Whiteside admitted to the City Librarian that he sent an incomplete account. He had lost the final page and added there was little on it 'worth preserving.'

An extremely moving letter was written by George Sommers who was helping to repair bomb damage after the blitz. He wrote to his wife from St Germans House in Pennsylvania. His letter shows how one ordinary man coped with extraordinary times and that, although caught in the midst of devastation, he continued the everyday concerns of life.

Darling Wife,
The Cathedral is still standing but burnt a lot inside & glass all out, around the shops are down and the center is badly, knock about, but there is a few miles of shops and houses left. There are a nice lot of shoes and boots at £1. 3. 9 a pair here, have you got to give coupons for them 'offe', say you have, I don't know about shoes. What do you think dear. How is Joan going on at school, a lot of children were killed this time it hurt me a lot to see them, no more I hope, I don't mind men, but.

I hope you had peace while I been away.

George William Sommers of Plymouth, 1942. He was then 44 years old.

Wed. We had <u>eggs & ham</u> for brakfast living high it the best we had yet. I hope you are allright dear you all & thinking of the M. O. H. has not told us when we return yet I will let you now dear as soon as I can but there is still a 'lot to get away yet. Hope Joan is looking after you, shall be glad to be home with you. The weather is grand plenty of sun hope you are having the same in Plymouth. It has been a lovery day we are here in the house by oursefe now. Help them to wash up and 'Affe' told the tale, and what to you think <u>eggs and baken</u> for supper when only this morning he was calling them everthing funey chap. Anyway it was a nice supper the best meal I have had here. The fighters are nowe overhead 6 of them they get on the nerves sometimes at night. I an thinking it will be a job to get my letters to you but I will write every day to you dear. It helps a lot when I am thinking of you and Joan. Its lonely to be away from home. I don't know yet when I leave it won't be too soon for me, but there a lot to do this time, tomorrow will see a lot done please God. We can't think of tomorrow without him. 'Affs' in yapping to the wimmen wile I write this letter I just post one 10 mins ago. But when I an writing I fell near you dear, and it helps me to forget it here. 'Affs' tell me now how claver he is, it feeds you up but I must take no notice. They are geting feed up with him here though he a good worker. Well dear I write more than I have done before since I been away from you dear. I an always think of you and Joan. You are all I live for. Glad when I all over and done with. Hope you don't want for anything as I am not home to help you dear. The plains and fighters are still flying over the city day & night. We are working until 9 oc tonight trying to finish it up, they seem very slow geting the boddys away witch is putting us behind. Look after yourself dear. All my love to Joan & you dear. George

The written accounts have an immediacy not possible to achieve in the oral histories. After sixty years it cannot be claimed that each detail is accurate. For example, several people remembered the blitz as having taken place in 1941 or 1943 instead of 1942. Some recall it as a reprisal for attacks on Dresden and not Lübeck. Also, some memories have been influenced by other factors. One memory which has not been used is that of a man who was not yet two years old in 1939 and yet remembers each word of Chamberlain's radio message of the outbreak of war. Questioning revealed he was a keen enthusiast of the war and, no doubt, has had his memory supplemented by heavy reading.

There is also a reticence on the part of some interviewees who remem-

First pages of the letter written by Mr Sommers to his wife, 6 May 1942.

ber people were considered to be 'going on' if they talked about their wartime experiences. The consequence is many have kept their memories to themselves. Some also feel that somehow their experiences are already known. The accounts appear exactly as they were originally written or spoken. No attempt has been made to change their tone or content. This exact use helps to bring out something of the character of each individual and is hopefully more accurate.

Some accounts concern the blitz but many others are of ordinary life. Some are of particular incidents. For instance, Bryan Bennett recalls a tip and run raid. He wrote of it 'I was on my way up Fore Street to buy myself a book when I heard the sound of a low-flying aircraft, and being a boy I stood and stared into the sky to see what it was when a man pushed me to the ground and laid on top of me, the next moment came the sound of machine-gun fire as it roared off into the distance, the man then got up and walked away, and I had no idea who he was and at the time never appreciated just what he did.'

Some memories pose particular questions. For instance, Rosemary Westell came to Topsham with her family in 1941. They had extensive views of the Exe from their house on The Strand. She remembers eight days before the blitz the army commandeered a derelict cottage on their property which they used to house a group of soldiers. They left on the night of the raid and were not seen again. Why were they there? Also, on the night of the blitz the family saw a big fire on Haldon and it was said later that incendiaries had been dropped to use as a beacon. Was this so?

Why a book of memories on the second world war? In the course of pursuing or conducting interviews this is a question I have been asked several times, nearly always by men and women who did not live through these years and sometimes by the children of those who were being interviewed. Some have disparaged the accounts as being stories of no use or significance. While this argument could be used to discuss the wider issue of social history in general, it needs to be understood that the war years were crucial in the history of Exeter. The city changed dramatically in that time. A similar book on memories of the 1920s, if it was possible, or of life in the 1970s, would be of less significance.

The war years are remembered as being particularly important in individuals' lives. This is seen in how some people perceive their memories and themselves. Sue Andrewes, for example, recalls 'although I cannot claim to be an Exeter 'girl' I do have this feeling that I somehow belong. Perhaps others feel the same if they shared the bombing of Exeter with the rest of the poor citizens as I did. One can never forget it, that is for certain.'

The war was a watershed in other ways. The destruction of the city has meant that many remember an Exeter before, during and after the war. Christopher Price was a young schoolboy who came four times a year to Exeter from Wellington. One of his great treats was a visit to Deller's Café and he vividly remembers the 'wedding cake-like shape and the decorations of nymphs'. His favourite memory though is of their Knickerbocker Glories. David Melhuish was also a young boy in 1939 and lived at Rosewood Terrace. He recalls 'the streets were devoid of traffic, just a few delivery vehicles. I remember our milkman used an old Austin Seven, but quite a few firms still used horse and carts. This meant that the streets were used as play areas without much trouble. Most kids went 'out to play' and the streets were treated as safe play areas with most damage done to neighbours' windows when a cricket match was organised!' Many recall being awed by the level of destruction for the first time.

More than a hundred thousand people were in Exeter during the war and this book comprises the personal experiences of only a small portion of them. Even so, each and every account is unique and helps to illuminate a period in which there is a surprisingly lack of information. The local newspaper, the *Express & Echo*, was limited in what it could report because of censorship, Exeter City Council minutes are sparse in their detail, spare paper was being salvaged through the war and very few people at the time recorded their lives in diaries or journals. Also, some of the accounts provide details on subjects on the history of Exeter which have never been examined. For instance, until now nothing has been written on the activities of British fascists at the start of the war or of the introduction of racial segregation by the Americans in 1942. These memories have, in effect, introduced new areas of historical research. This makes the recording of as many individuals' experiences as possible all the more important. This book attempts to show what kind of stories can still be told about the war years in the hope that the many hundreds of other people who have yet to record their experiences will come forward and do so. There is so much more which has not been recorded.

This book begins that task by telling the singular stories of some of the two hundred people who were here.

Deller's Café, built during the First World War and destroyed during the second.

LIST OF ABBREVIATIONS

A.F.S.	Auxillary Fire Service
A.R.P.	Air Raid Precautions
A.T.C.	Air Training Corps
A.T.S.	Auxillary Territorial Service
B.U.F.	British Union of Fascists
C.O.	Commanding Officer
D-Day	Deliverance Day, 6 June 1944, the date of the Allied invasion of Normandy
G.F.S.	Girls Friendly Society
G.I.	General Induction
G.P.O.	General Post Office
H.E.	High Explosive Bomb
H.G.	Home Guard
L.D.V.	Local Defence Volunteers
M.O.	Medical Officer
N.A.A.F.I.	Navy, Army and Air Force Institutes
P.O.W.	Prisoner of War
R.A.F.	Royal Air Force
R.A.M.C.	Royal Army Medical Corps
R.A.P.	Regimental Aid Post
R.Lo.M.	Radio-Location Mechanics
R.U.R.	Royal Ulster Rifles
S.D.	Special Duties
S.L.C.	Searchlight Control
U.S.A.F.	United States Air Force
U.X.B.	Unexploded Bomb
V.A.D.	Voluntary Aid Detachment
V.E. Day	Victory in Europe Day
V.J. Day	Victory in Japan Day
W.A.A.F.	Women's Auxiliary Air Force
W.R.N.S.	Women's Royal Naval Service
W.V.S.	Women's Voluntary Services for Civil Defence

PART ONE

LIFE ON THE HOME FRONT

WAR EVENTS

In the 1930s Exeter was a fairly small city. In 1931 the population stood at some 66,000,[1] with a limited amount of industry and a large rural hinterland that stretched to Devon's borders. The surrounding countryside was rural and the south coast and nearby Dartmoor had been tourist destinations for generations. Although Plymouth had a greater population, Exeter was the county capital in terms of politics, religion, education and culture. Even so, it was fairly isolated.

It had many everyday wartime events in common with other places. For example many have memories of watching dogfights take place high above the city; Edmund Forte was of many small boys who now recalls 'sometimes during the daytime I would see dogfights between aircraft taking place high above us. I could see as I looked up, there!

– a mass of white streaks. These streaks moved and changed shape. They weaved and made pretty patterns. It looked as if they had been scratched on the pale blue of the sky, all mingled and *higgledy-piggledy*. You could faintly hear the *whine* and roars of the aeroplane engines as they flew about up there. Often I could hear the faint *rat-at-at-tats* of their guns, but I never saw any smoke or saw one crash.'

Exeter also had several major occurrences in the war. The most notable was the blitz in May 1942. Many local men and women were away from their home city serving in the forces and heard the news while abroad. Doug Rowe was one. He was on a troopship when his home at 2 Isca Road was bombed 'and only heard on arrival in India through a letter from home. My mother was the lady who was wounded. She had gone to open the neighbourhood air raid shelter when the sirens sounded. She would have been killed had she still been in the house. My dad, Charlie Rowe, a well-known stonemason in St Thomas was away at work. My parents were re-housed in Isleworth Road and when I arrived back from overseas at St David's Station in the small hours of the morning, neither the taxi driver nor me knew where Isleworth Road was, no doubt to my mispronunciation of Isleworth. I was sad to lose all my belongings in the Isca Road house, particularly my collection of the Magnet school magazines and all my *Express & Echo* cuttings of Exeter City's famous cup run of 1931 – Charlie Miller, Happy Houghton etcetera. I remember all the names of that great team – happy days!'[2] Hundreds of other men and women also heard while abroad.

At the start of war Exeter was not considered to be in the front line. The diary of G.T. Harris, who was in the R.A.F., shows what it was like during the first months. He arrived on 23 May 1940 and wrote 'the station at Exeter is a place that was previously used as a civil airport. There are no beds but otherwise it is well-equipped. I slept on a wood-blocked floor with a ground sheet, a few old newspapers and four blankets.' The following day preparations were made to protect the airport. He wrote 'a lorry arrives with pickaxes and shovels. Soon we are filling sandbags. This done we threw up earthworks, a machine gun will be mounted in the centre. All over the drone similar posts are being built. It is quite a novel sight to see the R.A.F. in their shirt sleeves doing some work. A Flight Lieutenant who earlier in the day had been doing practice dive bombing at 300 mph with a fairy battle is swinging a pickaxe.' Three days later he noted 'in the evening I go to Exeter. People stare curiously, for down this way the war is still far away and it is not usual to see a man armed. As everywhere in England the women are smart, but in Exeter possessing more than average good looks. The atmosphere in the city is bright and friendly. Cheerfulness everywhere, one day I shall visit Exeter in peacetime.'[3]

Exeter, in common with the rest of Britain, experienced some key war events; there was the actual declaration of war, the coming home of men from Dunkirk, the fear of invasion during 1940 and 1941, D-Day and the celebrations for the end of war itself.

Declaration of War

War seemed inevitable during the summer of 1939: in July Prime Minister Chamberlain reaffirmed Britain's commitment to stand by Poland in the event of an invasion, in August a non-aggression pact

At the Territorial Army Centre, Barrack Road, November 1939.

was signed by Germany and the Soviet Union and on the first of September Poland was invaded by Germany. For many the first they heard of the outbreak of war between Britain and Germany was through their radio when the Prime Minister made his announcement at 11 a.m. on the third of September. It was a Sunday morning. Pat Salter, then only eight years old, thought the voice sounded ominous as her mother sat crying. Joyce Flack was only ten years old and remembers 'I was very frightened. I thought we would be bombed right away.' Elsie Wills recalled 'I was living just outside Exeter when the war started. When I heard the announcement on the radio, I went through to see my next-door neighbours and we cried together'.[4] As a nine-year old Sylvia Hart remembers 'being in my grandmother's room behind her shop [18 Sun Street]. It was quite a family gathering and a lot of worried talk about a war being threatened between our country and Germany, the worry being my boy cousins would all get called for military service.' Marian Wallen lived at 18 Powderham Road. She recalls 'I was ten years old walking along Cowick Street at Conneeley's with one of my brothers and someone came rushing out

The 'Catchline Girls' before the war, preparing mobilisation papers in Exeter.

of a courtyard saying war is declared. We ran all the way home we were so frightened – we had heard so much about bombs that could happen at the start of a war.' One woman, then twenty-five, recalls 'it was just a case of looking at one another and wondering what would happen. You knew the men would be called up. My husband was lucky in that way – his job kept him here. But he wanted to go. I had three brothers and they all came back.' Donald Sheppard was then not quite eight years old and remembers 'it was quite dramatic, this shaky voice of Chamberlain on the radio. That was it – we were at war. We knew it was coming. Everything had already been prepared with evacuees coming down.' Miss Olive Wakeham was working as a nurse and recalls 'I was working at Wonford House and I went to the matron of the hospital to report to her. I was a sister at the time. She asked *have you heard war broke out?* and I said *we'll just have to pull our socks up and keep our powder dry.*' Alf Wallen was living in Hawthorn Road and remembers 'I was in the front room of our house listening, on the wireless as we used to call it, with my father, mother and brother. I was fifteen at the time. The first thing I thought poor old Dad will have to go – he was in the first world war.'

Canon Michael Walsh recalls 'people used to ask *Where were you at the outbreak of the war?* Well, I have no hesitation in saying I know what I was doing and what I was saying at 11 a.m. on 3rd September 1939. It was a Sunday, and it was just at 11 a.m. and I was in church and just at the point of entering the pulpit to preach. Of course there were a lot of soldiers there and somebody handed me a note to say it has just been announced that we are at war with Germany. I stopped myself and I said *now this is a very special occasion.* I said to the people *we have no real experience of what going to war is like for civilian life here in Exeter, we may yet be pushed to the very limits, we may have to suffer quite a bit, we don't know how close the effects of the war are going to come to us – it may come right to your very door.* Course I didn't know then how prophetic the words were, that it would indeed come to everyone's front door.' W.L. McWilliam was one of those in the congregation. He later wrote that he recalled being there and hearing 'the grave news'.[5]

One woman, nineteen when war broke out, recalls 'at that stage I was thinking that pacifism was a good thing. I didn't approve of war at all. But at the same time you get carried away with it all. I wasn't party-minded but it seemed almost inevitable. I wasn't surprised by it. Course you remember all the tales of the previous war. There were those old enough to remember the great war because it wasn't so long before then that it happened. I remember saying to my gran *you are always going on about the war and it was years away* and I was thinking the other day yet here I am sixty years after this war and still talking about it.'

Dunkirk

British troops had gone to France in early September but little happened until the following spring. On May 10 1940 Belgium, Luxembourg and the Netherlands were invaded and by the end of the month those countries were lost to the Germans and the British began returning from northern France. In early June Winston Churchill, the new Prime Minister, gave his famous speech 'We shall fight them on the beaches'. The shocking manner in which the British Expeditionary Force came back from Dunkirk is also widely remembered.

Some of these men were sent to Exeter. Donald Sheppard remembers the early military use of the county ground in St Thomas. He recalled 'they turned the county ground stadium into a camp. The English were there first, the T.A. people had it. I think it was probably just before the start of the war. They were called up and I remember they were based at the county ground which is just behind where we lived. This must have been for France. I remember them queuing up for their inoculations because they were being posted. In what became a garage afterwards. They had a couple of medics inoculating them with dabs of iodine on their arms and one chap, I was down there with several kids watching, he said *do you live in that house where the back door is?* He said *do you have a telephone?* Because there were very few telephones then. And I said *yes we have*. And he came in and phoned his wife and talked to her. And that was the last she heard of him, he got killed early on. He was called Cann, they had a business in Queen Street. Years and years afterwards I met his wife playing bridge and it turned out that she was the one.' Exeter was designated to receive the men. D. Irene Thomas, who lived in Pennsylvania, wrote 'it was strange and dreadful to see contingents of the British Army, rescued by the flotillas from Dunkirk, marching, or rather shambling through our streets, gaunt exhausted men just landed from the Channel into the estuary of the Exe, without their arms or equipment, or even without uniform or adequate clothing.'[6] George Barnes remembers 'seeing the old Southern Railway trains with the soldiers rescued from Dunkirk. Not looking too smart, glad to be here. They used to hang out of the carriages and shout.' One woman from London, who came with her husband to Exeter when she was twenty-eight, recalls 'groups of them were just walking about – very poor, bedraggled. They came to Exeter to be sorted out – to re-clothe them. It was very sad.' Donald Sheppard recollects 'I remember seeing chaps come back from Dunkirk in the town. With sort of half uniforms, battle-dress trousers and any old jacket. They only had bits and pieces of uniforms.' Canon Walsh has similar memories. For him they were 'jaded out, dejected, disillusioned, the remnant of a defeated army. But soon buoyed up again. You didn't see many of them.' Christine Caldwell also remembers how the group of girls from the Central School of Speech and Drama were brought to the Civic Hall to dance with the still-shocked soldiers. Joyce Stabb recalls the train of soldiers coming back and how the women with her in the factory off Okehampton Street in St Thomas were allowed to stop their machines and go outside to wave to the men passing by. Olive Wakeham was another who remembers them. They looked 'devastated. It was amazing how they recovered. We used to go down and watch them come in by train, and give them cigarettes.' Colin Hopkins also saw them. He said 'I went over to the Royal Devon & Exeter Hospital where there were buses. A lot of them were, well, walking-wounded. They were taken out and brought into the hospital. They looked shattered, grey, ashen, frightened, like zombies they were to me.' James Bell was a young boy when they came home and recalls 'the Dunkirk troops were distributed all round the country, many came to Exeter and were laying on the grass in Northernhay and Bury Meadow, they might have been in other places. They were there for the best part of a week, with no shelter, fed by the Women's Voluntary Service. There were also French soldiers in the town at the time. As a small boy I went round the soldiers asking for foreign coins and received handfuls of French, Belgian and Dutch coins. I do recall the French soldiers giving me all they had. Some of the soldiers were injured and were bandaged up as the days went by. Army officers called out the names of the regiments and then names of missing men. There must have been at least 200 in Northernhay alone.'

G.T. Harris kept a diary during the war but, interestingly, some of the pages for his time in Exeter were torn out. He was a driver in the R.A.F. and wrote on May 31 'Exeter is packed with troops from the Flanders coast. Some of them have no more than they walk about it, dirty uniforms, tin helmets. Here and there is an occasional French officer. *Where's the Air Force been?* is the cry hurled at us in the street. *It isn't any thought of ours. Go see the Air Ministry* I reply truculently to one fellow in the fish shop. Seeing I am not taking it lying down the soldier becomes apologetic and hastens to assure us that of course the ordinary airmen had nothing to do with the scanty air support on the Western Front.'[7]

W.L. McWilliam was a Nursing Orderly who was sent with the Expeditionary Force. He worked at a store in the High Street and had been a member of St John's Ambulance Brigade. In 1973 he recorded

Spitfire crew at R.A.F. Exeter.

his experiences and wrote of walking along French beaches searching for living soldiers amongst the corpses. Fortunately he returned alive and noted 'the train was late in Exeter, it being nearly 8 p.m. I had hoped to meet my relations coming out of church from the evening services but it was too late so I hurried home and had much to relate before retiring to bed that night. In the morning the parish priest and congregation were very surprised when I arrived to see me at the 8 a.m. mass, and after this I went to the store in the High Street to see the staff and my employers who also got a surprise on seeing me.' Shortly afterwards he reported back to duty.[8]

Invasion

The quiet period of the first few months and the disaster at Dunkirk was followed by two years in which it seemed the Germans were unstoppable. The fall of France in June 1940 enabled the Luftwaffe to be based along the French coast, only a few miles from Devon. Suddenly Exeter was close to the Front Line and there were worries about being invaded.

May Balkwill remembered the prospect of invasion. She recalled of the collapse of the St Sidwell church tower 'it was so funny. They said *We will toll the church bells if the parachutists arrive.* And when the bells went I thought *Oh well, they'm here, let 'em come.* Nothing could be worse. At that time I didn't see any sense of danger really. I think the younger ones thought *Well, if it's coming it'll come. Live for the day* – so many of our friends had been killed. One of the women, Mrs Selly of Newtown, she was coming down to the shelter and she got shot up and this is the sort of thing you accepted.'[9] As a boy Donald Sheppard recalls thinking 'we all thought they would invade. We thought that being an island we had a good chance of keeping them out. But the danger was parachutists because the Germans did a lot of parachute operations. We did have great belief in the navy keeping them out.' Olive Wakeham thought 'we were afraid of para-troopers. Suddenly all the signs went at the start of the war. I remember once asking for directions and a farmer said to me *I baint suppose to tell you and I baint going to.* The place I was asking for was right behind me. It was very clever how we learned to get about.'

Many people have remembered how important the German attack on the Soviet Union on June 22 1941 and the Japanese on the Americans on December 7 1941 were. The Reverend John Benton, for instance, recalls 'it made a difference to know we weren't alone – there was a tremendous sense of relief when Russia was attacked and then again when Pearl Harbour brought the Americans in the war. We knew Stalin wasn't much better than Hitler but we weren't alone.' Alf Wallen remembers 'we thought after Dunkirk that we would be invaded. Then when the Russians were attacked – that was a real relief. We thought they wouldn't be able to attack both us and them. The Americans coming in was another turning point – then we had a chance.' Fears of a German invasion began to disappear.

D-Day

The Americans began to arrive in Britain early in 1942 but through 1943 Allied efforts were concentrated on bombing Germany and a ground offensive in North Africa while the Soviet Union struggled to repel the Germans and then advance. 1944 saw the long-awaited attack on the continent. Many Exeter people remember an increasing sense of anticipation of the Allied invasion of France. One woman recollects 'we knew D-Day was on from the wireless. We later heard of youngsters we knew being killed from the news people would get – a lot of young boys.' But many other people had some knowledge it was about to happen and were not surprised on June 6 1944. Olive Wakeham recalls 'we didn't believe it was happening and thought it was just another pretence, there had been several already. The week before D-Day we weren't allowed out of the city. At the exits to the city you had to show a permit, which you had to get from the police at Middlemoor. All the main roads were being used by troops, which we found out later. The night before D-Day the sky was black with planes.

SUPREME HEADQUARTERS
ALLIED EXPEDITIONARY FORCE

Soldiers, Sailors and Airmen of the Allied Expeditionary Force!

You are about to embark upon the Great Crusade, toward
which we have striven these many months. The eyes of
the world are upon you. The hopes and prayers of liberty-
loving people everywhere march with you. In company with
our brave Allies and brothers-in-arms on other Fronts,
you will bring about the destruction of the German war
machine, the elimination of Nazi tyranny over the oppressed
peoples of Europe, and security for ourselves in a free
world.

Your task will not be an easy one. Your enemy is well
trained, well equipped and battle-hardened. He will
fight savagely.

But this is the year 1944! Much has happened since the
Nazi triumphs of 1940-41. The United Nations have inflicted upon the Germans great defeats, in open battle,
man-to-man. Our air offensive has seriously reduced
their strength in the air and their capacity to wage
war on the ground. Our Home Fronts have given us an
overwhelming superiority in weapons and munitions of
war, and placed at our disposal great reserves of trained
fighting men. The tide has turned! The free men of the
world are marching together to Victory!

I have full confidence in your courage, devotion to duty
and skill in battle. We will accept nothing less than
full Victory!

Good Luck! And let us all beseech the blessing of Almighty God upon this great and noble undertaking.

Dwight D Eisenhower

*Morale-boosting letter from Dwight Eisenhower to the Allied
forces, D-Day 1944.*

We got up to watch them – they were flying from midnight until four in the morning. It didn't seem to stop. We were so thrilled when we heard. Almost immediately travel restrictions were lifted.' Canon Walsh recollects 'nobody really knew until the first announcement was made. The place was chock-a-block with airmen and soldiers. Every night they were practicing for the invasion, Americans mostly. You'd see them every night coming over.'

Many Exeter people remember how the Americans suddenly disappeared without having said farewell. The American airmen at the airport had notice of their leaving. One later wrote 'there were a few who couldn't believe the real thing actually was at hand when the 440th's base, at Exeter in Devonshire, was sealed on June 1. Military police saw to it that everyone who belonged on the field stayed in and everyone else stayed out. But the cynics recalled that there had been other restrictions before and they had been nothing but dry runs . . . crews of the 45 planes which were to participate in the first mission were briefed on the general situation, with more detailed instructions left for the next day. Then they were marched to separate Nissan huts surrounded by barbed wire. From that time until the completion of their mission they were severely isolated from anyone to whom they might carelessly let slip some vital piece of information. Similarly guarded were the map rooms, where diagrams and overlays of the course to be flown were being prepared.'[10]

Michael Payne was a student at Hele's Grammar School. He recalled 'I was fascinated by flying from my early boyhood and during the war would spend as much time as I could at Exeter Airport. The fact I wore my uniform as a member of Hele's Squadron of the Air Training Corps made me acceptable to the Americans. I am sure they thought that I was in the R.A.F. Squadron colleagues and I would cycle down the perimeter path, fetching up under any of the C47s which were undergoing maintenance. The crews allowed me to go on test flights with them, usually standing between the pilot and co-pilot . . . On the night they took off for D-Day everybody in Exeter knew that something big was on though it was a closely kept secret and we didn't know exactly what it was. There was a tremendous roar of aero engines as this air armada formed up over Exeter about 10 p.m. on June 5 1944. The sight and sound were impressive.'[11]

Evelyn Huxham was twenty-one years old and working at the radar post at Exminster. She later wrote on the 5th of June 'B Watch was on duty from 9 p.m. to 8 a.m. We were working our usual patrols (fighter planes from Exeter Airport) and watching on the radar equipment for enemy planes. The evening started rather quietly. I was in the operations room about 11 p.m. and we normally had to show our own convoy ships on the large table display map. We were informed of the position of many more convoys starting out from N. Scotland and then W. Scotland and gradually as the night wore on, more and more convoys were plotted proceeding south. The south coast also showed many convoys, many of these were the Mulberry Harbours being towed across the Channel.

We all became very interested as this was the first we knew of the invasion. By the morning, when we were relieved by A Watch at 8 a.m., there were excited murmurings to colleagues about what was happening. This, we knew, must happen soon as the roads, villages and towns were over run by American soldiers and their equipment – they were everywhere. I had been surprised to see American soldiers on the march from Plymouth to Exeter a few days earlier. We went on duty again at 5 p.m. and the 'picture' then was very dramatic. We carried on with our job of helping our fighter patrols who were flying from Exeter Airport.'

Dorrie Langdon recalls 'well after the war when my father had retired from London and was living in Somerset he would remark when driving around the countryside *that was where we had many American invasion troops hidden before D-Day*. His remit with the Ministry of Transport had included finding leafy country roads or lay byes where lorries, tanks or whatever, could wait well out of the sight of any reconnaissance aircraft the Germans might deploy.'

Victory Days: V.E. & V.J. Days

Victory in Europe followed eleven months later in May 1945 and on 2 September Japan formally surrendered. V.E. Day was celebrated with a great street party in London Inn Square, the meeting of High and

Sidwell Streets. Eileen Reynold's memory of V.E. Day was being nearly eighteen and dancing with her friends in London Inn Square. Christine Caldwell also remembers walking arm-in-arm with many others, singing and dancing, in great waves of people up and down the bombed High Street. It seemed to her that all of Exeter felt they had to go to the Cathedral where the authorities had arranged ten-minute services of thanksgiving for the crowds. Several former boys remember going up to the High Street and watching the adults dancing. However, at their age they merely observed activities of little or no interest to them.

Memories of the street parties are also vivid. David Harris recalls the celebrations in Exe Street. 'I remember V.E. Day – we had a big party in the street – with food that children liked. And afterwards us children formed a band with old oil drums with strings around our necks.' One woman, then thirty-one, recalls 'we didn't have our party until a week later. We had to collect food. But we have a nice party on Exe Island in the street on Rosemary Lane.' On that day the oldest son in Chanter's Bakery came down 'with a big tray of doughnuts. I don't think some kids had seen doughnuts before. He passed them all around.' It was, she remembers, 'inspired'. Nicholas Toyne recalls the celebrations at

A Victory Party in Exeter.

Argyll Road: 'very close to that seat [on Pennsylvania Road] on both V.E. and V.J. nights we all had the most magnificent bonfire. The whole road populace were there. Pop (lemonade) was given to all the children. I had Vimto! What an extraordinary time it was then.' Olive Wakeham remembers 'I loaned my gramophone and it was pulled along on my tea trolley. They had a party in the street in Princes Square and there was dancing and great excitement. Everyone brought out things they had been hoarding.' Marian Wallen recollects her street party at Powderham Road in St Thomas: 'we had a party in the road. Mum had her piano out in the road – with tables, bunting. Everyone brought out their own bits. I think we all stayed up. The gas would go out and then we had candles.' Elsie Wills recalls 'on V.E. Day people opened up their front windows onto the street and used them as bars. There was dancing on the streets and everyone was so happy.'[12]

Dorrie Langdon remembers the end of the war while living in Topsham. She later wrote 'my parents entered into the spirit of the day and we organised an impromptu party in the garden of Rosapenna. All friends from the youth club were invited, and some neighbours, Father produced a large red ensign flag (from the coronation of 1937) which was draped long the veranda railings. I remember distinctly I wore a blue pleated skirt with a white top and borrowed a red scarf from my mother, everyone did their best to wear some of the colours, if not all. Father opened the French doors and moved his big radiogramme as near as possible and I suppose chose his cheeriest records for us to dance and chatter on the big lawn. The news seemed difficult to assimilate and as dusk began to fall there were no lights visible as was normal. Blackout had been such an automatic part of our lives for years that there was a big pause in the jollifications whilst my father pondered on what to do. He and my mother decided that lights were in order and switched on all the house lights overlooking the garden. That sight just took us all by surprise and it was magical, how we cheered and laughed. A few moments later adjoining houses took the same decision and lights were coming on all around us. Mother found some refreshments for us and then we all walked down to the nearby tennis courts and then Matthew's Hall to find loads of people celebrating, with house lights blazing, a truly memorable night that Victory in Europe had finally had been achieved.'

The city gradually removed the physical traces of the war, although rebuilding took a generation. The war itself made indelible marks on local people. One woman's memories of the war's end was the sudden freedom from fear, of stopping that overwhelming feeling. For most of the war she felt they did not know which way it would go but finally there was a release from fear. Mrs Bette Simmonds was twenty-nine years old and working at a munitions factory when 'it came over the tannoy to say the war was over. I think the news came from the airport. When I got home my mother in law and neighbour were talking outside and said *why was I home, was I alright?* I said *No! the war's over* – so we crossed arms and danced around.'

These memories involved people in Exeter responding to events which took place outside the city. One event which was of great importance to the city was the return of H.M.S. *Exeter* from South America in 1940. The crew were entertained at the Guildhall and the Captain given the Freedom of the City. While war took place overseas the people of Exeter found their own lives also drastically changed on the Home Front.

The crew of H.M.S. Exeter *after their return from South America, 1940.*

CHAPTER

EVERYDAY LIFE

TWO

All facets of life on Exeter's Home Front changed in the war. David Melhuish recalls 'the war dominated every part of life, the phrase *after the war* or *when the war is over* was continually being used to qualify any plans that were being made. This was at the government, local government or at a family level.' Ordinary life was controlled by the needs of war.

Yet no single year of the war is representative; the character of the city continually changed with the course of events. The year 1939 was dominated by defence preparations, the quiet requisitioning of buildings for Whitehall civil servants and their removal to the city, blackout, the arrival hundreds of London schoolchildren evacuated in the first days of September, the number of unofficial evacuees who came privately, gas exercises and the 'phoney war' of the last four months of the year in which little or nothing happened. Some evacuees returned almost immediately to London. 1940 saw the start of food rationing in January, the return of men from Dunkirk in June, a growing disbelief and shock at the German occupation of all northern Europe, the Battle of Britain and the first bombing of the city in August. Throughout the year civil defence preparations grew and then intensified through 1941. In April 1941 a squadron of Polish airmen came to R.A.F. Exeter, there were also increasing worries that an invasion, particularly by paratroopers, might take place and while Exeter was occasionally bombed, the city was more concerned with two events overseas, the attacks by Germany on the Soviet Union in June and by Japan on the United States in December. There was a feeling that Germany might begin to lose the war. Many civil servants left and there was a second wave of evacuees when Bristol schoolchildren arrived at the end of the year. 1942 was dominated by three nights of bombing in April and then the Blitz in May. From this point, through to the end of the war, the city was preoccupied with trying to cope with the loss of lives as well as repairing and rebuilding homes and businesses. The Americans arrived in the summer of 1942 and for two years they dominated particular areas of the city: St Thomas was reserved for black troops and all Exeter east of the river was strictly for white servicemen. Exeter became a garrison town and was flooded with chewing gum, cigarettes and nylons. In 1943 the first of dozens of babies were born who had been fathered by American servicemen. 1944 changed the character of the city when in April it was included in a Military Protected Area with travel prohibited to non-residents and two months later the Americans left for the Normandy invasion. In 1945, finally after six years, war ended in Europe in May and in the Pacific in August. Exeter celebrated twice. Men and women in the services began to come home and the city concentrated on rebuilding.

The war determined who worked and how. Those still in full-time jobs in Exeter were in Reserved Occupations, jobs which were officially classified as being necessary for the war effort. All others who were fit and able were employed in war duties. Many were posted overseas. Other men and women were pressed into wartime service and many volunteered for extra jobs. Volunteer work took many forms. Ethel Harris remembers her mother 'registered with the Mayoress of Exeter's Hospitality Scheme, where some people would invite the Forces for a cup of tea, a rest, chat or meal, or would do some sewing for them. Mum had a very nice bunch altogether & as there were some soldiers guarding the bridge by the railway on the Dawlish side of Exeter some of them came & kept in contact after the war.'

Exeter grew accustomed to seeing men and women in uniforms including many foreign servicemen. Harold Cleave was one of the servicemen to whom a visit to the city meant merely passing through St David's Station. He recalled 'my memory of Exeter during the war is of the forces canteen outside St David's Station. It was open all night and I remember going from the pitch dark of the blackout into a haze, or fog, of tobacco smoke. Alcohol was not served (but might be supplied by the servicemen themselves) and the fare was basically beans on toast and cups of tea. I often travelled from the north of England leaving Carlisle at mid-day and would arrive in Exeter at midnight (the train passed through Bristol, where once during an air-raid it stopped in a tunnel until the all-clear was sounded). On arrival at Exeter St David's after a twelve-hour journey I would visit the forces canteen before travelling to my home at Yeoford via Crediton.'

The city changed its appearance. George Barnes recalls 'you knew the city was at war because it was beginning to get a bit shabby. There were foreigners about, you could tell it was war from the way buildings had their glass taped up, you could see some buildings with sandbags. But it was only when you became aware of planes flying overhead that you really knew it was happening. On occasions you would hear explosions or machine-gunning.' The Guildhall and other buildings were protected with brick walls and sandbags. Heritage items were removed from the city including portraits in the Guildhall, the city's archives and stained glass from the cathedral.[14]

The war greatly effected housing. It became a problem firstly with the influx of evacuees, refugees and civil servants, then with the great number of military personnel and finally, by the bombings and particularly after the blitz. The memories of Reg Southen, who joined up on 5 September 1939 in Little Castle Street, illustrate one example of the variety of housing needs. He was later posted to R.A.F. Exeter and all the men there were billeted away from the airport (the officers at the Rougemont, the sergeants at the Gypsy House Hotel and the rest of the men throughout the city). He recalls that it was said that every other house in Beacon Lane had billets.

Morale became an issue but not everyone now agrees on how buoyant it was. Canon Michael Walsh thought morale 'wasn't something that people expressed. It was a case of holding on. There was beginning to be a sense of weariness creeping in but that didn't last that long once there was hope, that the invasion was going to be successful and that the Allies would be victorious and the Germans would be pushed back.' Others have thought that there was a gritty determination through the whole of the six years. George Barnes does not think there was a great loss of morale even after the blitz: 'I think people took it in their stride, some were shell-shocked, but the main population grin and bore it, that was our attitude in those days.' Mr Glave Saunders, the city's mayor, thought his greatest memory was of the 'cheerfulness, courage and dogged perseverance of all our citizens.'[15]

One aspect dominated the lives of many adult women: standing in line became a way of life. Joyce Stabb remembers 'you had to queue for everything.' Another woman recalls how she queued 'for nearly one and a half hours for just one sack of Coalite and we burnt it all up trying to thaw ourselves out – Oh, happy days!'[16] Yet most men did not experience this part of the war years and some do not remember queuing, or rationing, to have influenced their lives at all. Moreover, women continued to queue for years after the war ended.

Rumours

It is not surprising there was a shortage of reliable news. Restrictions on the press and the questionable reliability of enemy broadcasts made it uncertain what was happening in the wider world. Eric Wheaton recalls 'there were rumours over the news – they weren't allowed on the news to say where bombings took place. They didn't mention Plymouth for instance, only saying bombing had taken place in a large city in the South West. People would guess where it took place.'

Many of the rumours related to food: news would go around that a local shop had items which were off the rations, such as batteries, and people would rush to form a queue. One woman, then married with a young family, recalls 'someone would come down from town and say *Woolworth's has biscuits* and you'd put on your hat and coat and out you'd go.' There were also rumours given to the police. One former constable recalls 'you'd get false information sometimes, nasty things that people were trying to stir up. That you'd want to watch so-and-so – that he was up to no-good.' Some rumours were not taken seriously such as one Arthur Blunt remembers: 'the only rumour I heard was that the top windows of the Rougemont had flashing lights – it was just a story.' Others were more serious. In the days immediately following the blitz the local authorities were sufficiently worried about rumours to issue warnings to local people not to believe what they were told: 'what somebody told you of something that somebody told him is probably a lie'.[17]

The course of the war was of legitimate concern. One woman, in her twenties during the war, recalls neighbours might be overheard saying *the war is going badly* or *things aren't looking up too well* but does not remember people actually believing the country was going to lose. In fact, 'Churchill would give a speech and that would cheer us up'. Few have memories of rumours of fifth columnists however many repeat the same story that 'there was a German spy in Pinhoe that used to hang out of his window to send radio messages.' The more common rumours involved German invasions. Donald Sheppard remembers 'people thought there was an invasion in progress when the Americans did some exercise off Slapton Sands. And several of their boats got sunk. And Americans were being washed up along the coast at Exmouth beach, Sidmouth. And people thought they were Germans. We heard stories from people that some Germans had been washed up at Budleigh. But of course they weren't, they were Americans.' Robert Crayford remembers soldiers who were billeted near Exeter suddenly being recalled to their barracks upon a rumour Germans had landed in Dorset.

Perhaps the most striking example was recorded by G.T. Harris, a driver with the R.A.F., who was on duty at the airport in May 1940. He wrote in his diary after one night 'in the guardroom we are given a lecture by the C.O. who is evidently three sheets to the wind. Unidentified aircraft have been seen flying near the camp. There are wild rumours of parachute troops, thousands, landing near Folkestone. *Shoot* says the C.O., *Shoot to kill*. We wander round the camp in a daze. Cold dawn is perceptively lighting the darkness. Black figures on the horizon which appear to advance towards me become visible as short stumpy trees.'[18] Fortunately, it was a false alarm.

It was understood talk could be dangerous. George Barnes recalls 'the place was full of rumours. There was one that German tanks were made of cardboard. That's what we were told immediately after the invasion of Poland, that the majority of them were there just for show. We would have rumours about fifth columnists. People were wary if you were approached by someone you didn't know who wanted to know something, say if they asked where the aircraft production was because they had a job there, you would say *sorry, I can't help you*. You only talked amongst yourselves, among people you knew, not in front of strangers or people on the bus who might overhear you.' Many queues had signs warning the wrong person might over-hear valuable gossip. Olive Wakeham remembers, like many others, the signs which said *Be Like Dad, Keep Mum* and how 'you learned to keep your mouth shut.'

Shortages

Many ordinary items were in very short supply; one woman, a young adult in the war, even reflects 'I have an idea we might have made our own toilet paper and threaded it through'. Another remembers how highly valued the tissue was in a box of new shoes. One difficulty was in finding soap; 'there was a shortage of soap – for your clothes, for washing your face'. Tissue paper and soap were just some of the items hard to find. One young boy recalls 'there were not toys or books, everything was recycled. We would sell our toys and buy other toys, get rid of childish things and get other ones.' He also remembers 'my mother turned sheets from side to middle. Cutting them down the middle and then sewed the two halves together because the sides don't wear out but the middle does.' Eric Wheaton recalls particular shortages. He said 'I remember in 1941 I went to Boots for film for my camera and asked if they had any. I said *I'll have two of those*. And she said *oh no you won't. You can have one.*' Helen Mann recalls being a child in Countess Wear when 'we were all very innovative – our carpets got very shabby & couldn't be replaced so my mother would get some dye & paint back the pattern over the worn bits, it looked quite good for awhile.' Olive Wakeham had a work car and the rare petrol to go with it. She was scrupulous in recording her mileage but on one occasion 'my cat once caught cat flu and it had kittens. The vet couldn't come out because of petrol rationing. So I put my cat in the car and went to St David's Hill. I was frightened of being stopped and thought, *oh my golly, how guilty I feel using the country's petrol to save my cat.'*

It is not surprising that during times of shortages there were exceptions to the community spirit. Many people remember how food was stolen from allotments. One woman recollects 'you almost counted your cabbages and carrots and what not when you left at night so you would know what should be there in the morning.' Gardeners stood watch to make sure there were no thefts. Desmond Dunn remembers how neighbours in Burnt House Lane stored coal in their baths because it was so valuable and did not think it was safe outside.

– Clothes –

Clothing was rationed in June 1941. Up to then it was possible to find clothes but supplies were limited. In the first year every man, woman and child had a ration of 60 coupons to purchase clothes.[19] It is to be expected that mostly women have memories of the lengths they or others went to find sufficient clothes. One woman who was in her twenties during the war recalls the great difficulties she had to clothe her young family and that it was a case of 'make do and mend'. One former teenager remembers 'the lack of clothes was very hard on a young girl growing up. It was very difficult to find anything to look attractive in'. Helen Mann recalls 'I got extra clothing coupons as a child, with 20 extra, because I had large feet! My sister was jealous. We queued for ages to get me some red shoes. I had a two-piece suit made from a square rug, obviously a dodge to get around clothes coupons. A lot of people queued to get one of these either green, blue or brown rugs.'

There was a need to be inventive and many ways were found. Joyce Stabb worked in a factory in St Thomas and her fellow workers calculated when the next husband would be on leave. The women would say *oh, you want something nice to wear for when he comes home.*' They loaned coupons and had others in return when their own man came home. She also remembers 'a young girl who worked in the same factory came in with a beautiful grey coat – made from one of the grey wool blankets the Americans had.' The Americans made a great difference. Patricia Stacey, who was a teenager in the war, had her first pair of nylons from an uncle who had been to the United States. She recalls 'they used to last so long. We used to wash them at night as my sister and I only had one pair each.' She also made under garments from parachute material. Another woman remembers parachute silk was valued 'if you were lucky enough and managed to get some – it took ages to unpick it and then you made underwear with it. You got some if you knew somebody who knew somebody who knew somebody. We would exchange it for something they wanted – a lot of bartering went on.' Yet another found another use for parachute silk: she recalls 'my brother-in-law had a car and it didn't have a hood on it. We would go out in it and get very wet. So we made a hood for it out of a parachute where we got it from I don't know. We still roar about it. We used to go out to Ide and had to start it with this great handle. Then we had to make sure the parachute was all right. We would have a few drinks, then the car wouldn't start and have to push it back. We called the car the Whipton Whippet.' Another woman, twenty-two at the end of the war, recalls 'in and out you would hear of someone in Fore Street in the market would have nylons. You would try to go up and buy a pair. They would get a hold of them from somewhere and sell them on maybe Sunday morning. You would do anything for a pair of nylons. Well, not anything . . . '

One woman's memories in particular illustrate the resourcefulness. Dorrie Langdon recalls 'another aspect of war-time difficulties for parents was providing clothes for us growing children. My Aunt Florence wrote to my mother asking for any clothing coupons we could spare as Alastair was growing so tall his trousers were always too short, hardly meeting his socks. Mother responded and in return a parcel of a skirt and two pretty blouses belonging to my cousin Joan were sent for me. I thought it a good scheme and I certainly liked my 'new' clothes. Eventually the blue tweed skirt was remade into a big floppy handbag and so it went on for years. *Make Do and Mend* was a slogan which seemed ever present; people good with their needle and sewing machine were very inventive and creative. My dancing skirt was made from blackout material, not on clothing coupons, and it was fully gathered with rows and rows of coloured bias binding at the hem. I remember I had brown agricultural corduroy trousers which were not on coupons and I wore them for years and years. When black school stockings became unobtainable Mother knitted me woollen knee socks made from seamen's oiled stocking wool. I can say they were warm, not at all smart and so hairy and scratchy, but there was no alternative at the time. Some girls at school would put black ink on their legs to disguise holes and ladders, but that was definitely not my mother's style so I learned how to darn beautifully neatly. She and I both knitted lacy, full-length stockings, from coupon-free thin thread, a long, long knit but again time and effort was used to try to compensate for the growing shortages. I certainly learned many practical skills which have always proved useful.'

She also remembers 'another area of shortage was that of footwear, I needed shoes badly and my father had somehow found out that a shoe shop was to have a delivery. He wrote to Miss Ragg asking permission for me to come out of school and meet him at the shoe shop; this was granted. School shoes were of course black but to my delight and consternation the only pair that fitted me in that consignment were red! Father bought them, flat wedge heels with a tiny laced-side vent, very smart and highly desired by me. Luckily Miss Ragg was not around to check. Soon after I got a pair of W.A.A.F. regulation black shoes so all was well. No Wellington boots to be found anywhere and I was lucky to get a pair riding boots instead, with canvas legs; I loved them and wore them for years. For my dancing no gym shoes or similar could be found and as my feet were still growing I needed something badly. Again my father came up with a solution. I can only suppose that in his lunch hour he would walk round the few shops to see what had been delivered, word of mouth spreading the news of something in short supply. He arrived home very pleased with a pair of boxer's boots, dark blue, high lacing up past the ankle with red laces, with beautifully soft pliable leather. They looked strange on a girl, but I didn't mind they were so comfortable.' She also remembers 'mother somehow bought a quarter of a parachute, pure creamy white silk, it took hours of patient work to undo the closely machined seams and with considerable skill she fashioned nighties, cami-knickers, French knickers, petticoats and a blouse. This I am almost sure was not on clothing coupons, so with lace from her sewing box or some dainty embroidery and a great deal of skill the triangular panels were fashioned into rather luxurious underwear. The plaited silk cords were put to other uses over the years and I still have some in my sewing box.'

– Food –

The rationing of food began early in the war; bacon, fats (margarine, butter and cooking fats) and sugar were restricted in January 1940. This was followed by meat in March, tea in July and cheese in May 1941. The amounts varied through the war. Consumers had to register with retailers. Offal remained off the rations but, like fish, became scarce. In 1941 some items were on a systems of 'grouped commodities', such as jam, syrup, treacle and mincemeat, and by 'points' rationing which originally was confined to tinned fish, meat and beans.[20]

Wartime bread had a bad reputation for its taste but was still welcome.

The shortage of food is one common memory. For one married woman, then with two young children, it 'was one of the hard things . . . sugar was ½ a pound per head. That had to be for everything – porridge, tea, cakes – it was never enough. Kids like cake. We could do with bread and butter but kids liked something sweet.' She had to make up puddings and 'nothing was wasted. Now when I throw away any crusts of bread I think back to it. We saved everything.' Canon Michael Walsh recalls life in the presbytery at South Street's Catholic church 'was very Spartan. Our housekeeper used to give us potato cakes – for breakfast, for supper. I didn't mind – I'd eat anything.' One woman, nineteen at the start of war, thinks food 'was terribly dull but we weren't hungry. You had to think twice about putting any butter on bread, at one point we only had an ounce a week. Well, that does two slices of bread. All the newspapers would have menus on using less sugar. It was terribly dull and tedious. Any woman with growing boys would have found it difficult but we didn't.' She also remembers 'if you saw six people standing outside a shop you joined it, you didn't ask what they were queuing for because you knew if you didn't want it the next door neighbour would. You had to think all the time about what you could have.' One consequence of rationing has stayed with her. She recalls the lack of milk 'course that is how I came to take coffee and tea without milk. And I still have it the same way – as black as your hat.'

Inevitably, perceptions were coloured by the ages of people during the war. Olive Wakeham was in her thirties and old enough to compare conditions with those of the first world war. She recalls 'the second world war was better than what you call The Great War for rations – we knew what we were going to get.' Iris Rice was sixteen when the first world war ended and recalls greater difficulties in getting food then rather than in the 1940s. Sidney Richards was a young boy living in Cheeke Street and does not remember feeling hungry. His mother was like many others: she gave up sugar and gave her ration to her two sons. Individual circumstances also made a great difference. Perhaps the most poignant is a memory of Margaret Ball regarding her father, then in hospital with cancer in 1941. He craved an orange and her mother was able to find a small tin of mandarins for him from a sympathetic grocer.

Doling out the rations was not necessarily easy. Ivy Facey recalls 'my mother had a shop in Beaufort Road and the three of us girls did the coups so we could get the right goods.' On one occasion her mother was ill in bed with flu and 'one old lady came in. And we put up her rations. She said *Oh, that's not mine – I get more than that.* She was a bit of a bully. But there weren't many people like that. A lot of people didn't take their full ration of tea and would say to my mother you know who to give this to. People would exchange things.' One local couple traded the bacon rations of their neighbour, a Jewish academic at the University College, for their tea. Tea rations were short, only 2 ounces per person but demand was still strong. Another person who remembers exchanges is Elsie Wills. She recollects 'with the rationing there was a lot of bartering went on. I knew a lady who was always short of cheese for her husband, and I would swap my cheese coupons for her soap ones, so that I could do the children's washing. Getting shoes for the children was hard and you always had to queue to get Start-Rite. There were shortages of many things but friends always helped each other out. When we went to the shops we'd take our own newspapers for them to wrap things in. We used the pushchair to go and fetch coal which there was always a shortage of.'

Bette Simmonds was twenty-four when war broke out and for her 'tea was a problem. My twin sister lived in Morchard Bishop and I would go home occasionally and they would give me some of their rations of tea. At the munitions factory I would put in an double tea-spoon of tea in the pot and the girls would let me have the first cup.' One American woman was puzzled by the English preoccupation with tea. She regularly passed through Exeter on the train from North Devon to London. At Central Station she wrote 'practically every compartment door bangs open, and figures, male and female, leap out upon the platform and hurriedly zig-zag through the traffic of people and porters milling about there. The platform tea-trolley or the Station Buffet is the objective of this race. The prize – mugs of hot tea. The return from this sortie for refreshment is like a triumphal procession. With a large white china mug of steaming tea in either hand, or a mug of tea in one hand and a couple of saffron coloured buns in the other, the returning contingent surges back in groups – one eye on the slopping tea, the other on the open door of a particular compartment, both ears cocked for the Guard's whistle. At its shrill screech there is a frantic dash of late stragglers. Cups in hand they leap into the nearest open door on the train. Bang – clap – bang – clap!'[21]

Inevitably there was some hoarding although many considered it disgraceful. One local woman recalls her aunt overheard a grocer explain goods being sold to another customer were nearly the last. She then insisted on purchasing every remaining item without knowing what it was. Later she discovered she had bought boxes of gravy browning – a little of which went a very long way.

Margaret Ball, seventeen years old when war broke out, remembers somehow people got by on their rations. She, like many others, went to the British Restaurant in Paul Street which served sausages and mash. One former constable recalls 'they served basics, you'd have say – a sandwich with Spam.' Pam Coombes recollects the British Restaurant she and the other girls in the railway office visited in Fore Street. They felt fortunate when Spam was on the menu but her abiding memory is of the pudding: something which didn't quite represent a sponge together with a custard synthetic which had a lurid yellow colour. Olive Wakeham recalls 'at the British Restaurant you could get a meal for ten pence. It was very well organised. Other restaurants had a limited menu which you could go to if you were a regular, but people would ask how could I start to be a regular?'

Many remember the efforts made at being inventive with food, some with fondness. Sonia Collins worked at the Allied Services Canteen at the Royal Albert Memorial Museum. One memory she has is of 'banana sandwiches' which were made from well-cooked parsnips flavoured with banana essence. Dorrie Langdon recalls 'war time recipes were broadcast on the radio and were topical, one actress called Mabel Constanduras made a jolly contribution to these programmes by having a 'conversation' with her 'Grandma Buggins'. Between them they came up with all kinds of food ideas, so if there were plenty of off-the-ration items they would suggest a possible recipe, for example rabbit stew or mushrooms to be gathered in the fields, rose hips to be picked and simmered into a kind of sweet syrup to go with sour plums or fall down apples. It was good, amusing listening even if there was no possibility of making a meal from their odd suggestions. One thing was Woolton Pie, Lord Woolton was the Minister of Food, but I have no idea now what was supposed to be in the pie.'

She also remembers how as a teenager 'on my Wednesday after-noons free at home there were usually some chores for me to do, helping to prepare the evening meal or some baking if we had sufficient ingredients. Two things I can still recall vividly, the first was the chocolate potato souffle. Wartime recipes were published in small leaflet form, or Mother had written them (in shorthand) from the Ministry of Food programmes on the radio, ideas for using substitutes or what there was plenty of in season. This afternoon I was left the recipe; peel and cook potatoes, mash thoroughly, sieve, then add cocoa powder, sugar, a little flour and baking powder. Not too difficult one would think. I put it in the tin, into the oven, then when the time was up I opened the oven (no see-through doors in those days) and to my horror the souffle had risen only too well, in fact right up through the bars of the shelf above! Disaster indeed, how to extract the wretched thing without ruining all of the precious ingredients? It took some time to cool sufficiently, then I painstakingly scraped and tried to reconstruct the pathetic thing, but I knew I could not deceive my mother. She didn't need eagle eyes. The other attempt I sometimes got wrong was to make the topping for the congress tarts, no ground almonds but 'use soya flour with a few drops of almond essence', well how few is a few? Too many and the whole tart tasted bitter and of chemicals, too few and the rather strong flavour of the soya became dominant. With practise I did get better. Dried egg was available from the U.S.A. and used in cooking, it had a very distinctive flavour making a horrid bright yellow scrambled egg, but we ate it. Once my mother tried to make boiled eggs mixing the egg powder with water then filling two eggcups, tying them together and putting that in the sauce pan. Out came solid, rubbery egg, no white at all so she did not try that again. For sweetness people tried parsnip or carrots grated in cakes and pies, today carrot cake is a favourite, but not at all attractive for our taste buds then.'

Many found the loss of sweets difficult. One woman remembers buying sweets a month or more before Christmas and putting them on the side so that her children had them. Dorrie Langdon recalls 'bread was never rationed during the war but it got greyer and greyer as the war continued and our jam-making certainly made it taste better. We also gave some of our sugar ration to one of the lady clerks in my father's office. In return she made delicious chocolate covered fondants. They were a real highlight when he brought them home, my favourites being the Parma violet creams.' Many former children remember they were supplemented in the war by gifts from American servicemen but even so rejoiced when they were able to freely buy sweets. Peter Philips was one young boy when sweet rationing finished who remembers joining a queue three-deep outside a sweet shop.

Perceptions of the availability of food differ according to other factors. Many men, generally not involved in queuing or providing meals, do not remember difficulties. Others differ if they themselves were involved in the food trade. Colin Hopkins worked at Exeter's leading grill. He recalls 'I was lucky working at the Chevalier. At the end of the evening the chef would say *Right Colin, what would you like?* I would either have it there or take it home. There could be steak or sausages or whatever was left over. So every night I had a hot meal.' Not only did he see more meat than most but the Donut Dugout was nearby at the bottom of Rack Street. Moreover, his mother worked there. The Dugout made donuts for the American troops and Mr Hopkins recalls 'when it first opened we would get this beautiful smell and we thought it was lovely. But after a month or so it was horrible.' The imperfect ones were not used and could be brought home.

– Stretching resources –

There were many ways to supplement food. Danny La Rue remembers how, after being evacuated to Kennford, he worked at a local farm and was regularly given eggs. Later he worked at Colson's Bakery where his perks included bread and tins of fruit.[22] Being near the countryside provided advantages. Brian Le Messurier recalls life in St Thomas as a schoolboy when he and his friends ranged through the countryside. He later wrote 'fish and pond life were not the only objectives of our country outings. We got to know the best places for mushrooms, blackberries, watercress and chestnuts, and these foods augmented our meagre wartime rations.'[23]

Many Dug For Victory. David Melhuish, who was a young boy throughout the war, remembers 'austerity was the overwhelming driving force of the time. We had to learn to live with rationing and a general lack of goods, from clothing to toys. I was largely insulated from these shortages mainly because Mum was such a good manager. Also Dad grew all the vegetables we needed at the allotment, even down to potatoes. Dad grew enough spuds to last the family for the whole year and these were stored in a big crate kept in the shed known as the washhouse. I was only five years old when the war broke out so I had not experienced living without shortages so I did not feel them too badly.' Helen Mann recollects 'every year a bit more of our lawn was dug up to plant more vegetables & we kept some chickens in our suburban garden.' Dorrie Langdon recalls 'I helped my mother in the garden, fed the hens we inherited. It was a completely new experience collecting the warm eggs from the nesting boxes. Cleaning the hencoop out was not a task I enjoyed at all but we did enjoy the additional eggs. For not having an official egg ration of one or two a week if available, we had a hen-meal allowance which we had to supplement with any vegetable peelings all boiled up in an old saucepan. The hens eagerly pecked up this mixture. I just knew it smelled disgusting and we were not too disappointed when Father found evidence of rats around the hen house and he decided they had to go. There was also an option to give up the jam ration for a little extra sugar and my mother made whatever fruit was available into jams and jellies. I was always on hand to help, picking, chopping up and stirring. The little house filled with the delicious aroma.'

Pat Salter, then a young girl, had a pet chicken among those the family kept in Pinhoe. Her favourite was called 'Dear Old Soul' and, luckily she thought, never made it to the table. Phyllis McGill and her younger brother Arthur remember their father kept poultry. They recall 'we had chickens and we would cry when one's time came. We couldn't bear to eat them. We named them all. One was called Hitler – he was white with a great tuff. There was only one pullet out of all them – and the rest were cockerels.' Others remember keeping rabbits including Desmond Dunn who had his in a hutch outside his family's home in Burnthouse Lane.

Christine Caldwell's husband John was head of Botany at University College of the South West, later the University of Exeter, and led the effort to produce all the food needed for the students and staff. She recalls he treated the campus as a farm and reared goats, rabbits, chickens and pigs. The lawns were used for hay-making and vegetables

Christine Caldwell, one of the girls from the Central School of
Speech and Drama, who helped Dig for Victory at the
University College of the South West.

The tennis lawn at Thomas Hall, converted to the use of goats.

were planted in the fields. A team of gardeners, mostly conscientious objectors, were assisted by a team of girls from the Central School of Speech and Drama who were evacuated to Exeter. They also had the services of Roger, the estate horse. One of the team was Christine's sister Sue who came down from Oxfordshire to help. She recalled 'at 21 years I was already working as a Land Girl. A tough life on a 1,000 acre arable farm in the Oxfordshire countryside. Although enjoying the camaraderie of the cheerful gang of other jolly girls I then heard of an official edict from headquarters saying that opting out of the service, to do other war work, was to be stopped. All right, but I still was longing to do training of some kind and this would make it impossible. Luckily for me, my brother-in-law, John Caldwell, had found out, in his capacity as Head of Exeter University's Botany Faculty, that there was a loophole – become registered as a full time agricultural worker & you had the freedom to change to other war work. Better still, he had, it seemed, started a scheme to make the limited grounds of the university campus as productive as possible and thereby to enhance the poor food rations of students in the Halls of residence. He could do with another 'female full time agricultural worker' come? *Oh! Yes! Indeed I would come.* I soon found myself a happy billet with the Short family up Streatham Drive. They had two dear small children & I was squashed into a nice little room under the eaves. They seemed not to mind or were silent about my dirty Wellingtons outside the back door. Nor, I now realised, did they kindly comment on the strong smells of my jacket and dungarees – goat laced with rabbit, pig & hen perfumes made it fortunate that they did not have to have me feeding at their table.'

Some institutions fared fairly well. For example, Sister Edward Mary recalls how well her convent at Palace Gate was treated by local shopkeepers. Their butcher would ring them if he had a supply of meat which was not on the rations and ask how much the children needed. Their good fortune was apparent when a guest from a Cornish boarding school was astonished to find meat served at lunch. 'This young girl exclaimed *you have meat? At school we never have meat because we have been told that you can't get it.*' When one of their pupil's fathers visited from his naval ship at Plymouth he brought a box of seagull eggs which, although fishy, were used in cooking or as boiled eggs for the children. They were fascinated by them. On one occasion the sisters had whale meat which they found tough and very oily. They decided they would rather go hungry than have it a second time. She also recalled that 'I couldn't say we were ever hungry but the food wasn't of the same quality as before the war.' There were young servicemen billeted next to them and these men had been given the choice of either military service or prison. The sisters became accustomed to the men raiding their garden. On one occasion the senior officer came by with a tin hat filled with money. He said he realised what his men had done and offered the money as compensation saying that given human nature he assumed that those who stole the most food had probably contributed the least amount.

Joyce Flack, ten years old when war started, also remembers eating whale meat. She thought 'it was horrible, fishy. My mother used to cook onions to take away the taste.' Like many others she had to try new kinds of food. Sylvia Hart was another. She was a young girl at the start of the war and recalls the tins of dried egg and how useful Spam was because it had enough fat to help make pastry. One local woman remembers pasties being in particular demand. Another recalled alternative recipes as being repulsive; while 'banana' sandwiches were popular at the Allied Services Club, Christine Caldwell disliked any of the imitation puddings made with parsnips which she thought always tasted of them. Her favourite food from the period remains pigs' trotters which she boiled, roasted and then served with mashed turnips. Joyce Stabb recalls 'there were foods that you ate that weren't very tasteful. You got used to eating stale cake. You learned to be economic and make the most of things you might normally have thrown out.' One woman remembers how she 'still managed a Sunday dinner and go to the butcher for a little joint. Through the week you'd have to do with liver (if you could get it). Fish was impossible, what with the war and fishermen. Beans on toast was a favourite.'

There was Black Market activity in Exeter as elsewhere. Sylvia Hart recalls 'rabbits, fish, sausages were coupon free and then of course there was the black market but to get you really had to pay.' David Smith remembers his father being a master butcher who had 'a typical Victorian corner shop with the house behind and above the shop . . . being a butcher he said on several occasions he was offered 'black market meat' by a certain character. My father was a very fair and honest man and he told me that he said to the person concerned he was not interested and that if he (the character) was caught he would be imprisoned, to which the person replied that he would never go to prison because he supplied several influential people in Exeter & he had made it known to them that if he was caught he would expect them to intervene and help him, if not he was going to 'sing like a canary' & 'take them down with him'. He was caught, he did not go to prison but was just given a fine.' One former policeman thinks 'yes, there was a bit of that. In the old civic hall you could tell what was going on. I think we had a special squad of 2 or 3 men for that. It was mainly cigarettes. There was also the innocent black market – small stuff with the wives trying to look after their families. Mostly it was that – nothing really naughty.' Another Exeter resident recalls the difficulties families had. He later wrote 'a lot of wheeling and dealing and Black Marketing went on at that time. People tried to make ends meet. So people would come and go. Perhaps they had been out trying to get some petrol, or food, or nylons, or candles or something. There was always much talk of parachute silk, I never saw any, but this was prized for wedding dresses etc. Family intelligence of what was happening on the streets, or in the shops was very important. You didn't want to miss a bargain after all! So, much time was spent exchanging information on what was happening and where and who knew a man who could get something (for a price).' But another woman, with a young family to look after, remembers that the black market was not for her and many others – they were too poor to afford the prices.

Good relationships with butchers were important. One woman remembers her butcher arrived each week with a parcel he announced as 'bones for the baby'. In it would be whatever could be had off the rations – sometimes pigeon but mostly offal. Another woman recalls her butcher gave extra food 'if they liked you and you were a good customer and kept your mouth shut – but you couldn't have it every time – they might say we've got a *rabbit* or maybe extra eggs. We'd think it was marvellous.' Farmers could also be important. Certain farms near Exeter provided butter or sometimes a chicken for one family. 'Sometimes someone would have killed a pig – very quietly. You never went short'.

Keeping in with grocers was also valuable. One woman recalls of a friend 'their mother was a dainty little woman and their father much taller, they were most kind. At some later stage his father was able to provide my mother with extra dried fruit for our Christmas cake, definitely under the counter stuff! We were lucky, the cake was as good as possible, no icing, but there was marzipan made from soya flour flavoured with almond essence. I can remember painting holly leaves and berries with food colouring for the decoration. Another occasional treat was to be given a few of Kemp's chocolate wafer biscuits, by him. As an area manager for a chain of grocery shops in Devon he seemed to have a few perks which he shared with some friends.'

Military contacts, whether Polish, American or British, were also crucial for some people. One man remembered food 'was worked on a racket. Most who were in billets would have the men there share it out – one would bring home corned beef, another bread, or Spam, offal, kidneys. All taken from military stores – pinched from the cook.' Americans were known for having the most food (see pages 146–8).

The end of the war introduced items which had not been known to Exeter children. One woman recalls 'things such as oranges and bananas kids never had them until after the war'. David Harris, only six years old when he arrived in 1944 from Middlesex, remembers the sudden appearance of new goods. He was living at Exe Street when 'a lady came running down the road banging on all the doors saying there were bananas in the local shop.' Sister Edward Mary remembers her convent in Palace Gate provided the pupils with a banana as a treat towards the end of the war. 'The youngest ones cried because they had never seen one and did not know what to do with a banana'.

Sixty years after the war many in Exeter agree with Christine Caldwell whose abiding memory is never having wasted food. She feels this is a hallmark of her generation.

Transport

Petrol restrictions made transport difficult and many remember the streets being empty of traffic and how easy it was for children to play street games. One woman thinks local people were devious in obtaining petrol and many others recall the lengths men and women went to for petrol. One woman remembers that her mother 'obtained black market petrol from the AA Man. This petrol was buried by mother in the bantam chicken run to avoid detection by Father who would have lost his job with the petroleum company.'

Another woman was working in the Timber Corps near the city and recalled lifts in an oxygen lorry and an empty hearse. She even accepted the use of the cross-bar of a bicycle.[24] Dorrie Langdon recollects 'we had no car in Exeter so the usual transport was by bicycle, I had for some years used my mother's special Chater-Lea which had three speed gears, but now she needed it herself and a new bike was purchased for me. Truthfully I never liked it because it was a wartime model, no chrome shining anywhere, a horrid back pedalling brake and no gears. However I cycled on it for years, once to Ladram Bay on a summer Sunday with my parents, but mostly it was to school. There were occasional bus trips but really we never went far from Exeter.'

Romance

For some romance was an escape from the general uncertainties of life. Even so it was difficult for some women to be glamorous with clothing shortages; one woman remembers how they wore trousers and kept their hair in scarves because of the shortage of hairpins and grips.

Many married including Bette Simmonds. Before the war she and her fiancée had planned on marriage but then her fiancée was called up. He was given compassionate leave and they married in 1940. She felt they were lucky; 'a sister of mine was in Cheriton Bishop and a baker out there said *if your sister wants to get married she'll want a cake and everything will be rationed. If you want I'll make it, put it away and put it in a special box*'. The following five days they stayed in Heavitree and during that time she recalls 'I was called up on my wedding day. Course he was home and took me. I did munitions in Willey's Avenue.' They 'had 5 days and then we went to Deller's on the last day and had a cream tea, about the last time we could have it.' Then they parted. 'It was pretty wretched, after having seen him off at St David's and walking back home on my own. I went back to my mother-in-law's house, she was in tears and we both sat there crying.'

Ethel Harris was married in August 1944 at Exwick. She remembers 'margarine coupons were at one time used for clothing and my parents saved & used theirs for my bridesmaids' 2 dresses, one pink and one blue. Mum made headdresses of wire covered with parachute cord material as someone had given her part of a parachute! My aunt and uncle saved their margarine coupons and had my wedding dresses made & gave me this as my wedding present. I borrowed a headdress and Mum made my veil of net. She also got a little extra in points to use for the reception and the Morrison shelter came into its own to lay out the spread. Ernest (my husband) was serving on a target tower out of Londonderry at the time and sent home butter, fruit, icing sugar, etc. as he could go (in civvies) to Southern Ireland. So we had a 3 tier

Inside of Deller's Café, fondly remembered by Exeter people.

cake, made by an N.F.S. Cook friend of my mother only the week before.'

There were unusual weddings. At Exeter's synagogue there was a double wedding. Bill Boam was a teenager during the war and remembers the two couples from London being married in about 1942. Joyce Stabb's wedding had to be arranged around her fiancée's time off as well as her own. A wedding cake needed much longer planning than they could afford – at least six months of ration coupons. She recalled 'I didn't have a wedding cake – it would have been cardboard for icing. My mother said to me *I don't like the look of that.* I must have shook my head no so she said *But make sure you have a nice cake for your silver wedding,* which I did.' She also remembers how in the factory the women supported one another. 'We were mainly married women, some with sons in the forces. Some had telegrams saying their men folk were missing or taken as prisoners of war. And of course we all felt sorry for one another. Even if we had news like that we still had to go to work, so we comforted one another.'

Canon Michael Walsh was an assistant priest at the Church of the Sacred Heart and recalls how in 1941 he married one couple. He recalls 'I intended on marrying them on Christmas Day and I was told I couldn't do that. But it was the only day the groom could get off – he was in the services – so I said *there is a war on you know.* I prepared them for the marriage and went to the reception afterwards. Annie was a nurse at Exminster and two days after the wedding she went down with typhoid fever. When I heard I hopped on my bicycle and went to their cottage in Exminster. I just arrived when the ambulance was taking her away to the isolation hospital in Whipton. I was

Miss Annie McGroarty and Mr Vivian Bussell on their wedding day, 25 December 1941, at the Church of the Sacred Heart, South Street, Exeter.

green then. They asked me to come in for a cup of tea, which I did. I then went to the hospital and they put a white suit on me – course I should have been quarantined myself. The doctor told me her chances of pulling through were virtually nil. So I gave her the last rites and halfway through she calmed down, fell into a deep sleep and when she awoke she was on the road to recovery.' Vivian and Annie Bussell have vivid memories of their wedding. They remembered 'most of our courting time was spent in Exminster eating fish & chips & drinking Vimto – being with other couples enjoying ourselves and making sure that no lights were shown to endanger our surroundings'. After the wedding 'we just came back home – mother put on a bit of a dinner etc. Course we only had one or two friends there. Then we went to my aunt's in Exmouth for a couple of days. That was our honeymoon.' Mrs Bussell recalls 'I was in white. I bought it in Exeter – even with coupons I got my white dress. I was only seven stone when I got married. Thinking about it now – there was already illness there, even though I was always tiny . . . later I dyed the dress. I had it for several years – I then couldn't go to dances because I couldn't go in a white dress and couldn't afford a new one so I dyed it a lovely green. Turned out lovely. I had it for a few years and gave up dancing later.' They also recall that several other members of the staff at Exminster Hospital were also struck down with typhoid.

Foreign servicemen played a crucial role in wartime romances. Canon Michael also remembers 'the place was chock-a-block with Americans. They had plenty of cigarettes; they'd throw a whole carton at you. The Americans used to parade from Topsham Barracks to here for mass – there were a high proportion of them who were Catholics. I performed quite a number of G.I. bride weddings. Before I could I had to communicate with their home town if there were any reasons I couldn't marry them.'

One woman remembers 'Deller's in Bedford Square was a favourite meeting place where you could have a cup of tea and a light meal on the first floor and look down over the balcony to the ground floor, where one could dance to a band. As most of the men were in the Forces and in uniform of some kind they were expert in dancing in heavy army boots'. For most young unmarried women the only option was a dance where alcohol was generally not served. It was not viable to go to pubs: one woman who was a teenager at the start of the war recalls 'decent girls didn't go to pubs. You would get such a name for yourself. Your name would be mud'. One woman who is remembered for having frequented pubs was known as 'Shilling Lil'. One former boy remembers how the adults used to whisper about three women in their street. He recalls 'the lady next door used to have an American sailor in. She was the talk of the road. We had three ladies of the night in the road – the lady down the road had the R.A.F. and the American air force and the third woman had them all.' According to one woman 'things went wild' when the Americans arrived. These young men, with their smart clothes and money, were sought after and Hoopern Fields became infamous as trysting grounds or, as one woman remembers, the Happy Hunting Grounds. They were, however, remembered by another woman to have been well stocked with condoms. Another remembers local people being both shocked and

A wartime wedding – Miss Christine Hayes and Dr John Caldwell, Dean of Science at the University College of the South West, at the door to the North Tower, Exeter Cathedral, 14 August 1941. Elsie Fogerty, the renowned founder of the Central School of Speech Training and Dramatic Art, is in the back row to the left.

titillated by the two brothels in the city: there was one in Longbrook Street across from the Black Horse and another in Pennsylvania Road near Union Road. One of these working girls was known for using her dog as a cover: she would take it for a walk and then pick up a soldier, often an American. Others have said they thought there was a brothel at Livery Dole and several in St Thomas. One former policeman recalls brothels were 'unofficial places' and not highly organised.

Canon Michael Walsh thinks morals changed. He reflects 'it wasn't as noticeable *during* the war as it became *after* the war. Life during wartime becomes very, very cheap – you were killing people. It's not easy to extract that attitude from everyone that didn't want to. Some individuals were used to killing – being trained to kill – this was one of the side effects of the war. Morals began to deteriorate but we didn't notice this too much, that life became cheap, of feelings of one person to another, until later. Morales began to fade particularly when it was felt that the war was going on for a long period, going on and on. With the wife at home – she is subject to all kinds of kinds of pressures and temptations, and sometimes succumbed to it. That we found. There were a lot more unwanted babies than before. If the mother was a Catholic we had no hesitation to have the baby baptised. We would help them as far as possible – we had organisations to help mothers. There was no hiding of babies going on really because the neighbours had a second sense of what was happening. It took some time before the local authorities were able to organise help to unmarried women. That was one of the effects of the war.' One former constable recalls how lonely many women were with their husbands away for many years: 'I myself had dozens of offers as a young policeman.'

Many have memories of beginning romances and discovering their new partner was already engaged or married. Some Exeter women remember how they finished these relationships but others carried on. Some women were already married and after D-Day did not hear from their American beaus again. Years later some still wonder whether these men survived the Normandy landings. Some women have remembered how married friends of theirs took up with married Americans for the duration of their stay in Exeter.

Women found they were expecting a baby and there were difficulties with absent husbands due to return. One resident remembers one particular woman trying to have a miscarriage and others have recalled women seeking abortions. One woman remembers being told that a friend was taken to London for one and subsequently died of peritonitis. Some babies were born and have grown up, it is said, not knowing their true parentage. This has been particularly talked about regarding fathers who were black Americans stationed in St Thomas.

One woman remembers coming home on leave to discover her fiancée was dating another woman. She found him at a dance and threw her engagement ring at him. Unfortunately for him the blackout made it necessary for him to crawl on his hands and knees to find it. She had some satisfaction in seeing him 'grovelling' in the dark.

Many Exeter men and women found their partners while they were serving away from home. For example, Lucy Bailey met her future husband while serving with the W.A.A.F. She recalls 'I went to see *Buffalo Bill* in Plymouth. We were told not to go to Union Street, but I was a bit of a rebel and I also didn't know what they were talking about. So I went. I was sitting in this cinema and had to spend a penny. I asked the gentleman near me if he could save my seat.

Wedding of Miss Lucy Bailey and Victor Kadzielska, 10 March 1945. She recalls 'my husband was dressed in his Polish navy uniform, I was in my W.A.A.F. uniform and the best man was in his American army uniform at the Blessed Sacrament Church in Heavitree.'

When I came out of the cinema he followed me. And I thought to myself, well I don't want anything to do with him. And then he started speaking, and I thought he sounded French. Then he said *Polski*, and *come back to our club*. I was excited then, because my sister was married to a Polish airman. So we went there, and everyone was so kind. Then he asked me if I wanted to go to his boat – a destroyer. And that is how our relationship started. I only saw him four times and then I married him. I was on duty and so was he. He swept me off my feet.' They married on 10 March 1945. She recalls 'my husband was dressed in his Polish navy uniform, I was in my W.A.A.F. uniform and the best man was in his American army uniform, at the Blessed Sacrament church in Heavitree.'

Although the war loosened morals for some, it should be remembered the times were more innocent than those today. One former schoolgirl at Bishop Blackall School recalls 'before the end of term we 6th form girls were to be allowed a leavers' dance in the school hall, this news was greeted with much excitement, for such an event was unheard of, actually boys were to be allowed on the premises! Georgie Combes was the organiser, everything was to be so very correct, dance cards, made by us. All the dances were numbered and noted as a waltz or quickstep etc. and boy partners had to write their names in a dance of their choice. I am not sure it actually solved the wallflower syndrome. In retrospect I think the Paul Jones was the most popular, it certainly was the ultimate in lucky dips with sweaty hands and pimples in our random partners. School desks were arranged down one side of the hall, covered

Mrs Lucy Kadzielska in her Going Away outfit.

with borrowed small tablecloths, and we each had our dance card on top, ever hopeful. Funnily I cannot remember who I had invited if anyone, but it was deemed an enormous success.'

News and entertainment

Romance was not the only diversion. Many went to the cinema and the theatre to escape the war. Pamela Taylor recalls her family having home entertainment as well as going to the cinema and theatre. They listened to the radio, particularly to the news and to light entertainment programmes. She remembers Churchill's speeches: 'we listened avidly to those'. Only once or twice did she think she heard Lord Haw Haw because 'he had a nasty nasal voice and he was a traitor and we disapproved of him . . . I suppose what he said was rubbish really and it was such obvious propaganda.' Another, who was married and in her late twenties at the time, recalls 'you just hated him. He had a very queer voice. How he could have done that, I don't know. Well, you'd listen to him, it was a German kind of news and you knew it.' She also remembers the uplifting effect Churchill had on them. George Barnes had his news mostly by radio. He remembers 'you weren't suppose to listen to Lord Haw Haw but I suppose some people listened to see what he had to say, to hear his angle on the news. He used to ask *where is the Ark Royal?* We didn't know but he did. We used to listen to him, he had a very distinct turn of phrase. We knew the newspapers were pretty strictly censored.' Ivy Facey, who was twelve at the start of the war, recalls listening to the radio and how at six o'clock the house had to be silent for the news and weather. The family would also listen to Lord Haw Haw but 'they didn't believe him. What he said around our place wasn't true. If he could tell lies about that we knew it was all propaganda.' She also remembers the rumour that he was last seen in England at Drewsteignton.

Many remember the importance of the radio and have memories of favourite programmes. One young boy, Sidney Richards, for instance, particularly remembers listening to 'Children's Hour' and 'The Man in Black'.

The cinema became an important escape. In 1939 some nineteen million people attended the cinema every week and in 1945 it rose to thirty million.[25] Even so when Ivy Facey went to the cinema there were occasions when 'very often you'd have to stop and go because the sirens went.' However, she would not see the end of that particular film. Margaret Ball remembers how she and her three sisters regularly went to see films, with their favourites being Shirley Temple, Deanna

A popular film with Dorothy Lamour, it played in Exeter during December 1944.

Durbin, Hedy Lamarr, Rita Hayworth, Betty Grable and their heroes Gary Cooper, Robert Taylor, Cary Grant and Clark Gable. This is mirrored by others; nearly everyone interviewed has fond memories of going to the cinema and particular favourite film stars. Some remember walking home afterwards at night was difficult due to buses having stopped running after nine p.m. Bombing made a difference: John Langdon, a teenager during the war, recalls 'in Exeter before the blitz we had many cinemas but were left with only the Gaumont, Savoy and Odeon. Programmes consisted of a main feature, a "B" Film and a News Film. A cinema organist played during the interval.'

One woman, who was born in 1914, remembers an alternative to cinemas and dancing: Deaconess Margaret and a young sister would come down to the West Quarter on Tuesday afternoons and from 3 to 4 they would have a mothers' meeting. A speaker would talk and then they would have a cup of tea.

Exeter was also full of music and Ivy Facey recalls 'there were a lot of dance halls around and the soldiers used to have their own bands. There was a dance on every night, what they'd call a disco nowadays, but nicer. My sister was the dancer in the family. If she could she would go every night.' Annie Bussell was one of many local women who loved to go the afternoon tea dances at Deller's Café. Eric Wheaton remembers 'I believe there was a woman-only band at Bobby's Restaurant but there were still chaps in the band at Deller's.' John Langdon also recalls his first opera was 'Dennis Noble and the Carl Rosa Opera company in *Barber of Seville* at the Theatre Royal. We had Symphony Concerts in the Civic Hall. The hall smelt of boiled cabbage because it was used at lunchtime as a British Restaurant! One member of the London Symphony Orchestra was heard to ask why they had to perform in a warehouse but that was the best that Exeter had to offer. On Sunday afternoons there were recitals in the cinemas. I remember hearing Moiseivitch, Louis Kentner and Rawicz & Landauer among others. I went to choral concerts in the Cathedral and the Mint. I was in the 2 school plays which were produced during the war, 'Ambrose Applejohn's Adventure' at the Kings Cinema, Okehampton Street and 'Henry IVth' at the Washington Singer Hall. I was also one of the 'Countess Weir Players' who performed plays in the old village hall. The Drama Mistress from Ashford (Kent) Girls' School which was evacuated to Countess Wear was the inspiration behind its formation. She also tried to teach us ballroom dancing. We also organised dances at School, music provided by the "Rapcats" from the Royal Army Pay Corps. No alcohol of course – except beer for the band. At home we had the radio but television was stopped at the beginning of the war. In any case by then it hadn't reached Devon. On the radio there were just 2 stations – the Home Service, a bit like Radio 4, and the Forces programme, like Radio 2. The main news was at 9 in the evening and everybody tuned in. Before this on Sundays the national anthems of all the Allies were played; my father was a soldier from World War I and very patriotic so we all stood to attention when "God Save the King" came on.'

School life

Life at school also changed with the large number of evacuees altering school times and some buildings had to be requisitioned. There was also war work. John Langdon was at Hele's School and recalls 'all large buildings and streets of houses had to have 'firewatchers' every night. We had a 'stirrup pump' (a bit like a garden syringe) and sand bags to put out incendiary bombs. At school there were 2 masters and 3 older boys on duty every night. For this we were paid a subsistence allowance so that was welcome pocket money. From school each class spent some days in autumn out on farms potato picking– hard work but that was also paid. We had no air raid shelters at school so when the air raid sirens sounded we had to disperse to pre-arranged houses round about. Later on our headmaster, Mr Nichols, decided that we were more likely to get injured by machine guns when walking the streets than by staying in our classrooms so we carried on with our lessons. Maynard School 6th form area was damaged in the blitz and as a result we had girls studying at Hele's for the first time. In return when our maths master left in 1944 Maynard offered their facilities to some of us in the science 6th. Children today, used to co-education, would think nothing of this but to us it was memorable.'

Many school children did not see their fathers for many years but other parts of their lives continued as before. The younger ones who did not know a pre-wartime diet also did not realise what food they were missing. Brian Le Messurier was a small boy living in St Thomas and used the nearby lanes and fields to play in. He recalled 'when my family came to Exeter in 1940 and took a house on the fringe of the St Thomas built-up area, the countryside on the other side of the hill became a natural outlet for me as a schoolboy. I found that the other children in the neighbourhood similarly regarded it as an extension of their back gardens, and soon we were making holiday and weekend outings to the Alphin Brook equipped with string-handled jam jars. Our fishing beat was anywhere between Rolls Bridge at the Pocombe end and the railway embankment near Alphington, and we did not seem to be troubled by farmers and landowners. This happy state of live and let live was probably due to the absence on war service of those who might otherwise have told us to clear out, but I do not remember that we ever abused the privilege. There was talk of an ogre-like farmer along one particular stretch, but he never manifested himself when I was around . . . I could go now to the spot where a German incendiary bomb fell and burnt itself out and I remember the road being blocked near Rolls Bridge by soil thrown up by a high explosive bomb which fell just over the hedge by the raised path curiously known as Doctor's Path.'[26]

Dorrie Langdon recalls 'my new school was a fee-paying girls' grammar named after a Bishop Blackall – unbelievably his Christian name was 'Offspring' which caused a definite hysterical reaction from us girls when someone found this out. We used to pronounce it in all manner of strange voices and it was guaranteed to be greeted with giggles. For me it was definitely not an easy transition from James Gillespie's High School. I only realised for the first time that I spoke with a Scottish accent and I was continuously being asked to 'say something'. It was a conscious effort on my behalf to modify my pronunciation. After a few weeks in the sixth form studying English, history and art, the paper work from Edinburgh arrived and I moved down a year into my correct age group. This was all very difficult; it was mostly a revision year basically for the school certificate exams (nowadays O levels or G.C.S.E). I had only ever studied Scottish history; every textbook and set book was different, I was not allowed to study my best subject which was science. The whole academic year was a huge struggle, to acquire new knowledge and I was feeling very inadequately prepared for the exams that were to come in June. Not only had the war produced a period of part time schooling but also a time when I was virtually an evacuee in an exceedingly mixed group at Ayr Academy, and now I was in a strange school in a strange country, my seventh change of school at the age of fifteen. All these factors compounded my situation.'

She was one of many hundreds of school children who were new to Exeter during wartime and kept strong memories of their previous schools. She recalls 'the girls in my form were for the most part local, but there was a small group from 'foreign parts' and I can only think of happy friendships. My parents were always aware that I needed friends of my own age and they kept open house and in turn I visited other homes gladly. I continued to wear my distinctive Gillespie's crimson school hat and there were a few other varying uniforms. On St Andrew's Day I wore my kilt and tweed jacket. Before long I was summoned to the Headmistress's room, this was such an unusual occurrence that everyone was wildly curious. It was with considerable trepidation that I literally stood "on the carpet" before Miss Ragg's desk. Displeasure showed on her face as I stammered out that it was the tradition in my Scottish school as a mark of respect to our Patron Saint. She immediately softened and acknowledged that my odd behaviour was understandable, but on no account was I to deviate from school uniform again. I retreated both shaken and mystified at her apparent ignorance.

By the summer term friendships were established, we went swimming on Saturday mornings, I had a bicycle and was able to find my way around. I cycled to school, to friends in Whipton, joined a country-dancing group, went to church and was allowed to go to an occasional 'hop' in the church hall. I became friends with some boys from Hele's Grammar School and Exeter School and we all attended 'citizenship studies' in the 'Post-war Society' meetings at our various schools. We learned about the roles of councillors, mayors, jurors, local government departments with seminars and various adult speakers. That featured highly in our estimation as our girls' grammar school was an entirely female establishment and we would laugh, saying that nothing in trousers ever passed through the portals. I think there gathered students from Hele's, Exeter, Blundell's, Maynard's, St Margaret's, Dover College (from Poltimore), Ashford School (from Countess Wear) and Blackall and we were assigned into to smaller groups to discuss various given topics throughout the day.

I took part in a debating society meeting at Hele's, speaking against the motion proposed by the boys, namely 'Modern civilization is degenerate'. Ivy Keene led for us, noting a promise of better health care and education with the hope of obtaining a good and lasting peace, my addition was to defend modern music, poetry and art. Cruelty, savagery and a lust for power characterised a too-feather bedded life style countered the boys. They lost the motion by 42 votes, however it is interesting to note the topics under discussion in March 1944 more than a year before the end of the war still appear on many agendas today.

The school day was rigidly structured, beginning with a full senior school assembly, all the staff wore their academic gowns, often teaching in them all day. We always had a record of classical music to come into the hall, then stood in silence until Miss Ragg appeared on the stage to lead prayers, then a hymn followed and any notices. We then were dismissed again in silence and walked to our form rooms for registration. School rules stated no talking or running in the corridors and as ' young ladies' we never disobeyed, there was a system of conduct marks which would appear on school reports and woe betide the few who always seemed to be in trouble. Detention on our free Wednesday afternoon was the penalty. Traditionally Wednesdays had been the games period, but our playing field was then 'growing food for victory' with crops like corn and potatoes. For games we had to make do with the tennis court; we played netball and I went on to do the referees exam so that I could be more involved. Tennis was fairly popular and we had some good coaching from our P.E. teacher Georgie Coombes. There were two gym lessons each week, one for Swedish drill which needed to be graceful as well as accurate, the other for apparatus work. I really liked the vaulting horse and box exercises, climbing ropes, parallel bars and the wall bars. I had great hopes of going to a physical training college, but no amount of persuasion on my part made my parents contemplate such a possibility for me, and I was very disappointed.'

CIVIL DEFENCE

On Exeter's Home Front an extraordinary amount of activity took place to make the city safe and to help win the war. There was a need for people of all walks of life to work together for a common cause. One woman remembers 'it was the war that softened class distinctions. We all had to work together.' She also commented 'they worked as hard as anyone. Everyone seemed to want to do something.' George Barnes also reflected 'I don't think it was a them-and-us situation. So many working class men became officers. It was a great leveller then – both up and down. We all realised we depended on each other. Together we could manage, but separately we would go under.' One man, a teenager during the war, recollects the class divisions then in Exeter. On one occasion he had played with the son of a prison warder but 'when my mother heard, she forbad me to play with him. That side of things was awful, but it was the way of things then, when I look back now it's horrifying, but it wasn't thought of then. There were no-go areas for me in the city, even Paris Street. I can remember being with another Exeter School boy and there were these council children who jeered at us and spat at us. They saw us wearing our school uniforms and called us snobs. That's just the way it was – it was horrid.'

It was necessary to include women as fully as possible. At the end of 1941 single women and childless widows between the ages of twenty and thirty were made liable for military service. This was later extended and many women volunteered their labour.[27] Mrs B. Clifton worked in the Still Room at the Bude Hotel before the war but then changed occupations. She recollected in 1977 'then the war came and I went to Wippell's and made the parachutes. I hated every minute of it.'[28] Dorrie Langdon recalls 'as I was an only child and over fifteen now, my mother was required to do some form of war work. It transpired that she became secretary to the Education Officer, a Mr Philip, at his office situated in Rougemont House. She worked a five-day week, full time, and naturally there were household duties to be performed, wartime shopping was difficult, a garden had to be kept in good shape and she had to cycle everywhere. It must have been a physically exhausting and worrying time.' For young women factory work could be difficult. Marian Wallen remembers 'I was just of an age when I had to go to work. In Ferndale Road there was a factory – I used a sewing machine to go all around the naval men's uniforms. Stitch all around, that was my job. It was such a mixed bunch there. I learned quite a lot – how everyone lived. Some were pretty tough, I was afraid

Staff of the Women's Land Army, Fairpark Lodge, Fairpark Road, Exeter, 1945.

Exeter Post Women.

Women at War marching through Exeter, 1941.

to talk sometimes – some of them thought I was a bit snooty. They didn't really like me very much – some of them.' Other women have similar stories of the rough character of factory life during the war. The population of the city was comprised of a changing number of children, including at times many evacuees, foreign servicemen, adults in reserved occupations, and younger and older volunteers. The need for workers gave rise to an unpopular figure in civil defence: one young women remembers the officious manner in which many wardens worked, similar she feels, to how traffic wardens are popularly perceived today. There were many roles to play to protect the city.

Early precautions

Mrs D. Irene Thomas wrote of the precautions her family took in Pennsylvania. These were echoed to some extent throughout Exeter. She recalled 'I had assembled an Air Raid Precautions case of essential foodstuffs as advised by the government, our safeguard against enemy interference with supplies. F.G. had buckets of sand and a stirrup pump on landings and stairways in case of fire from incendiaries. A heavy door at the back of the house in the courtyard opened directly on to the wide stone stairway down to the empty wine cellars under the kitchen and storeroom. The cellars were hewn out of the solid rock on which the house was built, clean and dry with electric lighting, and they made an ideal shelter with canvas chairs stacked in readiness in a corner. A joiner cut a large wooden trapdoor in the storeroom flooring and to it fixed a flight of wooden steps so that we could get below quickly in case of emergency without having to go outside to the courtyard. Moreover this gave us an alternative exit from the cellars in case the other was blocked. Besides the packed suitcase of baby clothes stood a dreadful 'respirator' with its mica face-piece like a small window in the top, and stout strap fastenings, designed for the protection of infants from poison gas; from now on every man, woman and child in the country was obliged by law to carry a case containing his grotesque gas mask whenever he went out, and to keep it always in hand in a known place at home. Our friends had become Fire Watchers and Air Raid Wardens who patrolled the streets to check the complete screening of lights and kept vigil at their posts. In September Great Britain and the Axis Powers were officially at war.'[29]

Edmund Forte remembers various precautions taken around his family home in Dunsford Gardens. He later wrote 'outside of our house in Dunsford Gardens was a broad swathe of grass, this swept all the way up to the top of the hill opposite the houses on Dunsford Hill. This lent the area a special feel of being in the *Country*, which they nearly were of course, being one of the last houses then, before the actual countryside began. One day men came and erected huge galvanised steel water tanks right opposite our house on the grass. This caused us much excitement. These were to be emergency water tanks, to be used should the water mains fail during an air raid, and our houses catch fire. At first some men began to use the tanks as their own private swimming pools, but wire netting was placed over the top so that put a stop to that. Another time they came and painted the roadway *Black* all the way up Dunsford Hill. This was, they claimed, because it was a light colour and reflected at night in the moonlight, and was used by enemy bombers as a run in to bomb the City. Some of the locals seemed to think that the road being white concrete was our fault. (People were prepared to be silly or pompous at the drop of a hat). Another source of much public concern was the prominence of Haldon Belvedere, a magnificent white tower which had been erected on the highest ground overlooking Exeter. There was talk of how the German Bombers used it to zero in on Exeter, so they wanted it demolished, which would have been a shame.' Thousands of other Exeter people watched a variety of efforts being made in their own parts of the city.

Blackout

Blackout began in the first month of war. For Olive Matilda Wakeham, thirty-two at the start of the war, blackout meant having only slits of light shining from car lights but 'the worst of all of it was the miles of cloth you would have to buy. We were afraid of letting out just a chink of light – wardens would appear at once.' One woman, who was in her late twenties during the war, remembers how she placed brown paper against the windows. They remained there throughout the day, and the several years of war, until they were blasted out. The Coombes family lived along what is now Longbrook Street but the size of the windows in the front room prohibited the buying of blackout material. They didn't use that room at night for the duration of the war. George Barnes recalls 'people were very conscious then of fifth columnists and worried about chinks of light.' Phyllis McGill was sixteen years old and remembers her family's efforts in Merrivale Road to maintain blackout. She said 'we had blackout curtains, so we could use our lights. Woolworth's use to sell it on the roll by the yard. We made the curtains ourselves. At first it was a bit eerie and frightening. I didn't like going out at first. With time you got used to it. And ventured a bit further.'

Many lived in fear of a warden knocking at their door and some got into trouble. Sylvia Hart was a young girl living with her family at 19 Hazel Road and on one occasion 'went into the passageway and put the light on. I hadn't realised the curtains hadn't been pulled on the top windows. An air raid warden saw the light coming through and my father was fined ten shillings.'

Pat Salter recalls the blacking of windows and the disappearance of streetlights. In Pinhoe a story spread of a ghost with a rattling chain but several of her neighbours were in on the joke: it was only Michael, the vicar's donkey, broken loose again. Joyce Stabb was sixteen when war broke out. She remembers her boyfriend whistling to her in the blackout so she knew where he was and found the right man. On one occasion he was leaving her home in Merrivale Road when he walked into a tree which caught his spectacles and whipped them off. He was then seen on his hands and knees trying to locate them.

Some got used to it pretty quickly. Revd John Benton remembers after the blitz 'my father said we better get away for a while. So we went to Milton Damerel and stayed at a farm. There they didn't worry about blackout at all. But we, having experienced the blitz and the sirens, we were perturbed that they didn't worry about it at all.'

Blackout made life dangerous for some. One woman, a teenager during the war, recalls 'we weren't at all nervous about it. It didn't worry me at all walking home in the dark.' Others did not feel so secure. Another woman recollects 'we as young girls then were taught to walk along the kerb, never go along the edge because you could be grabbed more easily even if there was a car coming. Some chap followed me home one time. The house had three steps up to the front door. Luckily someone answered the bell because he was on the bottom step by the time the door opened. It wasn't like today with all the yobs but in some ways it was just as dangerous.' David Melhuish, who lived with his parents at 9, Rosewood Terrace, close to St James Park football ground, remembers his father saying it caused stress to the bus drivers as they continually had near misses. He later wrote 'most nights I use to go to the fish and chip shop to get three penny worth of chips. In the winter this short trip to Thomas's fish and chip shop in Well Street next to the railway line, was quite difficult, as the streets were jet black.' Pamela Morgan's brother Jim dived into the canal to rescue a mother and her daughter who had fallen in because of the blackout. She recalls that the child was saved but the mother died en route to hospital.

Blackout had implications for the local police. Inspector Stanley Cole, who was a young constable in the war, recalls 'it was a bit more difficult to walk about, not so much in the main street, but in the smaller streets – in those areas where you had old-fashioned streets. There was a bit more crime, because the dark gave them better cover. But we knew the criminals then, not like nowadays where they can come up and down the motorway quickly. We would see them the next day here in the city. Blackout made things a bit easier for them.' He also remembers that they tried to ease people into the new regulations. He recalls 'you had to give and take a bit. You couldn't rush them and had to be a bit slow to get people used to the blackout.' He also remembers 'I was a young policeman on the beat just off Summerland Street there was an old-fashioned draper's shop with an old-fashioned lady that run it. It was very early days in the blackout. A light was showing above the shop, so I rang the bell. But there wasn't any answer. So I decided I had to do something about it, so I went up the drainpipe. With my trudgeon I smashed the window and put out the light. So the next day somebody must have seen her and told her she may be reported for the offence. And she came in that day, thinking

I was going to charge her – I had forgotten about the whole thing. She tugged on my trousers and she called me Inspector, and tried to pass me a three-penny bit.'

Blackout finished in the spring of 1945. When peace was declared one local woman remembered 'you were almost afraid to take down the blackout for a few days in case it was wrong.' David Melhuish recalls 'after V.E. day when the restrictions were lifted I can remember walking through the town at night and seeing all the shop windows lit up. I can remember thinking that this was quite wasteful as the shops were closed and there were no shoppers around. Just shows how conditioned I was.'

Gas attacks

At the start of the war there were general fears that the Germans would use gas as they had during the First World War. Gas masks were issued and it became mandatory to carry them. Eventually adults stopped carrying them. Eric Wheaton recalls 'in the early part of the war an A.R.P. warden came around to make us try them on and see if they fit. I remember breathing out and the air would come out the side. My mother had problems with her mask. She had had an operation a year previously and didn't want to smell the rubber but she got on with it alright eventually.' Sally Morgan remembers her baby sister being issued with a gas mask: 'she had a special contraption which was supposed to resemble Mickey Mouse, it was all rather frightening as you can imagine. Whenever we went, our equipment went with us.' Helen Mann recollects her father 'had a gas mask fitting session for numerous people in our sitting room. He had a corner shop at the time (1938). So it was pre-war of course. There were baby containers/masks, Mickey Mouse masks for under 5s and various sizes for youths and adults.'

Ivy Facey lived in Beaufort Road in St Thomas and was twelve years old at the start of the war. She recalls 'you had to carry your gasmask or else you would be told off. You would have to go home from school.'

Many former children remember carrying their masks in the early days of the war but that gradually they became complacent and stopped.

Public gas exercises took place in the city. Retired Inspector Cole recollects he trained with his fellow constables for gas attacks. They were then based in the city's police station in Waterbeer Street and went down into Pancras Lane where 'we had gas exercises. You had to go through the back of the Danish Bacon Company wearing the gas masks & helmet as exercises for gas – practicing where they smoked the bacon.'

Many people have remembered how much they disliked their masks but one woman who was in her late teens at the time recalls an amusing episode. She recollects 'on the night when the bomb fell in Saville Road there was a family called Chamberlain with several kids. The mother shouted to them *quick get under the table – it's gas*. They put on their gasmasks and when the warden came in and opened the door they were all huddled in under the table still wearing their masks. She just thought it was gas because I suppose things were blowing. We could laugh about that later because it was very funny.'

Wardens

Many volunteered to work as Air Raid Precaution Wardens: by 1944 the city had 1,266 general wardens and 74 shelter wardens.[30] David Smith, a young boy during the war, recollects the work of his father Emlyn as an A.R.P. Warden and on the night of the blitz 'each warden had their patch to patrol and my father put on his coat, helmet and picked up his gas mask and went out to walk his patch.' He also recalls an incident involving his father one Sunday evening when 'there was a violent banging on our front door. My father went out to investigate and came back to say *there was a flap on* and he had to report at once to his A.R.P. signing-on depot (which was at the bottom of Clifton Street on the area known at The Triangle). He went out and we did not see him until the next morning. He said when he arrived at the signing-on depot they were told that reports were coming in that *crack German parachutists*, many in disguise, were landing *all over the place* and that they were to help the local Home Guard protect and guard as long as possible vital places in Exeter from falling into enemy hands. He and another warden were each given a pickaxe handle and told to guard the City Swimming Baths in Paris Street which they did all night.'

Monty Force was an Air Raid Warden and was the first person to reach Blackboy Road which had the first casualty on the 17th of September 1940. He recalled 'a young policeman joined me and we saw the body of a boy lying in the rubble in front of the bombed house. The house collapsed like a pack of cards. The bomb took the house out of the terrace as if a giant had sliced it out with a monstrous knife. We had walked from Elmside A.R.P. Warden's Headquarters about 10.15 p.m. and I was on my way home. I was on the opposite side of Blackboy Road from the one where the bomb fell. I heard this plane, and then there was a thump. I got down by the high pavement for shelter. A young policeman joined me and we decided to get back to the headquarters and call out the rescue squad. Then we saw the body of the boy. We knew we could not do anything more for him, so I went to call the rescue team, in case there were other people still alive. Our training had been that as soon as anything like that happened we had to report right back and get the various services moving.'[31]

Another warden was A.E. Puddicombe. He recalled bombing in St Thomas and said 'I was an A.R.P. Warden and had just turned the corner from Buller Road into Cowick Street when I heard the whistle of bombs coming down and I dived for safety into the passageway of Davey's cycle shop. The windows of Webber's Furnishing Store were blown in. A stick of bombs was dropped. One landed at Shooting Marsh Stile, another at the back of William Brealy's building yard in Cowick Street and another in the back garden of a house in Wardrew Road.'[32]

On one occasion David Smith's father attended a lecture given by a retired colonel from the Indian Army on 'How To Recognise A German Spy'. His son remembers 'they were told if they suspected anyone they were to try & view them from the side because there was one thing no German could disguise — they all had *thick bull necks*. They were to creep up behind them and shout *Sieg Heil* when the suspect, if German, would immediately come to attention and give the Nazi salute. They were then told to employ the help of passers by to detain the suspect while they went off to bring back a policeman to make an arrest.'

Firewatchers

Many volunteered for fire watching, some with the firm they worked for. Others spent the evenings in public buildings. Pam Coombes, not yet fifteen at the start of the war, 'used to fire watch in old St Sidwell's church with my mother and when the Plymouth blitz was on we went with the verger, we shouldn't have done it of course, to the top of the tower and you could see the red glow so high where Plymouth was. At the church I used to go fire watching with mum. There were a small number of us, probably organised by the church. We had light in the vestry but not in the church. We used to practice at the bottom of Longbrook Street in the green. We used to take buckets and stirrup pumps into that green to practice putting out incendiary bombs. We shouldn't have been any good at it but we practiced.' She also fire watched at work. She remembers 'you were encouraged then to do some war work. Mum went to work in the railway office and that was a reserved occupation. I also had a job with the railway office at the end of Queen Street – in one of the row of tall houses that were later pulled down. They had basements, with rats in them. We used to have to fire watch there as well. The men were in the Home Guard, as they weren't fit for service. They used to do their practice down by St David's Station. And the girls we used to take turns fire watching. Just the girls at night, maybe once a week. It was a bit spooky, they were old buildings and were all joined up in the attics. We would sleep in camp beds. We couldn't have got at any incendiary bombs on the roof – I don't think we could have done any good but we were doing our best.'

Commercial buildings had teams of firewatchers. Vera Ashford was in her early twenties working at Marks & Spencers on fire watching duties. She recalled three women and one man would spend the night on duty and when it was quiet the women would wash their hair. When the sirens sounded they would go onto the roof with their stirrup pumps and sand and water buckets on the lookout for incendiary bombs. Eric Wheaton was in his late teens and fire watched at the family firm. He recalls 'I fire watched at Wheaton's at least one night a week. I slept there in a camp bed. There was one man and one woman – the women slept in the typists' room – the men slept separately wherever. I would spend the night reading – we had a large stock of books there.' Margaret Ball fire-watched at the Church Commissioners' office at Stoke Canon and was paid one shilling per night.

Other watchers were in the streets. Helen Mann remembers her father's work when 'a large part of the war he was responsible for organising street fire fighting rotas for a quarter of the city. It was compulsory to cooperate. Some people made bizarre excuses to get out of it. He would tell us funny tales about it. This meant he was always out during air raids checking.' Olive Wakeham, in her thirties during the war, worked first as a nurse and then with the blind for the county of Devon. But then 'after a year I was allowed to do voluntary work and I was a firewatcher at Marlborough Road working under a senior man. I can remember very clearly using buckets of sand on incendiary bombs. They were up knocking the incendiaries off the roofs and we were on the ground putting them out. Oh yes, I became very expert on putting them out. We would work shifts of two nights a week. I had a navy blue uniform and the skirt lasted me for years. Our headquarters was Church House below the cathedral. About 2 a.m. the head warden would ring us up and ask *are you alert?* We had a camp bed with a horrible grey-brown blanket. The night before the blitz I had been on duty.'

Brian Pollard began work in the summer of 1940 at Devon County Council's finance department and stayed there until 1942. He recalls 'by this time male members of businesses and local government staffs in the city, usually working in pairs on a rota, would spend a night at their place of work and be ready to react to any emergency which might arise. It was so at the offices of Devon County Council which were at the castle in the centre of the city. My usual partner was Ben who, although of conscription age, was exempted because of a medical condition. He was able, nevertheless, to take his turn at fire-watching, as it was called. Our night duties were mostly uneventful until towards the end of April 1942. The air raid siren was quickly followed by the sound of high explosive bombs. Ben and I went to the ancient wall of the castle to see what was going on and very soon magnesium flares came floating down on parachutes. Knowing there were many telephone wires criss-crossing the pitched roofs, gullies and parapets of the council offices and imagining the problems should any of the flares become entangled, we made haste to the roofs collecting a stirrup pump on the way. Water tanks, sand bags and various tools were already in places among the roofs. We saw where the main danger lay and were in time to extinguish a flare which had rolled to a gully and had already melted the lead. The fire did not penetrate and so the day was saved. Ben lived at Tiverton some fifteen miles away and usually came home with me to have breakfast. On our way we saw a good deal of damage to buildings and some were still burning. The folk at home were unhurt but we had lost most of the window glass at the back of the house. It must have been an exploratory raid because ten days later, in the night of 3/4 May, they came again and that was far worse.'

George Barnes, also at the Castle, 'went to General Accident Fire & Life Corporation – at Southernhay West. I fire-watched there and then I was at Devon County Education Office from 1940 at Bradninch Hall. We also had to cover the county's library headquarters – at Barley Mount in St Thomas. In the early days there was nothing to it. There wasn't much activity. We would fire watch in pairs, bring our supper with us, probably arrive by bicycle. We would settle down and wait for something to happen – which it seldom did. We slept as well as we could, in a chair or something like that.' Another local woman recalls her fire watching duties at Bradninch Hall where there was a rota drawn from the clerical staff, they had buckets of water and sand to put out the fires, used long-handled shovels and slept in sleeping bags. (see page 258)

May Balkwill knows the arrangements for fire watching in Russell Street. In 1977 she recalled 'you had one fire watcher who was responsible for the street; he came along with his rota and said *Look, you're on Thursday night*. And so on. I was out there one night with this little man and my next-door neighbour. The sirens had gone; the searchlights were on up at the airport and the old bombers going zoom, zoom, zoom. We always knew when it was a German one: I don't know why – they seemed to be heavier engines and be slow. They'd do zo-om, zo-om, zo-om. We were watching the searchlights and suddenly the gun at the airport opens up. I thought, *Oh, they're shooting.* I watched the shells explode and when I turned I was the only one left in the street.'

The fire fighting equipment was primitive. She thought it 'ridiculous. You had a bucket of water for the brave intrepid fire fighter that was going to be at the end of the hose. And we had what is known as a stirrup pump and it fitted over the bucket. The intrepid fire fighter was supposed to lie prone and hold the hose pipe over his head and sprinkle the incendiary bomb while the rest of the gang filled the bucket up with a chain of water. One doing the pumping, one on the end of the hose and the rest of the gang kept the bucket filled – about five on a crew with luck.' Many others remembered the stirrup pumps affectionately, particularly former school boys who used them to spray one another. May Balkwill also thought 'the fact that these incendiary bombs came down in hundreds they hadn't coped for. We were told not to put a jet on the incendiary 'cos it would explode. You had to spread it to keep it under control. You were issued with an ordinary shovel that you used to put coal on the fire and a broom handle. If an incendiary fell through the roof, you were supposed to go in this room, always presuming it hadn't set fire to the room and shovel up this thing. According to their theory it would just be lying on the floor, shooting out a flame but not setting fire to anything. You just had to crawl into the room on your knees, shovel it up, carry it through the house, put it in this bucket of sand and spray it with yer little stirrup pump, with a tin hat on which had F.W. for fire watcher. If they got caught in the eaves of the house, you were supposed to go to the highest room in the house, lean out of the window and unhitch it. In the meantime all the heavy artillery is coming, kaboom, wallop; all the high explosive bombs falling all around while you're fiddling around trying to get this one little incendiary off the roof. The incendiary bomb itself was about two foot long, maybe longer, with this great flame on the end: we'd never seen one up to then. Not at all the old idea of a little round thing marked 'bomb' with a fuse on the end which we thought of.'[33] Another firewatcher was also unsure of a bomb he found near Pollards Printing Works. Jack Southwood recalled that he and the other fire watchers said 'aha, some new type of explosive device Gerry is using' and 'so they covered it with sandbags. The police recorded it as unknown object, about 10 inches long, 4 inches diameter, shiny metallic, cold to the touch, rounded at the ends and emitting a slight hissing sound'. They called in an U.X.B. squad but before they arrived it was discovered the bomb was in fact a large tin of pineapple with the ends blown out.[34]

Canon Michael Walsh recalls the time he spent at the Church of the Sacred Heart in South Street. 'I was here for a period of just over 12 years, here in this house. We used to have a wardens' point in the cathedral school in the crypt of their building, which is just next to us. The wardens used to gather there every evening especially when we had a siren going. We would wait for the worst to happen – don our helmets, carry out gas masks and assemble. And if there was a siren we went out into the street to warn people to get off the streets if possible.' He was part of the group of men and women since remembered as the Holy Firewatchers (see page 249). Others were also successful. Norman Watts, then fifteen years old, recalls how a friend at Ladysmith School by the name of Tony helped save his family's home in Blackboy Road. During one of the April raids he found a ladder and climbed to the top of the house to pull incendiary bombs out of the guttering. Maurice Pike remembers his father, Tom Pike, was one of four firewatchers who successfully defended the Co-Op building on the corner of High and Paris Streets in the midst of devastation all around them. They were officially recognised for their efforts by their employers. Others, however, died while carrying out their duties in other parts of the city.

Mrs E. Curtis' work may have been typical. She fire-watched at Boots, on the corner of Queen Street and High Street, in groups of four and recalls they also slept on the premises, their camp beds were in the upstairs library. However, she, like many others, also had other duties. Mrs Curtis combined fire-watching with washing dishes at night at the Royal Devon & Exeter Hospital for the Women's Voluntary Service and preparing and serving food at the Allied Services Canteen which was then at the Royal Albert Memorial Museum.[35] There were a great number of jobs to do.

Many did valiant service but some deserted their buildings. Canon

Michael Walsh recalls very few firewatchers were on South Street on the night of the blitz and thinks this was why much of the street was destroyed by fire. Edward Greenwood was a member of the team of firewatchers at the Royal Devon & Exeter Hospital in Southernhay and was left on his own. He remembered 'when Exeter seemed to be burning all the way round, the fire watchers apparently thought that their first duty was to their own families, for which nobody can blame them and I was left on my own.'[36] It is not known how often this happened.

Perhaps the account by one firewatcher immediately recorded after the blitz illustrates the dangers. Mr M. Robins was on duty outside a woman's shop. He said 'my mates and I were standing in the yard at the back of her shop. She was standing in her doorway. We could hear a plane circling overhead. Then there was a rushing noise and a bomb fell in the middle of the road not many yards away. Some of us were knocked down and we were all covered with dirt. We picked ourselves up and none of us were badly hurt. We saw the house next door was damaged and the lights were blazing. We ran and put them out, then someone said there were seven evacuee children in the house. We hunted for them and managed to get them all out unhurt. Then we went back to find the owner of the shop, but the place where she was standing was just a pile of debris. The rescue squad found her buried underneath some time later.'[37]

Red Cross

One local woman remembers the Red Cross Nursing Association and working evenings at the Royal Devon & Exeter Hospital in Southernhay. Another, Patricia Stacey, volunteered at Mardon Hall where the American Red Cross ran a canteen. She recalls 'we could be picked up from the bottom of Streatham Drive in trucks and we were all taken home after our canteen duty. There was a whole team of workers. We served up coffee and doughnuts mainly. They also specialised in American cheese – my mother thought it was great when I could bring back a bit.' Inside the main entrance was a picture of Anne Shelton, the singer. Mrs Stacey remembers that 'they were nuts about her. And her records were always playing.' Two of her friends met American servicemen and later married them. Mardon had square dancing among other activities. She recalls various bands played on the college campus including the Glen Miller band at Streatham Hall. On one occasion she remembers that 'I looked up and there was Joe Louis. He was in the army and came in with the rest of the troops.' She served him coffee and, probably, doughnuts.

First Aid

Many people took part in first aid courses. Helen Mann recalls 'Dad was too old for the forces. He was a fulltime paid Civil Defence worker & attended first aid courses. He used to try & practice bandaging etc on me. I was upset and scared that he would make it real on me.'

Dr Charles Marshall, who lived in Sidwell Street, looked after No. 2

The staff at the First Aid Post, Shakespeare Road, June 1941.

First Aid Post. He recorded his experiences and noted there were four others in the city, No. 1 was at Bull Meadow Road, the Alice Vlieland Centre with Dr Harris, No. 3 was at Shakespeare Road Centre with Dr Tracey, No. 4 was at Merrivale Road Centre with Dr Murry and No. 5 was a mobile unit run by Dr Trevor Preece. Dr Marshall later wrote that 'the posts were administered by dental surgeons, as captains and deputies of the posts (2). There were trained nurses as well, Miss Edds from the Health Department and Mrs Joyner, a retired nurse. There were clerks, first aiders, stretcher bearers, including some men on the permanent staff, car drivers and ambulance men.

No. 2 Post was taken over with the others the day before war was declared, when, although the staff had been nominated for the best part of a year, we held our first combined meeting. The following morning we met and got down to work. The Hall had to be blacked out and stores drawn and distributed, but basically, we were ready to function the moment war broke out. The main hall was divided into two sections, male and female, and the cloakrooms provided for male and female dressing rooms, and also an office for the captain and his clerks. One of the adjoining garages was adapted as a mortuary, and though some people queried the necessity it was in due course made use of. Others were adapted for decontamination from mustard gas. Though the procedure was well practised it was in fact never used.

On the sounding of the sirens all personnel proceeded to the Post. This was known as a 'red' warning, a 'yellow' warning meant alerting key personnel as enemy aircraft were in the vicinity but not necessarily heading towards the city. As time went on when it was found that aircraft were passing over frequently, the personnel reported in a rota, only making a full turnout when bombs were dropped.

The training, under the M.O., was carried out on the lines laid down by the Home Office, and worked very satisfactorily. We practised among other situations as if the electricity and/or water supply had been cut off, which fortunately it never was, and as if there had been a gas attack. Some primitive casualty simulations were practised; the writer was gratified to hear that one of the personnel had answered, when asked what it was like when the post was functioning, 'just like a practice, only with real casualties'. It was always a pleasure to train such a keen unit; all were determined to do their best if the unfortunate necessity arose, and when in the event their services were called for, no time was wasted in reviving fainting first aiders, there were none. It will be remembered that very few had any experience at all of accidents or illness.

The first bombs fell in Saville Road, St Thomas, in the summer of 1940, only a few and those not heavy, but it was a salutary reminder of the possibilities of the situation. The next attack remembered was towards the end of April 1942. Though widespread it was not made with incendiary bombs but with high explosives heavier than previously experienced, and destruction was heavy in the Paris Street area. The casualty intake was small at Wrentham Hall, so leaving the post in the care of assistant M.Os, the M.O. donned his steel helmet, painted white with the letters M.O. on it, and wearing dungarees went to Paris Street with Mr Selley senior, a mobile dentist, and one of our post administrators. There was in fact little we could do, but I can remember carrying a lad who was a casualty pick-a-back over the rubble to an ambulance and the place where I had the car. Later in the R.A.M.C. I was to learn that medical officers were advised to remain in the R.A.P. (regimental aid post) where they could be found and could give help more efficiently.

This attack caused considerable alarm, and people started leaving their homes at night to sleep in the fields of Stoke Hill and the like. However, Sidwell Street had its main services intact and we stayed where we were. The procedure when the siren went was for us to rouse the maid and the billeted medical student and pick up the usually sleeping small children and take them down to the Morrison Shelter in the dining room (later combined waiting room and office), the older girl (born 1932) following. We would then dress and my wife would go down to the shelter with the others while I went to the First Aid Post.' He also wrote of the work of the Post during the night of the blitz (see pages 242–6)

Home Guard

The Home Guard is one of the best known of the civil defence services. It was begun in May 1940 as the Local Defence Volunteers. Men aged between 17 and 65 who were unable to enrol in the armed services were sought. The numbers reached over a million.[38] Alf Wallen remembers 'in 1940 my father and I joined the L.D.V. – we served together. At first we had broomsticks to guard the Countess Wear Swing Bridge, once a week. Not very long after, a month or two, we had rifles. But at first we used our broomsticks and pretended they were rifles for drill.' George Barnes recalls 'the Home Guard were first known as the L.D.V., the Local Defence Volunteers and also Look, Duck and Vanish. On occasions they would man places like Polsloe Bridge and ask for your identity card. Nobody thought very much of them. They weren't exactly a laughing stock but a source of amusement'. One former young boy remembers seeing 'the home guard drilling with broom sticks before they had rifles, marching down through the streets, it was humorous, there were all sorts of jokes about the Home Guard because they were all either very old or very young. A bossy chap in charge and the rest couldn't give a damn really.'

Many have memories of their fathers serving in the Home Guard. Patricia Purchese recalls her father guarding the waterworks at Upton Pyne and the reservoir at Barley Lane. Her father told her a story of

The Home Guard in Exeter: the 22nd Devon (5th SR) Battalion.

The Home Guard in Exeter: at the County Ground, St Thomas.

one of the unit having lost his dentures in one of the water channels. Likewise, Sally Morgan was told by her father of his trials and tribulations in the Home Guard and commented, like many others, that it was very similar to the television programme 'Dad's Army'.

Nicholas Toyne was only five when war broke out and recalled 'my father joined the Home Guard, and was issued with a 303 rifle and five rounds of ammunition, an air rifle and a pitchfork! There used to be Home Guard Exercises in Duryard. Half would have berets on and

Members of Exeter's Home Guard.

the other half would have those fore-and-aft forage caps the R.A.F. used to wear. Slinking through hedges and whispering *Shhhhh* to us boys and *don't tell anyone where we are!* About 100 yards in Argyll Road from where you leave Pennsylvania Hill, there used to be a slatted metal seat for people to sit on and look at the view across to Haldon. This was flattened by a bren-gun-carrier on one of these Exercises. Its left track went right over the seat. I went last year, in 2004, to see if it was still there. It was! Still there flattened in the hedge!' Douglas Newbery remembers following members of the Home Guard when he was a young boy. He recalls their attempts at installing barbed wire which would roll down a nearby hill and being amused by it. Brian Le Messurier was a boy during the war and had expeditions from St Thomas in the lanes and fields towards Perridge. He wrote 'the valley was sometimes used as an exercise area for the Home Guard, and I remember seeing a platoon of 'Dad's Army' creeping along hedges near Clark's Pond. They had a slit trench in the hedge at the top of Crabb Lane, another high up above the bottom part of Little John's Cross Hill, and a third, protected with barbed wire, just inside the field at the top of Constitution Hill.[39]

One tragic incident occurred at Stoke Canon. Sheila Pike remembers two of her brothers being in the Home Guard with the youngest being only fifteen. On July 5th 1941, she recalls, 'fourteen members of the Home Guard were travelling in a lorry heading for a tactics exercise. At Dulford village the vehicle was in collision with a lorry laden with coal. Three of those travelling in the lorry were thrown out and two died instantly, one being my brother, the third person died in hospital.'

Royal Observer Corps

Members of the Observer Corps watched for and reported enemy aircraft across the country: some 30,000 volunteers manned more than 1,000 posts.[40] John Caldwell was a Recorder and his widow remembers how he monitored planes crossing Exeter and reported them to the Control Centre. The planes were recorded at the head-quarters along the quay. It later moved to Barnfield Hall. Young women would track the planes across a great map on a table. The room was thick with smoke. His widow, Christine, recalls avidly reading his leaflets which described planes. She also remembers 'I was living in St Leonard's Road and then had a newborn baby. I suddenly heard the sound of aeroplane coming in rather low and I rushed over to the window being a keen plane spotter and saw a couple of planes which I had never seen before. I was trying to think what they were and suddenly it went 'crump, crump, crump.' It turned out to be a *Messerschmitt Me* 109. They were absolutely brand new, no one had announced them at that stage, and Holloway Street had a very severe raiding. My biggest embarrassment was that I had taken my new little baby to the window to plane spot.' Mr P. Stacey had a similar embarrassment: on one occasion he was returning home to Newton Abbot after working in Exeter and from the train saw planes flying low up the estuary. As he was in the Observer Corps he was asked by a colleague what kind they were and replied Hurricanes but they turned out to be German. When the train arrived at Teignmouth the air was full of feathers – a bomb had hit a house with a flock mattress.

Eileen Reynolds was one of the girls who plotted the planes crossing the Channel. It was, she later wrote, 'quite an experience'. Revd John Benton remembers how his father 'fire watched at one stage at the hospital but then he joined the Royal Observer Corps and used to sit on the top of Dunsford Hill where they had a lookup. I can always remember one night – my mother used to give him sandwiches at night in a package and he never knew what he was eating as it had to be in the dark. One morning he came back and asked *What on earth did you give me last night?* It was something which was probably pretty foul.'

A.T.S. (Auxiliary Territorial Service)

The Auxiliary Territorial Service was begun in 1938 to release men for combatant duty. They had support roles, such as cleaning and looking after supplies, but after a year they were given more operational roles.[41] Among those who served in the A.T.S. was Margaret Ball's mother.

She remembers that her mother and friends joined in 1939 but did not expect England would go to war. They enjoyed the social side of it. She later wrote 'imagine her dismay when a brown envelope came through the door with her 'call-up papers'. It was no use saying she had a family, but the army was sympathetic and allowed her to work in Topsham Barracks and come home at night. She worked as a cook in the officers' mess all through the war.'

Norma Lodge was in the A.T.S. at Charminster where she was told she worked in R. Lo. M. – she subsequently learned that meant Radio-Location Mechanics. She later wrote 'we were introduced to the cabins that housed equipment to be used on gun sites for tracking aeroplanes more accurately. The cabins were mounted on wheels with fixed aerials, the whole cabin rotating! There was also a small version called S.L.C. – Searchlight Control – for mounting on a searchlight. The work was very complicated and highly secret. All our notes had to be locked away each night and extra study had to be done in the workshops in the evenings. We were still unable to tell anyone what we were doing so we remained *Mickey Mouse Mechanics*.' Then 'it was decided to

The A.T.S. on parade at the Royal Army Pay Corps Centre in Belmont Park.

send our Calibration team to Exeter for a few days to attend to the gun sites around Exeter. It was about April 1943 and an officer, a craftsman, three girls and a driver travelled there in a mobile workshop. This was a three-tonner which had workbenches and equipment down the sides and one across the middle. Once again we girls had to travel in the back. We were told to take our own bedding in case we had to provide our own on arrival at the A.T.S. camp near where we were to work. There were just two stools in the back, which we tied firmly to the benches towards the back of the van, near to the double doors that went across the back. We used some heavy equipment to hold these doors slightly ajar and then tied them across the handles to stop them from swinging open. This was to let some air in and it gave us a bit of a view, even if it was only where we had come from. One of the girls made herself a bed on one of the workbenches and we two endeavoured to make ourselves comfortable with our pillows at our backs. We travelled from Charminster to Exeter like this.

When we arrived at the town, one girl, Ellen, was dropped off at her home which was near Exeter; Alice and I were taken right out of town to a village called Topsham. We were taken to a large house in its own grounds about two miles from Topsham. This house had been

The A.T.S.: Civic Leaders recognise their work, at Belmont Park.

turned into A.T.S. Quarters for a small group of girls. We were told that this house was full but that at the rear there were two Nissan huts used as storerooms. They had cleared a small space and erected two beds and supplied us with mattresses. We were allowed to use the facilities in the house and they could provide us with breakfast and an evening meal.

In the morning, the men and Ellen came to fetch us to take us all to our first job. This was a gun site on the side of a range of hills, looking down over a valley and river. On the hillside on the other side of the river at quite a distance, we could just make out the sight of another camp. The personnel at the gun site, including the Lt i/c were not at all pleased to see us and we soon found out why. We had the 'plane circling overhead, but before starting, we took a look through the rangefinder. It was trained on to the camp at the other side of the river, which was occupied by W.A.A.Fs who worked nights and slept days outside, the weather being fine. They had no idea they were being spied on as they got ready for bed. However the job had to be done so we proceeded.

At the end of the day we were taken back to our billets. As we had been taken right through the gates and up to the house we did not see the name of the place and the only way we could recognise it was by the distinctive gateposts. They were tall brick columns with big round concrete balls on the top. On the way back the lads mentioned that there was a very good film being shown at a cinema in Exeter, and invited us to join them if it was possible to make it. *Very easy*, we were told. We just had to go across the grounds to the back of the estate. There we would find a locked gate – climb over it – turn right along the road and walk along for about 2 miles and we would come to Topsham Station. We would then get a train to Exeter Station. To return we had to get the last train from Exeter to Topsham; there was however a HALT Station before Topsham. We had to alight at this station, walk along the platform and on to the railway line and carry on along this line until we came to where it went over a bridge. At the side of this bridge there was a flight of steps down the bank on to the road and we would see the house gates straight ahead. As it was blackout in the country, we were advised to take a torch. What they had failed to tell us was that this was illegal and had to be done secretly.

All went to plan until we got out at the Halt Station. It was about 10.30 p.m. and pitch black. We walked along the platform but as we stepped on to the track, a man's voice shouted *And where do you think you are going?* It was the porter. He called us back, gave us a lecture on the dangers on walking on the track, possibly being hit by a passing goods train, and made us go down the station path on to the road. There was a junction of three roads and we were lost. As we stood there, a jeep came along with four G.Is in it. They offered us a lift but as we did not know where we were stationed, we had to decline. To our relief, we saw the porter put out all the lights, lock up the station gates, and cycle off. We crept back up, climbed over the gates on the platform and set off. We hadn't gone far when my pencil torch flickered and went out and we were left in total darkness. After a time we became accustomed to the dark and could just make out the line to follow. All of a sudden, we walked into a gate across the line – we had gone down a siding. There was no turning back as we didn't know just where we had turned off. We could vaguely see a road at the bottom of the railway bank so decided to get down to it. The bank was steep and slippery, covered with stinging nettles and brambles. We were wet and torn and stung but arrived at the bottom more or less OK. We thought that we had better continue the way we were heading, then we heard voices, but our joy turned to fear. It was a group of drunken soldiers. There was a hedge on one side of the road so we pressed into it and hid our faces, and they staggered past.

After quite a while we came to a gateway, looked over it and made out the outline of a house. We knew it must be very late but plucked up courage to go up to the house and knock on the door. A very nice old gentleman poked his head out of the window and asked what was wrong. We explained our predicament to him and described the gateposts of the house. To our relief, not only did he know the place but said that it was only a matter of about ten yards further on to the bridge and the steps. Fortunately, as we were not on the strength of the camp we did not have to sign in. We crept round the back of the house, found our Nissan hut and got ready for bed. The time was 2.30 a.m. When the lads came to fetch us next day and we told them about it, they roared with laughter but it was very far from funny at the time. Soon after that we returned to Charminster, and were very relieved to be back.'[42]

W.A.A.F. (Women's Auxiliary Air Force)

The W.A.A.F. was reformed in 1939 from the disbanded Women's Royal Air Force of the First World War. At first the women did everything that men did except for flying. This later changed.[43] Audrey Randell volunteered for the W.A.A.F. in 1942 aged eighteen in her hometown of Grimsby. She wanted 'to have more say in the kind of job I would be doing, having seen my sister being called up and weeping all the way to the railway station. My friend Gladys and I decided on this course after having left grammar school and finished up working in the town's transport office doing a very boring job. At the town recruitment centre I was given tests in English, maths, geometry, trigonometry and algebra, having left school only two years earlier I was able to make a reasonable job of it. I was told that as a result of my tests I was eligible for the highest paid job in the service which was R.A.D.A.R. and which was on the secret list – very much so. Everywhere one went there were posters declaring CARELESS TALK COSTS LIVES and BE LIKE DAD KEEP MUM. When I asked what the job entailed I was told it was either watching a radar screen with an arrow circling and reading the location, speed, height etc of the blips which were aircraft, or plotting the routes of all aircraft, hostile or friendly on a large operational table. I chose the latter.' Once she finished training her 'first posting was to No. 10 Group in Devon. In a remote country house in Pinhoe (near Exeter) we donned earphones and learned how to plot aircraft on the large operational table, discs in black and yellow were hostile and gave details of altitude and how many. When we got the hang of it we transferred to the real operational room, many miles below ground, with a balcony where officers watched progress and decided when to "scramble" our aircraft in defense. We lived in a Nissan hut with a stove in the centre that never went out and ten beds along one side and ten beds along the other side. I was on "A Watch", there were three watches and I hated the night watch as I had difficulty in staying awake.'[44]

Evelyn Huxham came to Exeter from Sherford near Kingsbridge. She joined in April 1942 and after a four-week course she became a Clerk S.D. (Special Duties). In 1994 she wrote 'at the end of the course I was posted to Politmore Operations Fighter Command, and with others, we were billeted with families in Broadclyst and Pinhoe near Exeter. This was the early days of radar. After about ten months, a permanent building was finished near Exminster although we already had a very primitive radar station in the marshes. This building would need many more people to man it. I was posted to Exminster as a radar operator with other young women and we were moved to live in Clifton House, Clifton Hill, Exeter. We were divided into three watches, A.B.C., which covered the 24 hours each day.' She was working on the 6th of June when the Invasion of France took place (see page 28).[45]

The Mortuary Squad

Sylvia Hart remembers her father's work on the night of the blitz when they did not see him for four days. She recalled 'my father was on the Mortuary Squad. Exeter Central School was used as a mortuary. There was a lot of Exonians killed and injured. I remember my father coming home, my mother asked *What is wrong*? He looked at me and tough man that he was he burst into tears. He told my mother that having gone through the Somme, Ypres, and throughout the first world war it was picking up the bodies of women and children he found hard. The majority of the people killed were buried in Higher Cemetery. Some people that were blown to bits were taken and buried at midnight again in the Higher Cemetery. Lists of the dead and injured were posted on the railings of Southernhay West.'

Scouts

Many former schoolchildren have memories of contributing to the war effort. For John Langdon, twelve at the start of the war, it was through the 11th Exeter (Hele's School) Scouts. He recalls 'my first summer camp July 1939 – Marazion – swimming, visiting St Michael's Mount and a tin mine. A year later it was in Mamhead – 2 weeks' hoeing swedes – no excursions or much fun (apart from visiting the girls' school which had been evacuated there). We put up Morrison shelters in peoples' houses. Many old people were not able to lift the heavy steel sheet which formed the roof. We collected waste paper and delivered it to the Mill on the Exe which was then a paper mill but is now a pub. Some of us had volunteered as messengers for Women's Voluntary Services (W.V.S.) in case telephones were put out of action by bombing.'

Women's Voluntary Service

The W.V.S. was launched on 18 June 1938 in London. It was started at the behest of Sir Samuel Hoare, then Home Secretary, and aimed to more fully integrate women into war work on the Home Front. Its

Manning mobile canteens was one of the many jobs of the W.V.S.

driving force was the Dowager Marchioness of Reading.[46] The W.V.S. made a tremendous contribution in Exeter. Olive Wakeham worked closely with it and recalls they were a 'rather better class of women but everyone could be in it.' She remembers the local organiser, Kaye Goddard, as being highly organised. George Barnes recollects 'they were everywhere. They did a first class job, with the evacuees, emergency feeding centres, handing out clothes to those who needed it. They were accepted – well-to-do people who didn't naturally mix with the working classes but they had a serious job to do.'

Ivy Facey helped her mother who was in the W.V.S. and recalls other women in the team including Mrs Stringer and Mrs Gliddon. Not only did her mother help with evacuees at the reception area in Queen Street but 'another job was at Exeter Hospital washing up the supper things. In those days there were 40 beds in a ward. At one time they were very badly off for helpers so me and my cousin turned up. The sister said *Oh, I don't approve of this. I don't expect you'd clean up as I want things.* But later a lovely letter came to my mother with an

The staff of the Allied Services Club, at the Royal Albert Memorial Museum.

apology saying she had been too hasty about youngsters not knowing their job and that I was brought up properly.' She also remembered that 'Sister Sanders at the casualty unit was a great personal friend of ours and if they got stuck and wanted help a call would come down. Another thing we did was rolling bandages at the hospital.' The W.V.S. women also 'used to go up to the club at Lyon's Cake Shop at the back of which were the Swimming Baths. There were tables and chairs for the servicemen, sandwiches and teas and coffee, including lots of Americans. Somebody was there all day, sometimes the Salvation Army.'

Sonia Collins recalls the Allied Services Canteen and the work there of the W.V.S. It was located at the museum. 'It was for any members of the forces. They were really glad of it. Before D-Day the city was full of all sorts of servicemen – Polish, Canadians, Americans – they all came to the canteen. It was open seven days a week. Young people would come in to help. There was a big screen, with three or four panels, covered in blackout material. Men and women would give their badges which were put there. I have wondered whatever came of it? Service-men and women would come in, a desk was inside and there were usually two W.V.S. ladies in their uniforms. They used to serve food through to the night till 9.30 – hot dogs, banana sandwiches (out of boiled parsnips, finely mashed, margarine, with banana essence) and one woman used to come in on some nights a week and she would cook chips. I was fifteen or sixteen and helped in the canteen kitchen. Eight or nine of us were on permanent work, on shifts. There was a billiard room there but the dances were over at the Civic Hall.' One of those who helped the décor was Helen Mann. She recalls 'I was always top of the class for drawing and painting. I was chosen to go to the Allied Services Canteen where I helped paint a mural to put around the walls on screens.'

Messenger Boys

Trevor Searle remembers how he was a student at John Stocker School and 'after the blitz all of us boys with a bicycle were sent out with messages for a few days.' Maurice Pike, who lived in Albion Street, recalls 'I was at Hele's School and went back on the morning after the blitz. But when I got there the school was closed and they said to me *If you get this consent form signed by your parents you could be a messenger boy.* So, when an enquiry was sent to the control centre, you would go and find this such-a-such person at this address. This was provided you could get into the address, and then find out if they were all right. Some streets might be closed off if they still had U.X.Bs and policeman or a warden would tell us we couldn't get in. Sometimes you would find that the place would be badly damaged or the people even killed. You would try to find out this information from a policeman or a warden.'

John Langdon volunteered as well. He recalls 'after the "all clear" sounded we could see the flames from burning buildings reflected in the sky so I telephoned my W.V.S. boss. She said that as the 'phones seemed to be working I would not be needed until the morning so I went back to bed. At 6 o'clock I got up, had breakfast and cycled in Scout uniform and steel helmet to her house. Her husband told me to go and find her at a particular "dispersal centre" (for people who had been bombed out). By now the telephones were out of action (no mobiles in those days!). Many Scouts spent the next 2 weeks cycling round Exeter delivering written messages for various other organisations like the Fire Service and Police. I wrecked my cycle tyres on the glass and debris which was everywhere. We could not have gone back to school anyway as Hele's was used as an emergency control

Some of Exeter's Messenger Boys.

centre to replace those council offices which had been bombed. One day I went out in the W.V.S. van to Monkerton where there was a huge store of clothing to be given to bombed-out families. On another day I helped man the W.V.S. canteen van serving mugs of tea in Bury Meadow.'

Air Training Corps

Bill Boam was one of the young men who joined the A.T.C. He recalls 'we learned Morse code, navigation, gunnery – in a hall in Normandy Road. There were two squadrons in Exeter.' 1169 Squadron was formed in 1941. Fred Squire was one of the founder members. He recalled 'at the time I was a pupil at the former Exeter Junior Technical School in Bartholomew Street West. Harry Russell Smith, who taught engineering subjects there at that time, made it known that the squadron was about to be formed with himself as Commanding Officer. Several pupils joined, including myself. I was given the number 88B which indicated that I was the 88th Cadet to join the squadron. The letter B indicated that I was a member of B Flight. I still have the A.T.C. lapel badge issued to me then.'[47] John Langdon remembers 'as well as the Scouts I joined 13F squadron (Hele's School) of the Air Training Corps and learned Morse code and air navigation because I wanted to become a pilot. We also learned gliding and got trips in R.A.F. & U.S.A.F. planes from Exeter Airport. Our summer camps were held at places like the flying boat base at Mount Batten, Plymouth. Flying boats were used to attack enemy U boats and in air-sea rescue. We also learned to march, something Scouts never seemed to manage, and took part in many parades through the city during National Savings Weeks. At one rally in the Civic Hall after H.M.S. *Exeter* was sunk in the Java Sea I remember hearing Admiral Sir Murray Souter say that she would be replaced and that Exeter citizens should save enough to at least pay for the engines. In the event of course it was many years before a new H.M.S. *Exeter* was built.'

Work for the troops

Women throughout the city knitted for the troops. Dorrie Langdon recalls 'at school great parcels of knitting wool were delivered, navy, air-force blue, and khaki, all to be knitted into 'comforts for the troops', scarves, balaclavas, gloves, socks, mittens and v-necked pullovers; there was always a scramble for the two blue wools. We were expected to knit at playtimes and lunch times and indeed take whatever garment home to get as much achieved as possible. I don't think anybody objected, except those who made a muddle dropping stitches or who didn't know how to turn a stocking heel or make anything more complicated than a scarf. It filled us with quite a great deal of satisfaction to see the completed articles, knowing how much they were needed.

Another activity we undertook was the making of field dressings, this was a communal effort taking place on the large boardroom table we had in our 6th form room. We had lots of muslin gauze

A considerable deal of the voluntary work involved raising funds. One of the greatest efforts was made during Warship Week in which the city of Exeter raised £1,054,500.

squares, of differing sizes and boxes of dried sphagnum moss which had to be placed carefully on a square then covered with more gauze. These were piled onto a calico square which in turn was folded over neatly into a sort of cube. Nimble fingers soon made up these dressings. The sphagnum moss had natural anti-biotic properties. The task completed it was my job on my way home to cycle to the Convent in Palace Gate to deliver the parcels. I had to ring the bell outside on the Convent wall; that door would be opened and then at the front door a nun would peer through the small grill. Seeing who I was and why I was there, she would open the door only sufficiently for me to pass the parcel through. What happened then I have no idea, but hopefully our small efforts helped wounded service men on the way to a healthy recovery.'

There were also individual efforts. Marian Wallen remembers how as young girls 'we used to sew little bags and fill them with lavender bags and go around and sell them. All the money was put for the forces.' Others also recall the miscellaneous things that they and friends or neighbours did on the Home Front to help win the war.

Salute the Soldier Week at Central Station.

CHAPTER

S T R A N G E R S — B R I T I S H

FOUR

During the war Exeter was full of tens of thousands of strangers. Their number and makeup continually changed. These evacuees, refugees, civil servants, foreign servicemen and workers altered the character of the city. The impact was greater because many local men, and women, were absent overseas. They themselves sometimes became strangers. Sidney Richards remembers that after his father went to war he failed to recognise him three years later: he was told at St David's Station 'there's your father' and fled. Other children had similar experiences of greeting what were virtual strangers. The parents of evacuees could also become estranged and many families suffered from the separation. Eileen Reynold's mother came back to visit after returning to London with her three-year-old sister before Christmas 1939. 'I do remember Mum and Dad once coming down to visit in all that time. It was just a day trip. They came by coach arranged by the school. I couldn't really enjoy it as all I could think about was that they would be leaving me in a short while. It was sad.' Many others have similar memories of being upset from the disruption in seeing their parents.

Many hundreds of British servicemen passed through the city while on duty and some came to visit friends and family. Dorrie Langdon, who was a pupil at Bishop Blackall School, recalls 'during this time there were three very welcome visits from my 'big' cousins. The first was Bill Phillips, he had been in the territorials pre-war, had been evacuated through Dunkirk from France. He was commissioned in the Royal Artillery and had some leave and stayed with my parents for a few days, he travelled to Greenock and to my great delight I was allowed to travel with him to stay with Uncle John and Auntie Marie. It was very exciting for me, a real adventure and I recall the reality was of the overcrowded carriages and corridors full of service men and their cases and kit bags. To get to the toilet was like a weird obstacle race, clambering over sleeping bodies all none too fresh or sweet smelling. I was very self-conscious at the mild flirtatious remarks, and the fug of so much smoking. However I had a lovely few days of my Aunt and Uncle's, Bill and Alfie's company, Ian was elsewhere in the army. The journey home was much the same as that to Scotland had been, long, crowded but by then I at least had a little experience and the service chaps were polite and I had no problems.

David Irvine was also on leave and came to us in Topsham for a few days, he was in the Royal Engineers, commissioned and I suppose quite good looking in his uniform. We had visited Exeter on the Saturday afternoon, looking around possibly even shopping. Imagine my amazement when I was summoned to Miss Ragg's study and asked for an explanation of my behaviour in town on the previous Saturday. It seemed I had been observed, arm-in-arm with an army officer, with rouge on my cheeks and laughing; what did I think I was doing? It was disgraceful behaviour for a girl attending Bishop Blackall School for Girls. Oh, I can hear her indignation now! I had been reported by the French teacher, a Mrs Shorter, to the head. Well, let it be said that my explanation of my cousin's visit to stay with my parents was accepted, very sternly, no hint of apology. The red cheeks were certainly not due to any rouge, I have never used the stuff. What <u>did</u> the French teacher imagine I was doing? The mind boggles at what would have been a proper punishment, the thought of endless lines or perhaps 500 conduct marks or even expulsion! This incident was always a matter of great amusement to my parents in subsequent years.'

The city hosted a variety of temporary visitors. Revd John Benton memories illustrate some of the range: his family had five phases of guests. The first were evacuees from Westminster Bridge Road. He recalls 'we came back from holiday in Suffolk a bit early because of worry about the war. When we got back there were buses up on the road – with mothers and children from Westminster Bridge Road being debussed and being put into houses. And we were asked, because we were a family of 3 in a house with 5 bedrooms, would we take these people. So we took in a mother and her pre-school child. It was a cultural shock – the way they lived was very different from the one we lived. They used to go out all day – they had breakfast, met up with their friends who came down and the children got absolutely filthy. My mother used to say *but aren't you going to bath him*? I suppose they felt uncomfortable, and I suppose we did too. Because London hadn't yet been bombed, they went back again. There couldn't have been many weeks before the bombing in London started. Then we had my cousins from Wembley. I suppose by that time London was being bombed so my uncle Harry sent his two children. In those pre-war days the cattle market was in Bonhay Road and they didn't have cattle trucks like today. A lot of cattle were transported by rail and some were driven through the city, they came right down Sidwell Street into High Street. My mother used to get anxious – I can remember on one occasion being pushed into the doorway of a shop to get out of the way. When my cousin Philip saw the cattle he roared with laughter. I had been brought up in Exeter and was very proud to be an Exonian. And for this chap to come down and laugh at us I was offended, I was really furious and aggrieved. I could even say I bear a grudge to this day. I was mortally offended that he could laugh at us for having cattle in the street. My mother had to have an operation so my cousins went off to my aunt in Bampton. We then took in some students from the London School of Medicine for Women. We had one student and then we had another – an older student, a Miss Roscoe. Then the authorities said to us, would you like to have somebody more long term. So we had the secretary, Marjorie Allen, nearly up to the end of the war. She became a great personal friend of my parents. And finally we had an army officer who was a Scot and was involved in transport.'

Helen Mann's family also had a great number of guests. She recalls 'we always had someone billeted on us, first a lady Observer Corps member. Then an Ashford School girl, they had Clock House, Countess Wear, for their school from Kent and they did not have room for all their boarders. Felicity Atlee was a pupil there, her father was subsequently Prime Minister. I used to go and play in Clock House in the holidays. Then we had an American Army officer billeted on us. Then we were made, of course, because he would bring us cans of peaches, chocolates, and other welcome extras. We kids were fascinated because he would eat toast & jam with his bacon at breakfast, unheard of to eat sweet and sour here at that time. He also got me a drawing board, I have it still.'

As extensive as these lists are, Exeter hosted an even greater variety of visitors.

Workers

Many came to Exeter for work during the war. David Harris was only six years old when his family came from Hayes in Middlesex in 1944. He remembers there were already a great number of Londoners who were thought of as aliens. He recalls of his accent local people would point it out to him and 'they always seemed to call me a Cockney which I wasn't. They took any opportunity to make us look silly'. Even so, years afterwards he finds it easy to understand how the influx of Londoners unsettled Exeter people. He recalls one woman in Exe Street preventing his younger sister from walking on the pavement outside her house. She stuck out her leg and his mother told her to push it out of the way, which she did with force. There were differences between his school in London and that at St Mary Arches: 'we had exercise books in London but when I went to school in Exeter we had slates and chalk'.

Dorrie Langdon's father was appointed Transport Officer for the South West and arrived shortly after Christmas 1941. She and her mother came to Exeter a few weeks after the blitz and did not know 'what to expect as Edinburgh had only a small amount of damage. I was just fifteen, leaving my school, my relations and my friends for the second time to live in a foreign land, it was a difficult time for me! Add to this the strange sights of a recently bombed city which was barely functional. No shops, just barrows or old tables and hastily improvised stalls in the streets or a clear bit of pavement or from the back of small vans selling vegetables, bread and groceries. The rubble, broken bricks, timber, bits of pipes, glass were all being heaped into great empty holes where shops and houses had so recently been full of life and activity. It was a traumatic time for our small family; my father had been lucky to survive the blitz, and we had suddenly arrived in an alien situation. Obviously we needed to shop for food and as mother and I tried to find our way around Exeter we were assailed by the truly awful lingering stench of burning wood, rot and decay from many varied sources. The memory is with me as I write. The property that my father had been able to rent was a semi-detached, three bed-roomed house in Jennifer Close. In the front room nearly all the floor space was taken up with a Morrison shelter. The room was only used when my Father and I or school friends played table tennis on the shelter top, the additional hazards of striking one of the large bolts only added to our fun. Sometimes we did crawl underneath the shelter and pull the wire mesh sides in place to lie on the mattress, it was claustrophobic. This was all so extremely different from my parents' house in Edinburgh with its beautiful furniture. However it was comfort-able, clean and undamaged and we were grateful to be a united family again. The pace of life was slower, the climate softer, the Exeter people were genuinely kind and friendly. My mother was much amused to be addressed by shopkeepers, bus conductors and strangers as 'me dear' or 'me love' or even 'me lover'. The last was almost shocking to a very correctly brought up Edinburgh lady, but she knew it to be spoken naturally with no thought of giving offence.'

Very little is known of the hundreds of civil servants from London who came before the war. Even now some people are reluctant to talk of their war work because it was impressed upon them that it must be kept secret. Margaret Lander kept a diary of her experiences which included living in London while her parents were in Exeter working for Whitehall. She wrote nothing of their work here but the twenty-year old did mention on 26 March 1941 'Mum came home at 5.15 p.m. Her train from Exeter was machine-gunned by a Jerry – exciting! It's good having her back.'[48] The only one to be interviewed is a woman who came from London with her husband who worked for the Admiralty making charts in Bedford Circus. She recalls of Exeter 'I thought it was very nice. Though down there I was worrying about my family in London and I was the one that copped it. It was lovely when we first went there and I thought we were lucky to get away from London. We were able to go to places like Dawlish.' No other civil servant has yet been discovered.

Black Shirts

Another group came into Exeter from outside: Sir Oswald Mosley's Black Shirts tried to rally support for his British Union of Fascists at least four years before the war while he was campaigning for Britain to refrain from fighting Germany. There were several fascist parties throughout the 1930s but the British Union of Fascists became the largest when it was formed in 1934. Mosley became its head and modelled it on its counterparts in Italy and Germany.

While it is commonly held that Exeter, like the rest of the country, worked closely together for the general good and that it was a united front against a common fascist enemy, this belief overlooks the participation in far right politics. It is unclear how united Exeter was. Many have memories of the fascists. For instance, Lucy Kadzielska remembers 'my mother talked about the Black Shirts, she would say they were awful. She didn't think they were very nice, she was frightened.' Another woman, only sixteen when war broke out, had similar memories. She says 'I heard about them – always thought I shouldn't talk about it, like it was a secret. People used to say don't have anything to do with them.' Others have memories of neighbours being openly identified as fascists.

One former supporter recalls how 'Mosley came down to the Civic Hall and Joyce came down as well. He rented a hall to speak in. Mosley had tremendous presence. My father took me and my sister to Olympia to hear him. If you can imagine two young girls with all these chaps in their black shirts. I was then in a school in London and a friend of mine's brother was a Black Shirt and she also brought me to meetings. A tremendous number of people joined because of the theatrics. I think we were going through a funny time in the country, a bad time in the way of losing jobs. We were looking for a way out. I'm not sure people associated him with Hitler then.' Another remembers that some local people listened to what was said and felt that the party offered an economic solution to unemployment.

The presence of the fascists in Exeter is not universally remembered and is strongest among those who lived in areas which had open-air meetings. Canon Michael Walsh was in his late twenties when he came from Ireland to serve as an assistant priest at the Church of the Sacred Heart. He reflected 'Exeter was really not a place where they congregated. They didn't have many supporters here, at least I imagine so. Mosleyites didn't disgrace this part of England so much, that way of looking at thing didn't catch hold of the people as much – there wasn't as easy ground for them.' Yet others have particular memories. Michael Payne, who was twelve when war broke out, remembers fascists' flashes suddenly appeared overnight on the city's walls. He assumed schoolboys did them. One former boy remembers seeing them marching in Holloway Street. Reg Southen recalls how in the years before the war fascists used to gather at the Drill Hall in Bedford Circus to 'hold parades. They were quite orderly, like a glorified Territorial Army, not of any great trouble. They would then go through to Cathedral Yard, but not in great numbers.' George Barnes recalls 'my elder brother told me about meetings they used to have at Waterbeer Street. They always ended up in a punch-up. They were very extreme.' Eric Wheaton was only seventeen when war broke out and recalls 'I remember seeing the Black Shirts in front of Woolworth's in the High Street. They were marching up and down, giving leaflets. Not a great deal of them, perhaps 20 or 30 of them, in their uniforms. I remember taking a leaflet and throwing it on the ground. This was in the daytime, perhaps in the middle of the afternoon, before the war. People were not taking much notice of them. I believe there were speeches but I didn't take much notice of them, some treated them with contempt.'

Most memories centre on open-air meetings at the Lower Market and many local lads enjoyed the spectacle. Norman Watts was only twelve years old at the start of the war and remembers 'they were organised in Exeter and used to hang out on Market Street, outside in the evening between 6 and 8. They would have talks with a few leaders from the area. Some followers were there, in their uniforms – brown boots, dark brown shirts and a flash on their arm, with leather belts. There were maybe a dozen, or two dozen, of them. A crowd of people would gather – they would stay for about an hour. This was before the war, in 1938 or early 1939. They were popular at first.' Arthur Blunt was a teenager and living in King Street. He recalls 'they used to gather on the corner at the top of King's Street – we used to gather and the Black Shirts (men and women). Eventually someone in the crowd would start to shout at them and then there would be scuffles. There were, maybe, altogether – young women and men – six or so dressed in their uniforms with a lightning strike on their uniform. People were hostile – arguments would break out and fights. It was good fun at the time.' Colin Hopkins was only thirteen when war broke out and recalls 'I used to go up to see the Black Shirts as they were called. Oswald Mosley and his wife were in Exeter a lot. He used to ride a motorbike. At the top of Smythen Street, on Market Street, he used to always be there on a Saturday night. He had a van with a little railing that went around on the top. He used to get up on the top and speak and of course he would get a crowd. People would come out of the pubs and heckle. Invariably they had to get the police. Mosley would have his men with him, I suppose you would call them his henchmen, stood all the way around. If anyone caused any trouble the police were there. It always ended up with the police fighting. He used to get off the top of the van and shoot away on his bike with his wife on the back. She used to speak as well. This was possibly in the very early days of the war – there were not any servicemen around then. They used to have followers – you'd see them – the ones with their arms folded – and the people dishing out leaflets. I would say there was a bunch of a dozen or so.' Another local boy, who lived in King Street, recalls 'I used to love them. Entertainment, that was why. They used to meet at the top of Market Street, on the corner where Spec Savers is now. They used to wear leather trousers. You could go into the old markets and pick up the old tomatoes. Once they started on their stands, they would start shouting and blasting away, in black shirts, I'm not sure if some had brown shirts. All of sudden questions would be fired at them, they would get stroppy, there would be fighting and us kids would be ready. I remember one saying *we are peaceful people*. And there was a great knife in a pouch – on his side. And someone would start and that would be our signal to throw fruit. It was on Saturday evenings. We were very disappointed when nobody showed up – us loved to hate them. There were maybe half a dozen. One of the main men had a shop in South Street near Bear Street. Some of them would flit down there to his shop. It was great fun. Maybe 1939 or 1940.'

The history of the fascists in Exeter has never been written. One collection of papers from a regional member of the British Union of Fascists confirms the oral histories. The party had its headquarters in South Street by 1936 at Number 22 and in early 1938 it moved to Number 19. Number 22 South Street was the business address of Mr W. Trenchard, an umbrella manufacturer, and several people recall he was a party supporter. At Number 19 was W.F. Pearce, a chemist. The Party also used 7 Queen Street. The Devon organiser until the spring of 1939 was R.T. Cotton of Branscombe who owned the Fruit and Flower Farm there. He signed many of his letters with 'Yours in Fascism'. His foreman, W. Lane, was also a member of the party. In the spring of 1939 Cotton was replaced by H. John Forward who continued fascist interests after the war.

It was probably Cotton the former boys heard. On 2 March 1938 he wrote 'the people of Exeter are getting tired of hearing me time & time again. Also its confoundedly difficult to think of new things to say speaking most in the same street one can't repeat the same speech and I have such little time for preparing them. If only we could get someone else to come & speak they might take more notice, anyway it could give them the idea that there is someone else in the movement besides Mrs Cotton & I'. In a letter the previous month he wrote he was 'hammering on with meetings in Market Street'. He also noted the party's supporters in Exeter were hesitant to show public support because 'they are all engaged in some sort of trade which makes it a severe risk of losing their jobs if they were to stand with me in the street'.[49] His letters confirm the local branch used a loudspeaker van at open-air meetings.[50] By May 1939 meetings were held not only in Market Street but in Goldsmith Street and at Exe Bridge in Gervaise Avenue.[51]

Gauging the level of support is difficult. One former boy remembers 'it was all the rage at Hele's School' in the 1930s. This fits in with national support: the Black Shirts have been described as being particularly popular in public schools.[52] The Duke of Bedford, after whose family Bedford Circus was named, was one prominent supporter of fascism but while he visited his estate in West Devon he is not known to have had great influence in Exeter or then been a visitor. Another possible local supporter was the Earl of Iddesleigh who lived nearby in Newton St Cyres. He was a guest in 1933 of the January Club, a front organisation for the fascists.[53] The local organiser canvassed through the city. He later wrote that he met with apathy: on one occasion he noted 'we meet apathy on every side. Sort of Why Do You Want To Try And Wake Us Up attitude' while in another letter he complained '98% about are just too damned apathetic to express the least opinion or interest'.[54]

In January 1937 it seems there were few active supporters[55] and some organised local opposition. Yet the following month one member informed another that the largest meeting to date had been held in Exeter. Robert Saunders wrote 'after waiting an hour while the Salvation Army were at work, I opened the meeting and received my first really bad heckling, from the members of the Young Communist League. They had been holding a meeting on the only other pitch – down by the river – where one of the number had been addressing two swans, three or four Communists, but no human beings. We, on the other hand, and thanks to their heckling, had a really large crowd in no time. After a bit thankfully handed over to Captain Hammond. He was at his best and gave a fine speech. His biggest hit was when he said to a Communist woman who had been keeping up a running commentary of heckling: *I quite realise, Madam, that your husband will not allow you to speak when you are at home, but that is no reason why you should inflict it upon me now!* It made the crowd roar with laughter and kept her quiet for five minutes! Now that we have active opposition in Exeter I think that we shall make great progress there.'[56] That July the *Daily Worker* campaigned to disrupt Mosley's meeting at the Civic Hall in Exeter on the 4th. One fascist wrote that for three days the headlines were 'Mosley speaks (he hopes to)'. The branch expected 'an imported red front as well as the local'. Slogans appeared urging 'Smash Fascism Now' and the fascists chalked before it 'You can not'. Nearly a year later, in April 1938, one fascist wrote 'I am particularly anxious to have a good meeting in the St Thomas district of Exeter. We have been canvassing two wards there and had a large number of people showing a desire to learn more about us and then the local labour candidate has heard of our efforts & has had a meeting down there to try to counter our results. This district of Exeter lies on the west of the Exe and there are no cinemas or Woolworths or market places there & therefore it is almost deserted on a Saturday night . . . this attack by the Labour party has made it essential to return with a meeting there as soon as possible and as I believe I explained, Saturday is not the best day for this district.'[57] A month later, in May 1938, a speaker was interrupted by supporters of Millwall who were playing in the city that day. A crowd of 300 gathered and the speaker, A.G. Woodgate who lived at 58 Oxford Street, later wrote 'then one commenced deliberately to urge the crowd to attack us and it is a sad commentary on Exeter justice that the police, instead of arresting him as they should have done, made us close our meeting.' Woodgate had just moved to Exeter and became active in the branch at that point.[58] In December Mosley spoke once again and it was claimed that 'the Reds have given the Exeter members a rough time of late. And their police have not been too good, I am sorry to say.' The police appear to have altered their policy in 1939: it was claimed on May 23 they 'close down our meetings at the slightest hint of trouble these days'[59] but then, less than a fortnight later, it was reported 'the police turned the Reds off our pitch, so that was o.k. I had quite a bit of heckling and a really good audience. The police changed their attitude and were standing no nonsense from the Reds. One man was warned by them for pushing his cap down the loudspeaker, and later when he tried to climb onto the van, they arrested him. The Exeter members seemed quite pleased with the meeting and with the new policy of the police.'[60] The clash of Communists and Fascists was nationwide and it was at this time that the Communist Party began to challenge the British Union of Fascists in local elections.[61]

Exeter was clearly not a priority for the British Union of Fascists but it still attracted the national leadership. Mosley would have passed through Exeter when he campaigned for Lady Astor in 1919,[62] is known to have visited the West Country on lecture tours and to have been a guest at events put on by the National Union of Farmers. These have been described as being 'more relaxed and informal' than the violent marches and demonstrations in more urban parts of the country.[63] He was in Exeter on at least four occasions including 27 November 1936, 3 July 1937 and 9 December 1937.[64] Many in Exeter have remembered rumours that the mother of William Joyce, better known as Lord Haw-Haw, lived in Whipton. Joyce spoke in Exeter at a 'Speakers' School' in early January 1937. One member later wrote 'we had a wonderful time during the weekend. And also learnt much! About 25 at the school – a number which Joyce was very pleased with. Joyce was wonderful! Even those who use to think little of him now regard him as almost a demigod! The least one can say is that he is a very remarkable man.' Joyce left the Party shortly afterwards and fled to Germany at the start of the war.[65]

It is not known if local members were interned but there was some residual support and interest in the national effort to revive the fascist movement; the Duke of Bedford re-launched his British People's Party and Mosley also began organising a new party. While one Exeter supporter, identified only as 'Jack', possibly H. John Forward, wrote to a regional organiser that any local activity would harm his local business interests[66] there was continued local activity through the late 1940s and into the 1950s. One man recalls 'during the war I heard or saw nothing of these in Exeter. For a short period or so (1946–7) small fly-stickers appeared regularly on Fridays (market days?) along Gandy Street – self-advertising but neither offensive nor propagandist. I assumed that they were put up surreptitiously by persons coming in on market day. These stickers usually disappeared within 24 hours of being put up. I do not remember seeing any fascist slogans or graffiti.' In 1948 one local leading light was H. Jameson-Dixon of Silverton. He claimed to have been a 'pioneer' in the movement and had moved to Devon in 1939 to escape being interned. In February 1948, even before the city centre was rebuilt, a conference was held in Exeter to coordinate the re-launching of fascism in Devon.[67]

Evacuees

Exeter hosted thousands evacuees. In March 1941 it was estimated that there were more than 12,000 with the same number of refugees. The majority came from London, Middlesex, Croydon, Penge, Kent and Bristol. Some arrived with their mothers but many more were sent without any family members.[68]

Olive Wakeham is one of many who remember 'the vacs' and the profound impact they had on Exeter. She organised welfare for the blind in Devon and recalls a tremendous social effect the Londoners in particular had. She reflected 'the Londoners would teach us things – they taught us a lot including how to scrounge. They knew how to get money, they knew what they wanted. Devon had a reputation for being slow – slow to speak, slow to anger. They taught us that we had rights, that we could claim things – what we were entitled to. We were really simple Devon folk and we had been quite docile and mild and did what we were told to.' Another Exeter woman remembers the evacuation scheme as a great social exercise, of throwing different classes and generations together. In some instances, she felt, it worked tremendously but in others it was disastrous. Her memories are of Exeter householders desperate to have older students and not children who were often unsuitable for older people. She also remembers the anti-Semitism, particularly how refugees were sometimes called refu-Jews. Another resident recalls 'we didn't have evacuees. I remember a lot of evacuees were once brought into our road to find homes but my mother wouldn't have any. My father was quite annoyed by it.'

Children poured into Exeter in the first few days of September 1939. Nearly all came by train. Ivy Facey was only twelve at the beginning of the war and recalls helping her mother at the Civic Hall in Queen Street which was a reception area for evacuees. It was cold and drafty. On one occasion, for three days, she cut sandwiches and recalls her mother and the rest of the W.V.S. team would 'feed them sandwiches and soup. Then they took all their details and later new rations books would be given. They were supplied with clothes. They used to come down by the train-full'. Douglas Newbery was a young boy himself and watched the stream of evacuee children being paraded through the streets of St Thomas in search of accommodation. Columns of several hundred children were brought door to door with householders picking which child they would take. Kathleen Fletcher was only nine when war broke out and recalls 'what moved me greatly was when the evacuees arrived. It made such an impression on me. I was standing at the high street and traffic was stopped. They were walked down the High Street toward the Guildhall and I thought what a humiliating thing to do to them. People were very sympathetic and watching but it was as if they were Exhibit A – walking along with their cases, some with their mothers, in the midst of all these people.' Marion Waller also saw them come to St Thomas. She remembers 'you felt so sad – the dear little souls. People would say *I will have these ones*. I think it was down in Buller Hall. They came by train. We had quite a lot in St Thomas. We didn't have a lot in our actual street.'

Many have memories of their parents taking children in. Irene Lyne remembers the London evacuees at her parent's home in Willey's Avenue. She recalls 'two mothers had become friends on their journey here and wanted to stay together. So Mum, being good-hearted, took them both in. It was very cramped in our house but they were very nice. In time, as things calmed down, they went back to London.' Desmond Dunn was also then a young boy and remembers his mother taking in London evacuees at their home in Burnthouse Lane. They were infested with fleas and the house had to be fumigated. Several families stayed with them in the war. For one period he, along with his brother, sister and mother, shared one bedroom while the evacuees had the other two bedrooms. They shared the kitchen but largely kept to themselves. He recalls the evacuees arriving in a small bus with their labels and gas masks. Caroline Cornish lived at Culverlands in Union Road. She recalls that because it had seven bedrooms 'it was often occupied by many others during the war years, evacuees from London, medical students who lodged with us, army personnel (both English and American) who billeted with us, and friends who came and went 'on leave' or 'in transit'.'

Evacuees also remember their time in Exeter. Audrey Neville was fourteen when she was evacuated from London. In 2000 she recalled 'my wartime stay at 32 Duckworth Road in St Thomas was the start of 60 years of love and friendship. As a young girl, I was obviously nervous but I knew within minutes of meeting Mrs Lake that it would be fine. She took me to her heart straight away and was like a mother to me. During my two-year stay they treated me as their own, also welcoming my parents and relatives when the London bombing was bad.' She later wrote 'nearly 65 years later I am so grateful to the people of Devon . . . many good friends and relationships came from those dark years from both the evacuees and the foster families, and in my own friendship which has continued to the present day.' Her hosts had a daughter the same age, Joyce, who remembered 'I thought it was great when I was told there would be an evacuee coming. I didn't have any brothers or sisters and Audrey was like a big sister. We shared a room and had a lovely time.' They still remain close sixty-five years later.[69]

Brian Le Messurier is another. He was ten when he was evacuated from Guernsey in the summer of 1940 to escape the German occupation of the Channel Islands. He arrived at Weymouth in a Dutch bulb boat and then went to Oldham for three months. His parents settled in Exeter and he joined them at 61 Broadway in St Thomas. His first memory of Exeter was of seeing an abandoned bike in a hedge along the top of the garden – there to reinforce the hedge. His first thoughts were, while on a walk in Buddle Lane when an air raid warning sounded, that moves to make them safe were excessive. They took cover and went to a first aid station, in Merrivale Road, which was sandbagged. They were given air plugs to put in their ears and a piece of rubber for between their teeth in case bombs fell. This was all because it was so early in the war and it was a daytime alarm. 'We got a bit blasé after that – having once gone over the top – and then the blitz came and things really hit home.' On the night of the blitz they could see the cathedral from the flames and also the cupola on top of Cornish's on the corner of North and Fore Street. He remembers saying *Cornish's is still there and at least you will be able to get my school uniform'*. After the blitz they had a Morrison Shelter which became their dining room table. Next door there were two London boys living with the Bragg family. In the early evening before the blitz the Le Messurier family got off the bus in St Thomas, having just been to church, and the older of the two boys went off fire watching in the city centre. He was killed in the bombing that night.

Robert Crayford remembers how he was evacuated from London. He was 'hastily bundled on to a train at Clapham Junction at the age of just 10 with hundreds of other children, a cardboard label tied to one of my buttonholes and another to my small bag of possessions, for what seemed a never-ending railway journey to somewhere remote and unknown. For all we were told (was it for security reasons or not to alarm us?) was that we were going away somewhere away from air raids. We must have been on that train for almost 6 hours and so got used to being told we were not there yet every time it made one of its numerous stops. When at last we were told we were there, we swarmed around all over the platform like an army of locusts, certainly equally as hungry! When I discovered we were at Exeter I, at any rate, was overjoyed for I had relatives there and so did not feel, as many of the others must have done, so cut off from home, which in my case was with my grandparents with whom I had lived from the age of 4, just before my mother died. My aunt, uncles and cousins all made me feel very welcome but they could not put me up as they had several soldiers billeted on them already. However, if they had done then I would never had known the kindness, infectious good humour and mental stimulation of the people I was billeted on.' Not long afterwards, in November 1940, his grandparents moved to Exeter 'with the intention of making it their home and so, of course, to my unbounded delight, mine also. My grandmother was overjoyed at all the countryside so close around her and I walked miles in it with her along lanes which must have been as quiet and free of traffic in those wartime years as in her Victorian childhood.'[70]

John Mander was evacuated from Kennington to Whipton about the age of nine. He recalled 'I first went to Seaton for two weeks, returned to London, then to Somerset, then to Whipton having travelled from Martock, you were taken to the station all tagged up as to destination and put in the charge of the guard, no one came with you and given from guard to guard on transfer of trains and only 8 years old. We must have been tough in those days.' He did not know any other evacuees although there were refugees living with their relatives. He was separated from his sister, who lived in Heavitree, but their mother later came down and the three of them went to lodge, happily, with a Mrs Crees. Four children all slept in the same bed 'toe to toe'. He went to the local school and then to Ladysmiths School where he walked instead of paying the penny fare. His memories are of hay-making, catching rats and collecting shrapnel. The family returned to Kennington in 1946 when his father returned from the war.

A series of letters survives relating to the evacuation of a London girl by the name of Pamela Daymond. She stayed at 3 Baring Crescent and the correspondence shows the level of care some evacuees had. In one letter to her mother of January 1941 her host Miss Frideswill Every wrote 'I thought you might like a letter from me as Pamela is billeted here with her schoolfellow Jean Cocking. My mother and I are glad to have them, and they seem to be settling down quite happily. We had a siren yesterday evening but nothing happened. However we made up a bed for them downstairs instead of their own bedroom upstairs and they slept quite peacefully. I am going to keep extra specially careful watch on Pamela's health as she tells me she gets asthma and bronchitis and as that is the very same thing that I also sometime get badly I can sympathise and shall do all I can to guard against it for her without being too fussy! Please will you let me know anything special you want about her health . . . both girls are being so good and nice to have in the house. They are still a bit shy but that will soon be mended! I am interested that they are both guides as I am a Ranger Captain and have been a Guide for 27 years.' Pamela was brought to a farmhouse in Bridestowe after the house was destroyed in the blitz and then later remained with her hosts when they found a bungalow in Moretonhampstead.[71]

The letters also shed light on the difficulties caused by bombing. On the 26th of April 1942 a letter was sent to Mrs Daymond with the news 'I daresay you have heard through Miss Fox that Exeter has been receiving attention from Jerry. If not, would you please contact her, before making your arrangements to return Pamela here as I think Miss Rabson has written her full particulars. My position at present is that I returned with Jean from the country on Friday – found they had had a raid – slight on Thursday night. Friday night we had a fairly brisk raid, a lot of widespread damage & casualties. I drove all the morning for the 'Public Assistance' & we had a daytime alert & I guessed they'd come again so I took Jean (and Barbara as her hostess was glad I should do so) out to Thorn Farm again yesterday afternoon & left them there in charge of Mr Hill who are old friends whom I trust as if felt I must be here with mother & helping with W.V.S. & Public Assistance. I propose leaving them at the farm until Wed. if Monday & Tuesday nights have been quiet I shall have Jean back & Barbara will go to Mrs Gould also but if not I am suggesting they should come in to School by bus daily for a little while until Mrs Cocking settles what she wishes. Under these circumstances if you like you could phone thro' on Tuesday evening (I shall be out 7–10 but Mother would answer you). I expect if we get more 'attention' you will prefer to keep Pamela anyway for the time being. I forgot to say that this last night we had two sirens – but only one incident but it was an H. E. and incendiaries about 5 minutes walk from here. It shook the house but did it no damage. I was glad I'd taken Jean back to the farm tho' for her sake.

No more now – I must get some sleep, I've been driving again all this morning.' She added two postscripts 'of course we may be left alone now – last night's main objective was not us but 'the place at the <u>top</u> of <u>our stairs on the left</u>!' and 'give Pam my love & say I <u>hope</u> there will be no need for her to have an extended vacation'.[72]

However, only ten days later, on the day after the blitz, another letter needed to be sent. She wrote 'both girls are safe & well. Our house & all furniture burnt & most of our clothes – practically all except some clothes & what we stand up in. I evacuated the whole family early here & have been in Exeter to get Emergency Ration cards & forms to claim war damage compensation & clothes coupons. The Southern Railway is functioning today irregularly – just some trains when it can. Shall I send Pam back by Southern Railway approx. 12.50 train on which day I get your reply? Please try to contact Mrs Cocking so that the girls could travel on the same train. We are ten miles from Exeter.

No more now, thank God we are all safe. The girls have been so good – I shall be so sorry to lose my charges. But Exeter is no place for them. It is very badly blitzed tho' still not quite as bad as Plymouth.'

The young evacuee also sent a letter to her mother. She wrote 'dear Mummy and Daddy, we had a terrible raid on Exeter this morning. The warning sounded at 1.45 a.m. We got up and went downstairs. Soon the planes were over and bombs were dropped. Jean and I dived under the dining room table. Then Mrs Every went upstairs and shouted or rather screamed that the house was on fire. We all went upstairs and Jean and I took turns in pumping the stirrup pump and the water was coming out the top and Jean and I got soaked as we only had a nightdress, bed jacket, dressing gown and raincoat on. While we were pumping Jerry dropped H.Es and it blew the windows in and it blew Jean onto the floor in the pool of water that the stirrup pump had made. Then I went into the bedroom and just got the things which were on the chair by my bed and went downstairs and stood in the passage leading to the kitchen and Jean and I were awfully cold as we had wet things on and the window had been blown out. Then the roof fell in and H.Es still dropping near us and when it had quietened down again we went out the back door and gate and went across to the children's home where they were bringing in patients from the city hospital. Then we went to No. 9 The Crescent and then we were lent clothes. We stayed there until about 7.45 and then we came out to the farm which is about ten miles away from Exeter. We've hardly got any clothes left. I have lost my new hat and coat and also my glasses in the fire. All I have is a pair of shoes, also slippers, stockings, 1 pair knickers, 2 bodices, 2 vests, 1 nightdress, 1 bed jacket, 1 school blouse, 1 dressing gown and rain coat. That's all I've got . . . Don't come down to fetch me because you couldn't sleep here at the farm. It was absolutely a nightmare as we were having dive-bombing. Mrs Every hasn't a stick left of her house except 2 pictures. The house is absolutely gutted. Nothing left of the house except the 4 walls. Hope you are all well. See you soon, love Pam'.[73]

Some adults only knew evacuees in a professional capacity and thus have particular memories. Canon Walsh recalls the evacuees coming to the Church of the Sacred Heart in South Street. He said 'there were a certain number of evacuees. I'll tell you now, there was one particular school billeted here in Exeter. There were a number of Catholics amongst them. Some used to come to mass and one day I picked up one of them, who must have been seven or eight, and said to him *now will you preach to us? What are you going to say to us all today?* as a bit of fun. I didn't realise how prophetic it was going to be – that young chap later became a priest.'

Sylvia Hart has particular reasons to recall the evacuees arriving from both London and Bristol. She later wrote 'they came around asking for people to take evacuees. We had two boys at first from Fulham. I ended up marrying one of them in 1951. Let's see that is 54 years this August. No wonder I've got the V.C.! or should have, Ha! Ha!' He was only with them for six months but the romance blossomed later while on a visiting holiday.

Not all memories are pleasant ones. One woman used to come to Whipton when a young girl to visit her grandmother who had three London evacuees. Her principal memory is that one of the boys used to expose himself to her. Another woman remembers her brother took exception to their evacuee because he thought she had 'most awful habits'. Nevertheless, for a short while the family kept in touch with her after she returned to London. Afterwards communications stopped and they continue to wonder if she was killed in the subsequent bombing of London. Conditions could be hard. One family found that the prim spinster with whom they were billeted objected to any noise so they played 'Happy Families' as quietly possible in order to keep their daughter, and hostess, happy.[74] One former policeman recalls some evacuees were involved in crime. He remembers 'just a few of the older ones, particularly if they were in houses that didn't care for them – that pushed them out all day. If the householders weren't the caring kind, there were problems. They got up to petty crime. But the ones that treated evacuees as part of the family, they fitted in'. Donald Sheppard recalls Percy, the London evacuee who his family hosted in their home in Cowick Street. He remembers 'they came down the street. These poor kids had labels. We had one for a short spell but he had something wrong with him. He went into my room and I went into another. That was a dramatic event. My mother went into his room in the morning and she came rushing out saying *he's not there – he's gone, his bed hasn't been slept in.* And he was underneath the bed, he had never slept in a bed, he had always slept underneath his parent's bed. It was what he was used to. He became ill, went to hospital and we never saw him again. A lot of them went back home again, masses of them came but gradually drifted back. For a short spell there were masses of kids around.'

Some hosts also had bad experiences. One woman, sixteen when war broke out, recalls she was living in St Thomas and 'a coach came up the road. Most people had said what they would have, either a boy or a girl, that is if you could fit them in with bedrooms. There was one girl sat there alone – called Lily. Our house was full. I was looking at her and said to mum *no one wants that little girl. She could come in with me, in my room.* The four boys were in the big room with two big beds. Mum said *she will have to go in with you.* She came from London, had a rough upbringing – never heard from her parents. I had the worst nights I ever had – with bedwetting. I tolerated it for so long, a few weeks. And said *Mum this is awful.* And we had trouble at school – taking things. It went on for some time. Her birthday came and there were no presents or card come. Eventually she went back to the authorities and I suppose she went home to London. We never heard from them. I would imagine her life was pretty rough.'

Some evacuees continued to live in Exeter after the war. Others did not return to their own homes for less happy reasons. Doreen Walker was a young girl living in Isca Road during the war and remembered two London evacuees who had been playing near the railway line in Bonhay Road. One stepped into the road and was killed by passing traffic. She thought 'how ironic that he left London to escape death by bombing and lost his life so tragically here in a road accident. The whole neighbourhood of Fortescue Road where the boys were staying were deeply disturbed by the tragedy.'[75]

Refugees

Many hundreds of people came to Exeter on a private basis and some stayed with friends and family to escape danger perceived back home. They were known as refugees. Two have since become well known. Rabbi Lionel Blue came as a young boy in 1939 and later wrote 'I learned a lot at Exeter. I did learn manners, which were much admired in the ghetto when I got back later. I opened the door for ladies, and was specially polite to skivvies and charwomen. I doffed my school cap . . . in Exeter I also learnt to tap dance. I was getting obese on a self-chosen diet of faux doughnuts with false cream. The school doctor suggested rugger or running from lamppost to lamppost. But Aunt Poppy said there was a Jewish family in Exeter, and their daughters ran a dancing academy. So I became a hoofer instead and shuffle-hopped along with the chorus, occasionally tripping up the whole line . . . I also had a special turn and a sweet plump girl called Sarah with a very nice nature who was appointed my partner as we shuffle-hopped across the stage warning rabbits in song to Run, run, run! Now that the farmer's got a gun, gun, gun.'[76] Bertha Glynn was fourteen at the time and recalls 'Lionel Blue used to come into our shop on Sidwell Street with the people that he was evacuated with. He was a brilliant little boy, they used to fire questions at him – he was a clever little boy.' Her sister Sarah was his age and recalls 'he was evacuated to a family, I think the Grangers. My sister Stella had a dancing school and Mrs Granger brought him to our mother's shop in Sidwell Street. As we were a Jewish family Mrs Granger thought it would be nice for him to meet us. We went together to a fete once in Exeter. He was a very clever boy and they billed him as the Wonder Boy, and I was the Wonder Girl – I was known as Exeter's Shirley

Temple. And people would fire questions at him over geography. We used to sing a song together 'You Can't Black Out the Moon'. The second is Daniel Patrick Carroll, an Irish-born thirteen-year-old who left London to live at Kennford during the war. He later changed his name to Danny La Rue. He wrote that he enjoyed his time in the countryside around Exeter and later worked at Colson's as a window dresser.[77]

Some refugees had Exeter connections. Eileen Reynolds' father was from Topsham and her mother brought her and her three-year-old sister from London to stay with her uncle and aunt. They had a difficult start when they left on September 3rd. She later wrote 'my Dad took all the family on the bus to the Elephant & Castle tube station. The tube would take us to Waterloo Railway Station for us to board a train to Exeter. As we were descending on the escalator over the tannoy came the famous words of Neville Chamberlain *this country is now at war with Germany*. There was total panic: people collapsed and the next thing we knew we were all falling on top of each other down the escalator. Fortunately no one seemed to be seriously hurt. My mother's thoughts at that moment, as she told me later, were that the skies would blacken over with German planes.' The three of them travelled safely to Exeter but arrived late. 'No one had come to meet us. We asked a man where we would find Mr Rutter, 18 Rugby Road, and luckily for us he was their window cleaner and kindly took us straight there.'

She also remembers celebrating Christmas in 1939 at the evacuees' Rest Rooms at the cathedral and later wrote 'we went into the cathedral where there was a huge Christmas tree, almost touching the ceiling, crammed full of wonderful presents. The Bishop of Exeter (I believe his name was Mortimer) was there to present us all with a gift. It was so exciting and the most wonderful thing to happen to us since leaving London. I remember a photograph being on the front page of the *Express & Echo* of the huge tree and the bishop giving my sister and me our gifts.'

Like some others her time was not at first a pleasant experience. 'It was a very unhappy time at Auntie's. She had never had children of her own, and wasn't fully prepared to take us on. We were treated as if we were in bed & breakfast and evening meal. We had to be out of the house by 8.30 a.m. in the morning in all winds and weathers and were not allowed to return until the evening meal, which we ate separately in the kitchen. When I wasn't at school, like weekends and holidays, we spent most of our time in the shelter in St Thomas's Park which was almost next to the house, or we would go to the rest rooms for evacuees – which was a building next to Exeter Cathedral. We had happy times there. The people in charge were kind; we had cheap meals and played games.' She, her mother and sister were there for only a few weeks and then lodged in another house. By Christmas her mother returned to London with her sister and Eileen was brought to Pinhoe where part of her school had been billeted. For two years she lived with Miss Wills who owned the local bakery. She later wrote she 'loved going in the bakery room to deliver cakes and bread with George, one of the deliverymen. The 'maid' called Stella was so nice and kind. She cooked the breakfast for us and the deliverymen, and also served in the bakery shop. Another girl called Jane was billeted with me. One day we had a lovely surprise. Stella took us both to the huge restaurant in Bedford Street, Deller's, sadly bombed in the Exeter blitz of 1942. It was a wonderful experience. We went up in the bal-cony where we had silver service tea and assorted cakes, looking down to the Palm Orchestra below. I will never forget it.'

Nicholas Toyne was another refugee. He arrived in Exeter at five years old and later wrote 'my father, Wystan Toyne, was a solicitor in Birchington, Kent. In July 1939 he decided that because of the "war clouds gathering" he would take his family, my mother and myself, down to Devon to live. We arrived in Exeter in our little open Morris 8 Tourer after 8 hours travelling. We moved into a top floor flat in Heavitree just below the garage on the main road. My father found a job with Exeter City Council as Assistant

The interior of Deller's Café.

Town Clerk under Mr Newman. After a couple of months we moved into a rented house in Marlborough Road. I went to "Miss Johnstones" junior school in Polsloe Road. After a year in Marlborough Road my father bought "Farthings". It was the third house down on the right hand side in Argyll Road at the top of Pennsylvania. This gave us a marvellous view over the whole city. Being in the private estate of Duryard the road was unmade-up with large pot-holes. Several times a year nearly all the owners of homes in Argyll Road got together and bought lorry loads of 'clinker' from Exeter's coal-powered Power Station and with garden rakes and rollers made the road a little easier to drive up and down. Petrol was severely rationed, but my father had an extra allowance for his job with Exeter City Council to allow him to travel all over the city. At this time Devon had air raids and we would see the occasional German plane flying about. For me at 7 or 8 years old this was very exciting. Imagine the sirens sounding and giving their awful up and down cadence, then my mother would say *I think we had better get under the kitchen table now*. If it was in the middle of the night, to get up and have a picnic and cocoa with your parents and Labrador dog under the table and hear big bangs outside was great fun for a small boy! We did have an Anderson Shelter dug into the garden. It made a great 'den' during the day. Daylight raids on Exmouth happened sometimes. And on one occasion German fighters or fighter-bombers, three of them, obviously saw our hill-top and sighted our row of houses going down into the valley. They came across our view going over Exeter, turned to the right and aimed in line astern straight at us. My mother didn't like the look of this and so we ran for the wooden kitchen table and dived under it with the dog. At this moment there was a high-pitched whine from a, as I later found out, Rolls Royce Merlin engine. Coming out of the sun a Spitfire with R.A.F. roundels on its side and tail shot after them. They immediately broke off their dive and shot out to Exmouth, dropped their bombs and went out to sea. Minutes later the Spitfire came back and did a double victory roll; telling all of us cheering people in the street that he had got two of them! I was told later that it was very frowned upon by the powers that be for the plane to do this. It said *look what I've done* and used up precious fuel. But I'm glad he did. It is something that is etched in my mind forever.'

Another was Thelma Baker. She came to Whipton from Southampton in 1941 and recalled 'outside school hours we children used to play together in the street which you could do quite safely in those days and even go roaming around the area. Nobody stopped us. We went miles and in the autumn often helped ourselves to apples from people's orchards. Despite the war, they were very happy times. We had a lovely childhood. Like me John remembers the wizened old lady who lived in a cob cottage which used to be in Hill Lane but which isn't there any more now. We children all thought that she was a witch and we were terrified of her. We would always run past her cottage.' She had come to Exeter to escape the bombing at home and recalled 'it was rather ironical that having come to Exeter to escape the bombing in Southampton, I should find Exeter also being bombed. I remember how, during the Exeter Blitz, we slept aboard an Exeter Corporation double-decker bus out on the Exeter by-pass.'[78]

Schools and other education establishments

Entire schools from Bristol, Kent and London were evacuated such as the boarding school from Bexhill which was sent to Topsham.[79] The evacuees had a tremendous effect on local schools particularly in finding them places. Patricia Stacey remembers how her schoolroom in Pinhoe had to be divided into two – by blankets – to accommodate all the children. Like others she attended school half a day – either in the morning or afternoon. John Langdon recalls 'at Hele's we had learnt to cope with large numbers of evacuees and classes were held in all sorts of nooks and crannies until the old St David's Vicarage was taken over. Many boys stayed with us throughout the war.' Helen Mann remembers 'the school doubled in size with evacuees and their teachers. After the blitz for a week we went to Bishop Blackall School for half a day so that Maynard girls could use our building, as their school was damaged by bombs.'

There was also the need for religious instruction. Eileen Reynolds was evacuated from Walworth in London and remembered 'the first Sunday at Auntie's (in St Thomas) the bell rang and Auntie said *I have someone to take you to Sunday School.* I went to the door and standing there was a very strict-looking lady in a Salvation Army Uniform, with a bonnet on and a big black bow on the side of it. I was happy to go, as I had been going to Sunday School, Church of England, in London. Auntie seemed to have the impression that I had never been to Sunday School or even knew what religion was. How wrong she was. The Lady Commissioner at the time was Ellen Tinkham who had a large draper's shop in Cowick Street, and a school for handicapped children is now named after her. I loved the Salvation Army band and the women with their tambourines. The hymns were so joyful. I was only 12½ but really liked one of the boy drummers, Derek Trebble. I suppose I had a bit of a schoolgirl 'crush' on him.'

Some householders preferred to have older students in their homes rather than young evacuees. The Central School of Speech and Drama was one institution which came to Exeter. Christine Caldwell remembers 'it was one of London University's subsidiaries – they dispersed their colleges throughout the country. Exeter got the Royal Free Hospital students and the Central School of Speech and Drama. As a third-year student I came down in September 1939 by train. I had never been in the West Country before. It was an adventure for all of us. The lucky thing for us was that the families of Exeter had been told they would have evacuees, and they jumped at the chance to have older drama and medical students because otherwise they would have had young children from the East End of London. So we were all welcomed in. There were maybe a hundred of us. The University College [later Exeter University] was very depleted then, only 400 or so, and there were not many men because of the call-up. The students already in residence were extremely disturbed by our arrival – we were all rather sophisticated and personality girls. And we were called instantly, a name which we never overcame – the Glamour Girls. It was absurd really and probably meant as derogatory, but this was the name we were given. The students there were pretty hard working and destined to become teachers. After the first year we took over the whole of Reed Hall – we lived in it and had our classes there. We banded together and formed a Troupe Concert – we used our talents and training in singing and dancing to perform for the local troops. We went all over locally and was enormous fun for us. We also went to the prison – rather a mistake. Prisoners got extremely excited, they weren't used to having a group of nubile young women entertaining them. The School went back almost immediately after the blitz, thinking if they were going to be bombed it might as well be in London as Exeter.'

Even though the students were older and with fewer problems, not everyone welcomed them. Mrs D. Irene Thomas wrote 'I was firmly committed until Easter to accommodating three medical students from the college – had felt unable to refuse since with the accommodation available I was lucky not to be put in charge of 'evacuee' children, a difficult assignment for a parent with my special cares and responsibilities. All the same, I had been reluctant to accept these students although they all – Pamela, short and dark, business-like and brisk, Catherine, fair and gentle and soft-spoken, and Seeta, shy and silent, a beautiful young Indian – made me eager promises if only I'd be persuaded. *No wonder they were so anxious to come*, said Kaye: FG's study to work in and two large airy rooms upstairs, a beautiful house and sunny garden – compared with the digs they had probably inspected elsewhere Maryfield must have seemed sheer luxury. I told the girls frankly of my difficulties and for their part they offered to make their own beds and keep their rooms tidy, said they would be out from breakfast until dinner at least five days out of seven, and would in all ways give the minimum of trouble.'[80]

The city accommodated these British strangers but there were many more others to come.

CHAPTER

STRANGERS—FOREIGNERS

FIVE

Thousands of foreigners passed through Exeter. Perhaps only during the First World War had the city seen so many different types of men and women and from so many places. At least one was less truthful about himself than the majority: one man was found to be a spy. Val Eaves was a child in the war and remembers how her family had moved from London to 51 St Anne's Road. Although their house was full with family members they had two male lodgers. She recalls 'I can't remember what reason we had these two gentlemen in the house. One of them apparently had a gun and he asked the other to hide it under his bed in case anything happened. So when the police came it was under the wrong bed.' He was arrested as a spy and sent to the Isle of Man.

The vast majority were 'friendly aliens', mainly from the continent, the Empire or the United States, but some Exeter people, who were born in combatant countries, were sent away to internment camps and there were several local camps for prisoners of war. The war gave the city a cosmopolitan air it lacked before.

Exiles and Refugees

Thousands fled war on the continent for Britain and Exeter hosted some of them. One local woman recalls 'there were a number of refugees from Germany and Austria here at the time and I think they were accepted. A lot of them were intellectuals and earning their living going around giving lectures. I think they were accepted by the population . . . My mother went to Music Appreciation Lectures and was very fond of her teacher who was Austrian.' The Thomas family, who lived at Maryfield in Pennsylvania, had an Austrian in their household. Mrs Thomas wrote 'Trude Ehrenberg, a Jewish refugee from Hitler's Austria, came to live with us and to help me as one of the family. Short, stout, spectacled and nearly always cheerful, how welcome this homely Austrian girl! We tried to help her build her new life by giving her a pleasant room where she could entertain her fellow exiles and her English was so fluent that it was easy to feel her as one of us.' She also remembered how on one occasion 'she made one of her rare allusions to her recent experiences in Vienna, adding to my astonishment, *And yet, you know, I could not help but applaud Hitler as he rode down the Ringstrasse!* She spoke almost complacently and though I could perhaps understand her being momentarily carried away *then*, I simply could not understand her tolerance now; no use asking her to explain. I simply gave her up with the unspoken cliché that human nature is often very mysterious.' She subsequently left the household when her 'linguistic gifts had been requisitioned.'[81] Dorrie Langdon also recalls 'an unusual school friend was Zenis-Ria, or Trixie as she preferred to be known. I believe the family to have been possibly Jewish, her father, a scientist, from Germany or Austria, having left before being persecuted. He was in some sort of research project, dealing with charcoal pellets for chickens! It does sound unlikely, but he perhaps was not at liberty to divulge fully the nature of his work. I stayed for a weekend at their house in Cheriton Bishop and was amazed to find her mother spoke not one word of English. Trixie spoke English well as did her father. Indeed she was very intelligent and had outstanding results at school certificate, especially as English was not her first language. The strangest thing about my visit was the borsch or beetroot soup, totally unknown to me at that stage and not to my liking at all. But that was what there was for supper, so I had to eat it.' Bertha Glynn's family had two evacuees with them. Their home at 159 Sidwell Street was destroyed during the blitz and Miss Glynn recalls that 'these two German ladies who were evacuated had all their belongings in our shop that was also bombed. After that they went back to London.'

The Czechs and the Polish

No. 307 (Polish) Squadron of the Royal Air Force arrived in Exeter on 26 April 1941 and stayed for nearly two years. One former constable recalls 'they were nice lads, very orderly, very correct.' One woman remembers 'we admired them tremendously' while another thought they looked 'absolutely immaculate, so smart'. Part of their appeal seems to have been not just their appearance but their bearing: the Poles 'would say hello and click their heels'. It has also been said they were 'so well-mannered and did very well. We felt so sorry for them for being far from home. And we were always worried to death if we would not see them again for a few days.' One woman remembers they were very popular until the Americans arrived. George Barnes recalls 'they had a reputation for being a danger to the ladies.'

The 307 (Polish) Squadron R.A.F. on parade, 1942.

Michael Payne recalls he 'was watching airfield activities from the far side adjoining the old A30 Exeter-Honiton Road when Jan Michalowski's Mosquito fighter came in running on only one of its twin engines. It think he saw that his approach was off centre for the runway and he opened the throttle on the engine which was still going, apparently intending to circle for another approach.' Unfortunately the plane crashed. Mr Payne remembered 'I was told that Stanislaw Sxkop and he had been school friends in Poland and chose to fly together in 307 Squadron. They were both killed in the crash and buried side by side in the Higher Cemetery which has quite a section devoted to the graves of Polish airmen. During the blitz the Polish airmen shot down four German bombers.[82] Len Willis recalled 'in off duty time I used to go to dances in the old Exeter Civic Hall with three of them who were all ground crew. I think the air crews mostly used to spend their off duty time at the George and Dragon, Clyst St George. I was very impressed by the Poles. They were absolutely brilliant. If an air raid warning siren sounded while they were at a dance or some other social function, they would drop everything and rush back to the airfield at Clyst Honiton to report for duty. It was tremendous dedication. They leapt to the defence of our country just as if it was their own.

I saw one example of that on a Sunday night early in 1942 when I was out for a drink with some mates in the centre of Exeter. Around 9.30 p.m. we were at the junction of Magdalen Street and Holloway Street not far from where the new Hotel Barcelona is now, when I heard the unmistakeable sound of the engines of a Junkers 88 enemy bomber going overhead. It was dark and we couldn't see the aircraft. Then I recognised another sound, that of a Rolls Royce Merlin engine which I judged was powering one of the Polish squadron's Defiant night fighters. Then I heard guns firing and saw flames coming from what I could see was the Ju88. I discovered later that the bomber crashed near Longdown and that all four or five of its crew were killed. Their graves can still be seen today in the Higher Cemetery.'[83]

Sister Edward Mary at the Palace Gate Convent recalls meeting many Polish servicemen and that they often went to the Heavitree church. She remembers 'being at Rosary House one time and we wouldn't know if the sound we sometimes heard was a Pole at the controls of a plane or a passing motor bike – they flew so low.' Sylvia Hart recalls 'you would hear them returning. The Polish and Czechs, if they were shot up on mission, would rather try to make it back to base than bale out of their craft over enemy-occupied territory. At odd times you would hear an explosion and you knew some poor souls didn't make it.'

One Pole was Joe Wasniowski who remained in Exeter. He recalled in 1988 that on one occasion 'twelve of our aircraft had been out on patrol over the English Channel and were in an engagement with enemy aircraft. The fog came down as they were making their way back. They were going round and round trying to find their way in, and some began running out of fuel. Only two came down without damage. Some of the pilots were forced to bale out and we lost 10 aircraft, several of which crashed in the fields near the airport. Our squadron leader was killed, and three of the pilots were injured.' They were at the airport until April 1942 when they moved to Northolt.[84] A considerable number of Polish airmen continued to live in Exeter after the war.

German prisoners of war

The city also had German prisoners. One former schoolboy remembers them being marched around the city under armed escorts and the large triangular patch on their trousers. Some remember the patch as a shooting mark in case of escapes. One Exeter man recollects hearing as a teenager the rumour that went around Exeter that the head of a German pilot had been used as a football.

Maureen Smith remembers as a young girl seeing the German prisoners coming every day to Calthorpe Road where they had a camp of wooden huts. From there they helped build Prince Charles Road. During the winter months her parents gave them tea and the family made friends with them. One of them, a young man named Fritz, carved two wooden hearts for her. Rodney John Coles, then a young boy, also remembers the Germans and their toys. He knew a party of about twelve prisoners who helped repair bomb damage. They lived in a hut in Homefield Road near his family home. He recalled 'the Germans used to make wooden toys and give them to us and other local children. They had a brazier to keep themselves warm and used to toast food against it. I know they were supposed to be the enemy, but I got on all right with them'.[85]

Colin Hopkins, then a teenager living in Stepcote Hill, recalls there were 'Italians mostly and some Germans. They seemed to do well in Exeter. They had brown suits with a patch on their backs and possibly on their knees. They were polite. They used to make things. They didn't want money but cigarettes or chocolate. I saw them walking down the streets with girls. To start with they were shunned a bit – and so were the girls – catcalled. But after a time things quietened down. They weren't doing any harm. They were allowed the freedom to walk around.'

Annie Bussell was a nurse at Exminster Hospital and recalls 'the German boys were quite nice – they couldn't help being German and going into their army. I nursed ordinary soldiers. They were treated well, as well as our soldiers. And they were quite nice really. They were in the military part of the hospital. Some spoke English but we never mentioned the war.'

Canon Michael Walsh was a priest at the Church of the Sacred Heart in Exeter and recalls 'towards the end of the war there was a lot of German Prisoners of War interred at South Molton for a long time after the war. We had a little church in Crediton. They were brought to Crediton to join in our services. Once a year on the 6th of June, on the feast of St Boniface, who is the patron saint of Germany, we used to go to Crediton every year because it was his birthplace and we had a solemn high mass in this small hovel of a church, I used to call it the black hole of Calcutta, in the morning. Then we would gather round the Buller statue in the evening for another service, and afterwards the Germans would give us an impromptu concert. God, they could sing.'

Italians

There were many Italians in Exeter before and during the war. John

Mander was a young boy evacuated to Whipton and remembers the Italian prisoners at the top of Summer Lane. They worked on the farm with no sentries and walked about on their own. Douglas Newbery was only six years old when the war broke out but remembers the Italians, in their brown uniforms with a yellow patch, who late in the war walked unescorted from their camp at Nadderwater near Whitestone into Exeter. He got to know several of them. Barbara Shute remembers her brother working for Smale's Garage in Alphington Road and how he picked up Italians from Cleve House to bring them to Tiverton. She sometimes accompanied him and one prisoner made her a present of 'a square piece of wood with wooden chickens on it, underneath was a piece of string and when you pulled it the chicken would peck the board.' Another woman recalls how a friend 'became friendly with one of the Italians. He made her a ring and broach from Perspex that came from a crashed plane. The Poles made them as well.'

There was also distrust. Pamela Morgan was only ten years old when the war ended and remembers the Italian prisoners of war working at the gas works near where her family lived. They were allowed out for lunch and one very young man picked blackberries for her. She threw them in the canal thinking they might be poisoned.

In 1945 Lady Aileen Fox supervised a small group of Italians who helped with her archaeological dig. She wrote 'the only labour obtainable was six Italian prisoners of war from Poltimore, who needed close supervision; I found two of them asleep under a buddleia bush one warm afternoon . . . the city officials were helpful with the loan of equipment, including an old air raid shelter in which the Italians cooked their midday spaghetti.'[86] Alison Maslen remembers as a teenager watching an Italian helping to excavate the Roman mosaic in Catherine Street following the bombing.

There were also Italians in Exeter before the war. Some were rounded up and interned. In 1977 Mrs E. Dolman remembered Fungo Morelli, an Italian who had an ice cream business in the city as well as a restaurant in Summerland Street. She wrote 'I really was upset when I heard that they'd interned him. He was such a nice man. We were all upset; I don't think 'e would have done anything'.[87] Another was arrested and sent away, presumably to the Isle of Man to be interned. One former policeman recalls 'an order came down that this particular man was to be arrested. I brought him in from Berni's in High Street, took him in and took away his shotgun. He was then taken away.' It was probably no coincidence that the British Union of Fascists met at Berni's Continental Café at 7 High Street before the war.[88]

The Fortes were another Italian family living in Exeter and with a business in South Street. Several St Thomas residents remember them with affection and how accepted they were during the war. Edmund Forte was a child during the war and lived with his family at 2 Dunsford Gardens. He remembered 'we did face problems with some people. There was a certain degree of resentment about the success of the Forte family as a whole, having started from nothing. And also because of Italy's participation in the war on the Axis side. Anti-Italian feelings were running high at that time, and several of our relations, some quite elderly, were interned. My grandmother put an advertisement in the *Express & Echo* to say that two of her sons had enlisted to fight in the Army, and others might be called to do so at the appropriate time. To avoid trouble, members of the family saw to it that things were kept as discreetly simple as possible. Everyone tried to avoid being gossiped about. And we all tried to behave properly, respectability was all at that time.' Their ice cream shop in South Street was destroyed by bombing. Their home became 'pretty crowded at this time. Apart from us, there was Grandma Pacifica, Aunty Mina, Uncle Tommy, Aunty Louisa and Uncle Alfred her boyfriend, and god knows who else? But I remember it as a happy time, full of food smells, cigarette smoke, damp washing and *pasta faciolla*.'

Americans

For two years American servicemen had a tremendous impact on the city centre and the areas in which they were stationed particularly those in St Thomas as well as the naval men in Countess Wear and the army at Topsham Barracks. Airmen were stationed at Winkleigh and Dunkeswell. The Americans first arrived in the spring of 1942 and most left two years later for the invasion of France in June 1944.

Two popular sayings regarding the Americans fairly well describe their impact on Exeter.

– Effect on children –

Colin Hopkins was a teenager and said of them 'I remember when the Americans came. I was in the Cadets and we were parading through Queen Street and in the crowd were these chappies with strange looking uniforms on. These were the first Americans I saw.' Tom Rookes was another young boy when they arrived and recalled when three regiments of the 29th Division paraded through the city. It was 'held almost exactly a year after the 1942 blitz on Exeter, the parade did much to boost local morale.' He remembered that he 'was a boy at Episcopal School when the Americans arrived. My family had been living in married quarters at Higher Barracks, but when my father was posted overseas we had to move to Longbrook Street. We were, though, still getting our rations from the N.A.A.F.I. at Higher Barracks and when my mum sent me on errands there, the Americans befriended me. I used to spend a lot of time up there and used to go for meals with them in their canteen. They would sometimes fill a pillowcase with leftovers and I would stagger off home with it. It was very welcome because food was so severely rationed so far as we were concerned in Exeter.' These men were later killed in the landing in Normandy on D-Day in 1944.[89]

Local people took some time to get to know their new arrivals and the newcomers had to become accustomed to Exeter. Donald Sheppard remembers 'when the Americans first got their English money we were at Sunday School which was right nearby. They were fascinated by these huge shiny pennies. They rolled them on the pavement and kids were running after them. They were all sitting around on the church-yard, the churchyard wall and the park wall.' He also recalls 'seeing an American football match once in the county ground. They were all padded up, we didn't know what they were – they looked like spacemen. And they had hot dogs and hot doughnuts.' Many others remember the Americans having a great deal of money compared to the English. Some recall that they found it difficult to deal with the currency and occasionally were short-changed. One man remembers an American being taken advantage of at a fish & chip shop: 'he placed a pound on the counter not appreciating its value and said *I'll have a pound's worth of fish and chips* when fish was tuppence and chips a penny.' Two others have recounted similar tales of how this particular shop was sharp with Americans. Eric Wheaton recalls 'when I was on leave I saw quite a few Americans. The airmen were stationed at Winkleigh. They would come into Exeter. My father was a Special Constable at the time and he met a couple of Americans walking around Alphington area. One of them asked where the nightclubs and restaurants were. He told them they had to get on a bus and go back into town. They said they had just got off one – it had said Broadway on the front.' It would be difficult then, or now, to find many similarities between the St Thomas neighbourhood of Broadway and its American counterpart.

The most common memory of the Americans is of local children asking 'Any Gum Chum?' Sidney Richards was a young boy living in Cheeke Street and kept an autograph book of signatures from foreign soldiers, including not just the Americans but New Zealanders and Poles as well as many others. He was the guest of American soldiers at two parties given at the Odeon Cinema. These were for children whose fathers were stationed abroad and for those whose homes had been bombed. He remembers asking *Got any gum, chum?* and was given the reply *Yes, have you got a sister, mister?*' Peter Philips was a young boy living in Redhills and one day called out to some Americans going by in a jeep. To his surprise a packet of cigars was thrown at him but his father was far from delighted. M. Godsland remembers that his first doughnut, with holes, came from the Americans. Sally Morgan stood as a very young girl with her friends and watched the Americans come in from Countess Wear to meet local girls at the Civic Hall. The children would call out to the Americans who would give them gum and chocolate. Her mother would tell her off for 'begging'. Colin Hopkins also reflected 'they gave children sweets. To think if you did that today, what trouble you would get in. How times have changed.'

Edmund Forte saw many Americans while growing up in St Thomas. He later wrote 'people were generally pleased, except those men who lost their girlfriends to some handsome 'Yank' with plenty of money and access to nylons, chocolate and coffee. At this time huge convoys of American trucks would be passing up or down Dunsford Hill. Teresa and I would go and sit on the wall and wave to the Yanks, and shout *GOT ANY GUM CHUM?* And *Hooray*, we would then be showered with sticks of chewing gum, or bars of chocolate which they called candy. It was lovely. Teresa and I would sit on that wall by the main road and swing our legs and watch the convoys go by. If a convoy should happen to stop for a rest by the wall, which they sometimes did, the soldiers would get down off their lorries and make a fuss of us. Without exception they were friendly, generous and kind. They were easy to talk to, straightforward and uncomplicated, very unlike some of our grownups who seemed to take being grown up very seriously indeed. The G.Is, as the grownups called them were mostly big men, or they seemed big, compared to the average men that we knew. They all had suntans, even in the winter, and big white teeth. They always chewed gum, and smiled a lot, and called each other Joe or Chuck or Sam in loud voices. That is something else I remember about them, they weren't afraid of being loud and noisy. Several times I remember identifying soldiers of Italian descent (on my Mum's orders) telling them who we were and where we lived, and they would then scamper across the grass to our house to talk to Mum in Italian, and often gave her some extra food, or other goodies. I remember some of the soldiers paying us a visit when they were on leave later. They were really nice. They came to thank us for our hospitality and, like all Americans, they offered a genuine invitation to visit them at their homes in America and stay for as long as we liked.'

Trevor Morgan, then a young boy, remembers the Americans working near Central Station on Richmond Road where they sorted out the mail. They too gave out chewing gum and embroidered U. S. Army shoulder flashes. Maureen Smith recalls the Americans arriving and one lodged with her family. One memory which has stayed with her is of the tins of peaches he gave them. She later wrote 'I have loved them ever since.' John Langdon recalls 'my father's work took him all over the county and he always gave lifts to hitch-hikers in uniform. One day he invited a very pleasant American soldier for a meal. In return he said he would send us a book; it turned out to be the Book of Mormon! We used to take our summer holidays at Widemouth Bay and in 1944 a US supply ship was sunk in the Atlantic and crates of American rations came ashore which supplied us with tinned meat and Hershey bars that winter. The locals who, were expert beach-combers, buried large quantities of Bourbon for future use.'

Many families got to know particular Americans very well. Gerry Linnell was a young boy living in Wykes Road. He recalls 'we went into Northernhay Park for something like *Make A Friend With An American* – with a band playing. There were loads of people there. We talked with them and one in particular we invited to Sunday tea – which wasn't brilliant in those years but Mum fed him well. He was based at Dunkeswell. He used to come round when he had leave. Then D-Day came along and they all went. He was a nice chap – tall, lanky, I think he came from Kansas or somewhere like that. A farm boy I think.' Rodney John Coles was another young boy when the Americans arrived. Two of them, who he only knew as Pat and Goody, also visited his parent's home. He remembers 'the G.Is were always very friendly towards the English kids and used to dish out chewing gum and various sweets that were hard to obtain in this country.' He wrote of them 'they seemed to have an endless supply of gum and candy, to name a few – Hershey Bars, Baby Ruth, Lifesavers (like our Polo Mints but in hard fruits), Beeman's Gum, Wrigleys. *Got any gum chum* was the catchphrase of the time. The big thing with boys was collecting American shoulder patches and kit, we would swap with each other. Pipe torches was favourite if you could get batteries, we obtained kit from U.S. dumps and G.Is, some brand new. They seemed to throw away everything not like our families (*Make Do and Mend*). We had patches on jumper elbows, shirt collars were turned, an extra seat was put on trousers to last longer. No designer clothes then. The two American soldiers that befriended our family, Pat & Goody, were members of the 4th Infantry Division. Their shoulder patch was the ivy leaf which they gave to me before leaving to prepare for the D-Day landings. We were all very sad to see them go, we never heard from them again. I found out later the 4th Division fought at Cherbourg, and Bastonge.' He also recalled that 'several times Pat and Goody took my cousin Ray and me out to their camp on the Exeter By-pass in their jeep and we were served slap-up meals in the canteen there. That was a real treat for us in those days of food rationing.'

They knew the family because his father 'met them at the Ship Inn pub in Heavitree. He said they looked lonely and lost. He brought them back home for supper. I remember Mum had sausage rolls all hot. She also had jam on the table, they spread the jam on them. Mum noticed from the scullery, wagging a finger at me – I knew what she meant. They were regular visitors at weekends, Pat & Goody would turn up in their Jeep with a box of goodies – tin fruit, peanut-butter, Spam, powdered egg, cigs for Dad, candy for us kids. It all came to an end – Dad went overseas, Pat & Goody gone. I felt lost for a while. Roll on peace I thought.'[90]

– Effect on adults –

The most common memory for adults is of variants of the saying of Americans at the time – 'over here, over paid and over sexed'. For two years these servicemen had a significant effect on the city's social life. The Americans were here in great numbers, several thousand passed through the city. Sister Edward Mary, who was at the Palace Gate Convent, remembers them coming to the Catholic church in South Street as does Canon Michael Walsh. They also went to the synagogue, which was otherwise quiet through the war, for Yom Kippur: Bill Boam recalls about half a dozen being there. One local woman remembers Clark Gable being at Exeter's airport and staying at the Royal Clarence while another recalls Gary Cooper was there. One woman, who met many Americans as well as French, Polish, Czech and Russian servicemen, is Ailsa Loaring. When she was seventeen she started work at the St George and Dragon at Clyst St George. Her father was the manager and among those at the pub were Clark Gable and Joseph Kennedy. She remembered 'we had some good times in those days and there were sad times. The Americans always used to be flash with their money and buy a round and say have one yourself as well. And beer was only pence a pint.' Some of the aircrew stayed in the pub. Mrs Loaring recalled 'we took them in and all the people from the operations room. The ops people slept upstairs and all the aircrew were in the ballroom at the side of the pub which was turned into a dormitory. If we wanted to have a dance we pushed all their beds to the side of the room.' The bar's ceiling was signed by hundreds of these airmen.

The Americans were kept in check by their own military police who were called 'snow balls' because of their white hats. Colin Hopkins, then a teenager, remembers 'if there was any trouble in a public house between the Americans and the British. The American police would come on the scene and they would wade in and hit only their men. They wouldn't touch anyone who was British. Sometimes there would be trouble in the streets – fighting and kicking. But up would come an American jeep – with their batons – and hit them in the back or the legs. Every now and then there was trouble – drink related. Or, over a girl. You could go into a pub and see sitting on the seats an American, then a girl, an American, then a girl. Our chaps didn't stand a chance.'

The Americans' success with local women was partly due to their spare cash. Whereas a British private was paid fourteen shillings per week his American counterpart had £3 8s 9d – nearly four times more.[91] The Americans also had access to food supplies and other goods denied to British soldiers. This had an added attraction for women in a city where these items were in short supply.

Retired Inspector Stanley Cole was a young police constable in Exeter before he joined the R.A.F. He later wrote 'at the time I was a young police constable. Police service in this country was declared a reserved occupation, and policemen were unable to be called up, and I recall that we youngsters in the force, much to our disgust, were involved with filling sandbags and issuing gas masks to the citizens of Exeter. This account however is not about me, but about an unknown American soldier, who was among the first American troops to be sent to the United Kingdom prior to the planned invasion. This unknown G.I. was stationed in tents with his colleagues on the surrounding fields of the Exeter by-pass which in those days was undeveloped.

I was on my last week of police duty before reporting to the R.A.F. to commence my Air Crew training. My tour of duty for the week was the late night shift of 10 p.m. to 6 a.m., and on the Monday night at about 11.00 p.m. I was patrolling the Cathedral Green area when a G.I. approached me, and in his full American accent said *Say Mr Policeman I like your hat. My folks back home would just love to see an English Bobbies' helmet.* And with the same he produced a packet of 20 American cigarettes and offered to swap them for my helmet. I told him in no uncertain terms that is was impossible for me to give away part of my uniform in such a manner, and I continued to patrol my beat. The next night I was again approached by the G.I. This time he entreated me to let me have a packet of 200 American cigarettes for my helmet. I did smoke at that time and for a married man on a young Policeman's wages the offer was tempting, however I again turned down his request.

It perhaps should be mentioned at this point that America's contribution to the war against Hitler at this time was not exactly received with open arms by the British Public and the American Authorities endeavoured to win over support by instructions to 'woo the British' with lavish gifts of sweeties – goodies to the children who overwhelmed the American Camps, and such luxurious-hand outs of sheets and other bed linen etc to the females who besieged the American camps in war-time Britain, tied with rations and clothing coupons.

My American G.I. made at least two more attempts to part me from my helmet until the Friday night – one more day to go before I swapped my police uniform for the R.A.F. Blue, and it was then I succumbed. I must have had a least 3 or 4 police helmets on the top of my wardrobe at home. There seemed to be no requirement to hand in an old helmet for a new one. The American was dangling a beautiful fountain pen in front of me. Such an item I had never seen before or even heard of a Sheaffer white spot. I questioned our Yankee friend as to what he would do with the helmet should I let him have it and his reply was *the folks back home would just love that Bobbies' Helmet. I shall stuff it away in my kit bag.*

Feeling assured and with no thought for the future I arranged to meet the G.I. after my tour of duty was complete and the swap was made. He had my helmet and I had his Sheaffer white spot fountain pen. I went off to my bed.

Sometime during that morning, and I being fast asleep at the time, my wife woke me to say that a policeman had called to check if I was all right and safely home as it appeared that the Commanding Officer of the U.S. Army stationed on the by-pass had telephoned my Chief Constable, and in the words as our Chief later liked to relate, said *Hi Mr Chief, have you got all your bobbies safe and sound as I have got a drunken G.I. wandering around the camp wearing one of your bobbies' helmets.*

As a result my Chief instigated an enquiry to ascertain if all of his Force, a small one in those days, could be accounted for, especially those on the previous night shift. I kept very, very quiet hoping for the best and saying nothing and with a war on hand the enquiry fizzled out when we were all accounted for.

I got off very soon after to commence my flying training in the R.A.F., but my 'friend' the G.I., what was his fate? Did he make invasion of France together with my helmet? We shall never know whether his folks ever saw the English bobbies' helmet. I shall take my story to my grave and my family will keep and cherish Dad's Yankee pen, but sadly I believe it is too much to hope that my unknown Yankee friend reached his home safely, and even too much to hope my helmet, <u>the</u> helmet, survived.'

— American perspectives —

Few Americans have recorded their impressions of Exeter. American airmen with the 440th Troop Carrier Group were based at R.A.F. Station Exeter for five months in 1944. One of them recalled 'on April 26th the 330th moved to Station No. 463, near Exeter in the county of Devon. This was the base slated to be the scene of our take-off in the Normandy Invasion. It was an enormous change from Bottesford, for Devonshire is England's modest approximation of the Riviera. For the first time the 440th discovered that England could be attractively green, fairly dry and quite warm in the month of April. Right off the field the countryside descended into a pretty valley and then rolled on up into hills with villages and towns visible for a great distance. After a cold winter, Devonshire looked good to us. The field itself, a civil airport before the war, lies five miles east of Exeter, the pear-shaped perimeter encircling three asphalt runways, 2040, 1,450 and 940 yards long, respectively. Line offices were the usual camouflaged stucco huts scattered around the perimeter, while a modern control tower building dominated the southeast corner. One area was reserved for a small R.A.F. Spitfire unit. On the south side a narrow road with embankments led up to the different squadron sites. It was much too narrow for military traffic, but somehow the American six-by-sixes managed to scrape past each other. About half way up this hedged lane were the mess halls and N.A.A.F.I. to the left and the station cinema to the right. Beyond the last squadron are, the road branched off into other lanes leading to the little villages of Aylesbeare and Rockbeare. All along the tree-lined route were farms, haystacks and orchards.

Recreation on the base itself at first assumed the usual pattern of snacks at the N.A.A.F.I., the station cinema and soft ball games but before long Special Services swung into action with dances and E.N.S.A. shows (British equivalent of U.S.O.). The N.A.A.F.I. tea truck, did yeoman service for the men on the line and later an American Red Cross club mobile put in a welcome appearance. They say that smells help to prolong memories of places. No doubt the station cinema at Exeter will long be remembered for the rich odour of sheep and fertiliser that accompanied the stroll along the path to the show.

The charming rural area due east of the field beyond the barracks held favourite haunts of many of the men. A short bicycle ride took one to the much-frequented Halfway House or the Blue Anchor where the drinking of mild and bitter was a far more leisurely affair than the mad scramble of Nottingham. In these pleasant out-of-the-way pubs even Scotch whiskey was usually available. The Devonshire pubs in particular had the interesting feature of being divided up into a number of separate lounges, with the taproom as the nucleus. Usually, there was a dart game in progress in one room, a piano in another should the drinkers care to raise their voices in song, and they usually did. Few G.Is mastered the complicated scoring system of darts, and those that attempted a game with the skilled local gaffers always met defeat.

They were comfortable places and it was no effort at all to sit there all evening drinking beer. It's a headier brew than the American beers, and returning bicycles frequently took spills . . . Not far away lay the town of Broadclyst, which housed the W.A.A.Fs who worked at the aerodrome. There, the approved hangout was the Red Lion when a W.A.A.F. dance was not going on. It was all very pretty country and thoroughly explored by the tireless Yanks.

From the base a civilian double-decker bus could take you into Exeter if you didn't care to thumb your way. But many didn't care to go all the way to Exeter, for approximately midway was Pinhoe, the site of 'B' Camp, home of the A.T.S. girls. And just outside of Honiton Clyst was the modest Black Horse Inn where you could eat a pretty good meal for a couple of shillings.

But most of us took our off-duty passes to Exeter itself, a bustling city of some 70,000 population with many old houses and red limestone churches. A large area, especially in the shopping district, had been practically levelled during the German blitz . . . With their respects paid to British traditions and history, the 440th settled down to their usual pub-crawling. And there was no lack of them in Exeter. Each found his favourite haunts, even into the far-flung corners of the city. In the center of the town, the Ship seldom failed to attract the eye and the dry throat. Popular bars were located in the Rougemont and Royal Clarence Hotels. One remembers the Clarence for its pictures and elaborate decorations, while the Rougemont calls to mind the sharp-eyed barmaid who very firmly let you know when you had had your quota of gin. Some liked the Shakespeare Inn but here the Navy offered serious competition in drinking.

There are so many uphill, downhill and winding streets and lanes in Exeter that comparatively few got around to exploring them all, but the sum total of the 440th effort was commendable. Some like the little uphill park that afforded a short cut between the Rougemont on Queen Street and the Savoy Cinema. Others preferred the more out-of-the-way lane that led down stone steps to the Exe River. At the Allied Club, opposite the bus depot, British and American uniforms mingled in queues for tiny cheese and fish sandwiches with the usual tea or foul coffee. Or if you preferred doughnuts there was always the Red Cross Dugout. For a night's lodging the elegant Red Cross Club

Residents of Mardon Hall in wartime before the arrival of the Americans, including staff of the Air Institute at Farnborough.

at Mardon Hall would take care of you. And for shows there were the Gaumont, Savoy and the Odeon cinemas. At the Odeon you could also get a pretty decent lunch according to British wartime standards. Late snacks were difficult to find. Usually, there were a few fish and chip shops open after 10 o'clock and you queued up to get yours, all nicely salted and vinegared in a piece of paper. Some of the boys were amazed to find that 'chips' were merely good old French-fried potatoes.

As far as possible the 440th found an Army home for itself in Exeter. They got to know the country and the people there and the people got to know them. When at your departure British citizens temper their sighs of relief with honest regret, you've unquestionably left your mark there . . . It'll be hard to forget Exeter for many reasons. From there we took off for the D-Day missions. From there we made our first landings on hastily constructed airstrips on the Normandy coast. There we celebrated the first anniversary of 440th Troop Carrier Group. And from there the air echelon took off for the flight to Italy.'[92]

Another American who recorded his experiences in Exeter was John Moon. He was based at what turned out to be the largest supply depot in Southern England. It returned to British control by the end of July 1944. One thousand personnel worked at the site which comprised some 578,000 square feet of storage.[93] Moon later wrote 'I was one of the hundreds of American sailors shipped into Exeter to serve at the U.S. naval supply base, code named JOWL-93. My group arrived in September 1943 and were billeted for a short time at the Royal Marine Barracks in Topsham and then when some Quonset Huts were built we moved onto what had been a beautiful golf course. We turned it into the epitome of a mud hole. In my Quonset Hut of 28 men, 25 were either immigrants or first generation; one lad, Bob Huntley, was born in Bristol. In the adjacent hut were two men who had won German Iron Crosses in the First World War and their mates never really trusted them.

For the next eighteen months we worked long hours doing logistic work for the D-Day invasion. Recreation for enlisted men was mostly non-existent. Most nights I got a ride into Exeter and found a seat at the Ship Inn and after a few pints went over to the area of the railroad station for the greatest fish and chips ever produced; this was followed by a long walk back to the supply base.

We had two British technicians installing our communication equipment and they drove our people crazy. We wanted them to do a fast bare-bones job that would get our communications up and running, but they insisted on perfection for every minor piece of work and every union-sanctioned tea break. The cultures didn't clash, we enjoyed the differences.

One family, as I recall Chick, invited me to their home. Their attractive blond daughter was rather interesting. They were an exceptionally nice family and they took my mate and me to Torquay for the day. I enjoyed it, but looking back it had to be difficult for my hosts – they really did a nice thing, but there was a generation gap, and a very wide cultural gap in that they were well-mannered and we were, for the most part, too young not to eat pie with our hands. It must have been a tortuous day for them.'

– Local romances –

The Americans were also regarded as being over-sexed although many remember this in more delicate ways. Phyllis Hawkins recalls their impact on 'the iron railings outside Boot's on the corner of High Street and Queen Street. The Americans used to sit on it, waiting to pick up the girls. The railings eventually had a bend in it caused by their weight.' One woman remembers her sister telling her 'they used to pick us up in their trucks and take us to dances – they would show the girls a lovely time. And absolutely shower them with cigarettes, great big packets. And sweets. And what we were most impressed with was their uniforms – this was the standard thing girls would say – look at their lovely clothes. Ours looked a bit tough. *They* were very impressive.'

Dorrie Langdon recalls 'one spin-off from the dancing was for a group of us from school, with Georgie Coombes, to attend a Square Dance on Wednesday evenings at Washington Singer Hall. This was one of the university halls of residence occupied by American soldiers waiting for D-Day. It was a good evening of dancing, with genuine 'calling' by different Americans. We quickly had to learn the new calls, and dancing seemed faster than our usually more sedate form. The young soldiers were extremely polite, enjoying the experience of a relaxing, homely sort of entertainment. I believe many of us thought

Two cartoons by 'Stil', George Stillings of Exeter, 1944.

the apple pie and ice-cream served at the end to be a real treat and reward for our squashed toes that our sweaty partners inflicted upon us.'

Marian Wallen who lived in St Thomas recalls 'they came full-force. There were a lot of them, en masse in lorries. I remember the first time I saw them was during the summer in an open lorry. They would throw out chewing gum and cigarettes. Some people were lucky and got DuPont Nylons.' She also remembers that 'down Tin Lane was my dancing school and I saw ever so much that was going on down there. My mother nearly stopped me going because of it.'

One local woman, who was a teenager during the war, recalls 'they were all over the place . . . Oh, they behaved reasonably well I think. I remember one tried to pick my mother up one night and she said *oh, don't be so silly, I'm far too old for that sort of thing*. But apart from that, I think they behaved reasonably well . . . He was walking along besides her and trying to chat her up. He said, *say, do you ever make dates?* But it was all fairly harmless.' Another remembers her mother forbidding her to date the Americans and encouraged her to see the local Marines at Lympstone. Yet another remembers that as a teenager she went to dances at the American navy camp where the Sam Donoghue Band played and that the Americans also came to Topsham dances.

Olive Wakeham was in her thirties when the Americans arrived. She reflects 'the Americans were like they said *over paid, over sexed and over here*. We welcomed anybody. We thought they were jolly nice, they had lots of money. The young girls liked them. Very handsome they were too. The women fell for them. They were very fine soldiers. We were most grateful that somebody was trying to help us. We never resented them, we looked upon them as our saviours. We were getting worn out by then. They were always so nice – if you were merely pleasant to them they would give you a bar of chocolate.' She recalls one incident when she 'had an Austin 10 for work and was allowed to only go 30 miles an hour because of the petrol. I would only give lifts to soldiers because I was on official business. I gave a lift to an American from Georgia who said *What a quaint car*. I said it was very reliable and he answered *You British and your reliability*. He didn't believe me when I told him about only going 30 miles an hour – why would we obey the rules? He was also surprised that we had proper roads.'

Sister Edward Mary recalls a lunch at the Palace Gate Convent where a husband was visiting his wife and children who were staying with them. The convent was used to having Americans visit who had family ties with them and often they asked their female guest to show them the cathedral while the sisters taught the pupils. At lunch their male guest asked his wife *just what do you do all day?* to which one of their children innocently answered *She goes out with American soldiers.*

One woman remembers dating an American who went off on D-Day and never heard from him again but not through him trying: 'he was very nice, handsome. He was from Tennessee. I think I met him at Emmanuel Hall. My mother told me years afterwards when she was dying in 1962, that she had burnt all the letters and cables that he had sent. I never had them. It was terrible now that you think about it. He must have thought I was killed in the blitz.'

Norman Watts, a young lad during the war, remembers the impact of the Americans on Exeter. Local women, particularly in Burnthouse Lane, would be paid to do their laundry. He remembers going into Northernhay Gardens with his friends on bicycles and shining their torches on the courting couples there which included many Americans. The servicemen would chase the boys, into Queen Street, who were then pedalling furiously. He also has memories of seeing the Americans with the local girls against the shop fronts in Sidwell Street. He recalls 'the girls used to meet them in Paul Street – at the bus depot. At night they would all come in – women from twelve to sixty it seems they would come in and get all sorts of things from them – from nylons to chocolates.' One woman remembers 'course some of the girls used to go out with the Yanks. I knew of them but not in my circle. They used to get nylons and things like that. And the Yanks had the money'.

Mardon Hall was run by the American Red Cross and had a canteen for servicemen. Patricia Stacey was one of the girls who volunteered. She recalls 'we would be picked up from the bottom of Streatham Drive in trucks and we were all taken directly home after our canteen duty. There was a whole team of workers. We served up coffee and doughnuts. My mother used to think it was great when I could bring back a bit of American cheese.' One of the men she remembers was Joe Louis. Just inside the front door was a picture of Anne Shelton, the British singer. 'They were nuts on her and her records were always playing.' Mrs Stacey's father was strict about her coming home on time but several of her friends met American servicemen and later married them. Another woman remembers the romances at Mardon Hall and yet another of the courting which took place in Hoopern Fields. One woman remembers how her friends married Americans and how one couple, both married, enjoyed a romance that included various gifts such as a skirt made from the American's officer's spare cream-coloured trousers. She also had a platex corset sent over from the United States. Her husband was then on service overseas.

– Black Americans –

Through the two years of the American occupation of Exeter the city was divided into two parts: on one side of the Exe river were white Americans and on the other were blacks. This followed national procedure in which the British government allowed, and even sanctioned, the introduction of segregation into the country. This was done to accommodate the feelings of those American soldiers who could not accept black Americans being treated as equals. It was felt blacks would expect the same treatment at home. The official policy of the American government was one of non-discrimination – because it was important to mollify black opinion in the United States with regard to forthcoming elections. However, the actual practice was the complete segregation of American servicemen on racial lines. Not only were they placed in separate regiments but there was to be no mixing in social circumstances.[94] In September 1942 Devon's Chief Constable, and presumably his counterpart in Exeter, received instructions that British police were not to enforce any American 'order to prohibit certain places out of bounds to coloured troops'.[95] That job was given to the American military police.

The black men were sent to St Thomas. This part of Exeter was easier to control movement in: only one bridge needed to be guarded. It is also interesting because this part of Exeter housed the greatest number of evacuees in 1939. Segregation meant black soldiers were denied the centre of Exeter which not only included dances at the Civic Centre but also the Allied Services Club and the American Red Cross facilities at Mardon Hall. In October 1943 a representative of the city council attended a meeting in Bristol with representatives of the United States Army to work out arrangements for American troops in Exeter. One of the agreements was there was to be no billeting of 'coloured troops'.[96] They stayed in the County Ground in St Thomas, in tents throughout the year. In contrast, many white Americans were housed in homes in Exeter. The rugby ground in St Thomas was also an easily defined area in which to confine men.

Sister Edward Mary remembers the first Americans she met were black and questions whether they were the first to arrive. On one day a pupil asked *Sister, I met a black soldier, what are they?* This question was later superseded by another – *Sister, I met a soldier and he had a funny uniform.* On hearing its description the child was told he was an American and she responded *Oh no, he's not – he isn't black.* The student had never seen a white American. Dorrie Langdon recalls the first time she saw black Americans. She later wrote 'walking to a friend's house in the blackout, I passed a group of American soldiers, they politely said *Good evening ma'm.* I was startled not by the greeting, but by the sudden rolling of the whites of their eyes, which was really the only visible part of their faces.' Others remember white Americans arrived first.

Most remember Exeter people having readily accepted black servicemen. Ivy Facey recalls their colour 'didn't make a difference. They were accepted. My mother always had someone in for Christmas – the first year it was two Frenchmen. Later they were Americans, black

The Old Bridge which crossed the Exe between St Thomas and Exeter.

or white. One year it was six Air Force men, just before D Day. Our house was an open one.' Douglas Newbery, then a young boy, remembers black Americans not only at the County Ground but also at a small camp on the St Thomas side of the river near Cowley Bridge. He has no memory of there being any negative feelings about their being black. The men would give local boys gum on condition they were allowed to ride their bicycles. One Westcountry farmer was quoted as saying 'I love the Americans but I don't like these white ones they've brought with them.'[97] However, one person recollects resentment. One local woman recalls 'my father didn't accept them, he hated them.' On one occasion she remembers 'my father and I used to have to walk along Tin Lane about half past seven. One of the men looked over the wall and said that morning *oh, an Angel from Heaven.* My father shouted *shut up your row, you black bugger, go back to America.* He didn't like blacks.'

Trevor Morgan, then a young boy, remembers his father having a meal with the most famous black American serviceman in Exeter – Joe Louis, the boxer, came to Topsham Barracks. Tom Rookes remembers going to the barracks and watching Louis fight. He was then World Heavyweight Champion. Louis was given permission to go to parts of the city that other black men were refused and others remember him walking about in Exeter. Still, not everyone was supportive of him: one resident recalls a local publican refused to serve Louis and demanded he leave her pub. In other parts of the country Louis faced similar problems.

Donald Sheppard, about twelve at the time and living in St Thomas, remembers 'the place was full of Americans, they were all over the place. When the black ones arrived they were confined to camp. They weren't allowed out for about a week. Our first sight of them I remember was when I walked up Tin Lane, which runs between the churchyard and the county ground. And all you could see was a pair of hands and a face all the way up through looking over the corrugated iron fence – two hands and a face all the way along. We hadn't seen too many black people up until then.' Historically the number of blacks in Exeter had always been small. In 1939 Exeter still had very few resident

(On following page) Tin Lane, between the church and the County Ground, 1939.

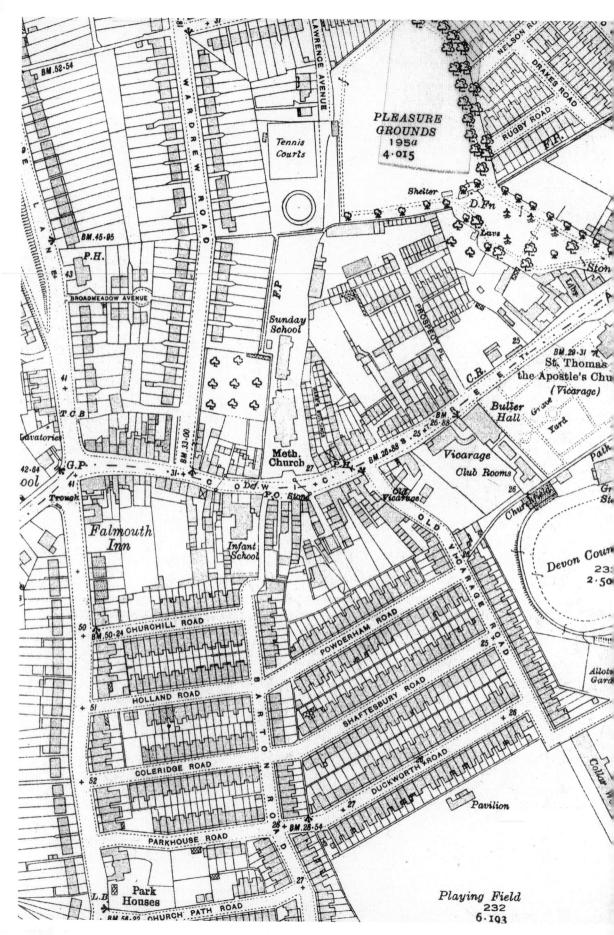

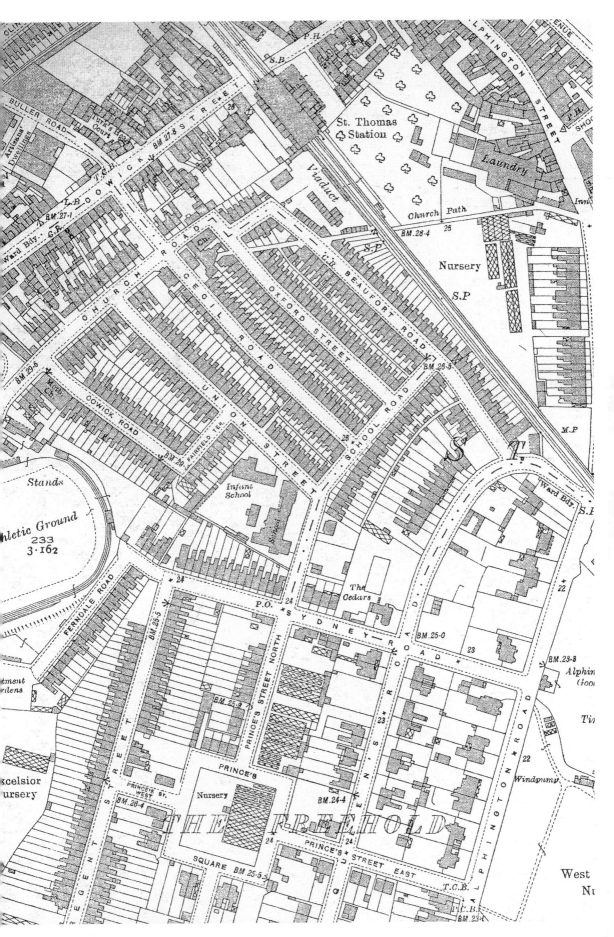

and this influx of black Americans was the greatest it had known. No doubt they would have been the first some local people had seen. Interestingly, one woman recalls that Leslie Hutchinson, the well-known black musician known as Hutch, was not allowed to stay at the Clarence.[98] This might have been in deference to American wishes regarding its' own black soldiers. American policy resulted elsewhere in the country in introducing segregation for British citizens who were also black.

It did not take long for Exeter people to realise the level of discrimination. John Langdon was a teenager during the war and recalls 'I had very little contact with them but the engineer at Digby Hospital, who was a friend of my father, reported that the U.S. Army, which had taken over the hospital, treated its coloured soldiers very badly. Hollywood didn't show us that aspect of American life.' One woman, who was in her twenties during the war, recalls her husband meeting white Americans at the Bishop Blaize pub. He 'liked some of them. He didn't like the way some of them treated the black Americans – they ignored them and thought they shouldn't be there.' Many were shocked at the treatment and sympathised with them as the underdogs. They may also have found the black Americans more congenial company: it has been shown that a greater number of black soldiers liked the British than the white Americans did. This may have been because of their surprise and gratitude in being treated as equals, for many this was the first time white people had done so.[99] White Americans also had a reputation for being ostentatious with money and some resented they had so much food whereas the English were severely restricted in comparison. John Langdon also recalls that a friend of his father's 'reported that the US engineer in charge of the construction of the U.S. Navy supply depot on Topsham Road made huge demands for water on the city water undertaking' with the excuse 'we Americans are a clean people.' In comparison, many remember black Americans generally being more modest.

The segregation arrangements were strictly adhered to and many people have remembered, like Sylvia Hart, that 'white American personnel were separated and had different camps around Exeter to avoid trouble between them'. Colin Hopkins also remembers the trouble between the white and black Americans. He recalls 'the blacks were over in the county ground. The whites were on this side of the bridge. On one end of the bridge were black military policemen and on the other were white military policemen – to make sure the whites and blacks did not cross over. On the corner of Exe Bridge was a big hotel – which was a military post. One white and one black military policeman would go together through the city, I guess if they found a black they had to be represented.'

It appears as though occasionally black and white Americans managed to cross the bridge and fighting was common. Phyllis Hawkins was only nine when war broke out. She recalls 'we lived in Alphington Road opposite Crawford's Hotel. At that age we had a lot of fun with the Americans. I remember one day going up town to meet some friends. Exeter had a toyshop called Webber's on High Street. Two Americans, one white and one black, were very drunk and fighting. A crowd gathered and all of a sudden I could see my uncle, a very jovial chap who was pretty short, under five foot. He got between these two great big drunken men and separated them.' Ivy Facey remembers 'the night when an American, I can't remember if he was black or white, was stabbed in the Assembly Hall in Cowick Street. After that the blacks weren't allowed across the bridge, or the whites over to St Thomas, at night.' Donald Sheppard recalls 'all their officers were white and we used to think they were very harsh to them. There used to be problems at dances in Buller Hall. I remember the fights. We never experienced fights, they used to carry knives. Some English chaps were on leave one day and one of them got stabbed by a black American. There was a great carfuffle. It was very dramatic.' Black soldiers were known to carry knives, perhaps they faced a greater chance of being attacked.

Disputes seemed to be set off by black men being seen in the company of British women. Pam Southen recalls 'white Americans were not happy when the black Americans came. Blacks would go to dances. It was the white ones that objected and caused trouble. It wasn't caused around drink – it was racism. They would start a fight because they didn't like to see a white girl dancing with a coloured man. In those days, the best ones for dancing jive were the coloured fellows and the girls liked to dance with them.' Donald Sheppard remembers there was interest in his family: 'my sister was in the land army and used to cycle out to the market garden in Pinhoe every day. They used to see her on her bicycle and this one black sergeant wanted to buy my school blazer. *I'll give you five pounds* he said. And he said to me *is that your sister? I would like to get acquainted with your sister*. But, no he didn't. She was about twenty at the time.'

Other girls soon became friendly. One former teenager remembers passing through Chudleigh Knighton where the Americans had a great ammunition store which was guarded by black soldiers. It was, as she remembers, 'commonly said that if you looked into a local pram a baby of mixed ancestry would look back at you'. Colin Hopkins recalls 'people loved them. They soon fraternised with the girls or at least the girls would with them. Quite a lot of coloured babies were born. I don't think people really cared. I don't know what happened in their families, but on the outside no one was bothered. I don't think there was any fuss.'

There were worries of these liaisons at the national level and whispering campaigns were initiated to instruct the British in how to associate with black Americans. In other parts of the country the Women's Voluntary Service tried to discourage British women associating with black men: rumours were spread that black men were likely to have venereal diseases. They also introduced segregation: elsewhere they had separate facilities for black soldiers.[100] There is no evidence for the W.V.S. organising this in Exeter. Elsewhere whispering campaigns were initiated against these British women; they were derided for being working class, poorly educated and too old to attract a white man. It was also suggested that they were lascivious and attracted to black men because of their reputation for being well-endowed: one Somerset man said they were 'prick-mazed they be, prick-mazed'.[101]

In Devon at least 83 babies were born from these romances and they were well known in Exeter.[102] Another woman recalls 'I used to laugh – I thought it was funny to see a great big fat black man with a little white woman. You would see them in the churchyard – they treated it as if it was a park. They thought nobody could see them there. That was where it all happened – they would leave all kinds of bits and pieces there in the churchyard. But it used to happen. A lot of the babies were adopted. I didn't hear of any abortions but many of the coloured babies were adopted. There was a babies home here on the Alphington Road.' One man who was a young lad at the time recalls that he would climb up the trees to look down on the soldiers and their dates: 'that's where I had my early sexual instruction'. There was some dissention. One woman recalls that 'we had a back lane and the black men used to take the girls down there. My father threw a bucket of water over them one night.'

There was a great difference in the potential romances between British women and either white or black Americans. Many white Americans brought home their girlfriends as G.I. brides but this option was not open to many black men: in many American states mixed marriage was illegal.[103] The result was that white babies could be born to married parents but black babies were likely to be illegitimate.

Parliament passed the Visiting Forces Bill in August 1942 which established that the Americans had sole criminal jurisdiction over their members.[104] Local policemen in Exeter were still however aware of crimes committed by American soldiers. Retired Inspector Cole recalls that as a young bobby 'we gradually got to know them and they didn't really give us any trouble. Occasionally the Americans would steal bicycles – take them back to their camps. We lost some of our yobos when they got called up, so I suppose the Yanks took their place, but they weren't ever nasty. You could get trouble in the dance halls when a local boy had left his girl to get a drink and then a Yank would move in – that's when some trouble happened. There was daily stuff, but nothing serious. Blacks would be inclined to keep to themselves, the men altogether. The whites treated them with contempt. We wouldn't do that, we'd talk to them. Terrible. We hadn't seen anything like it before.' Another man recalls a serious crime. He remembers 'there was an incident along the river with a 15 year old girl on the banks, got mixed up with the black Yanks hanging around, they jumped her, a dozen or so, and raped her and then threw her body into the river. She drowned.' Another former policeman recalls 'they were well policed by their own snowballs – the military police named after their white hats. The Americans did everything to look after their own people. The coloured people were on one side of the river and the whites on the other. A post was on Exe Bridge. I remember going in there once and a suspect was being interrogated – he was sitting on a chair, with a light directly above him and men were walking around him in circles. He had stabbed a marine. There were three murders – all by black men. Generally there were more problems in St Thomas with coloured men and knives, some fighting and disturbances with local people.' American black soldiers were more likely to be found guilty of crime than their white counterparts.[105]

Dutch

Among the continental visitors was one notable Dutchman. Leendart Jonker, a turret gunner with the 320 Dutch Squadron of the R.A.F., wrote an extraordinary account of his experiences in the city during the autumn of 1943. He recalls that on 25 October 1943 'it looked like any other day so ordinary – but!!!! 52-Crew members of the 320th squadron of the Netherlands Fleet Air Arm had to report early in the morning for a special bombing-mission over enemy territory across the Channel. The target was the airport Lanveoc-Poulmec . . . In all 133 airplanes would take part in this operation. The airfield to be bombed, was being used for long distance reconnaissance enemy planes which operated with the German submarines (creepy assassins, no wonder they were called the Wolf-pack) on the Atlantic route during the last war.' However, the plane and Mr Jonker were badly hit but managed to get back to England. He recalled 'although tormented by appalling pain and loss of blood I crept out of the turret as I wasn't able to stand up. I looked at my right arm and became dumbfounded, it was nearly severed by the elbow and the underarm was hanging on by a strand of my skin. I also suffered immensely of a severe wound in the thigh of my right leg and of lesser cuts and lacerations on back and legs. While I laid down there, I somehow succeeded to put on an emergency dressing around my arm or what was left over of it. To accomplish this I had to open a package of emergency first aid kit. Our navigator, Claassen, did his utmost to assist me in my efforts but to no avail. Neither did he succeed in injecting me with morphine to soften my pain. Do not ask me how, but during this spell I noticed that the panzer-windows of the fuselage had disappeared, apparently blown away. Beneath me was an enormous hole on account of having lost our bottom-turret. Above me the blue sky. Through all the holes cold air readily found its way into our plane and probably the cold air acted as an anaesthetic and made me feel numb and drowsy, most presumably it also stopped the flow of blood from my numerous wounds. Just over Exeter where the landing was set in I accidentally looked to starboard side of the plane and to my most astounding horror I saw that the tyres of both wheels of the landing-gear were ripped apart and hanging on the landing-gear. The moment Jan landed the plane or what was left over of it, he slightly pulled the plane backwards, this to achieve a soft landing. When the wheel-rims hit the ground the engines stopped. The pilot managed to clear the take-off strip of the airfield by steering it into the field where it came to a standstill. All I can say after all these years, to me it was the most successful landing I ever encountered in my whole career and I am still in awe and amazement. At that moment the time on my watch read 15.27 hours. Immediately nurses came running towards the plane to rescue me out of the wreckage. They did not succeed in reaching me on account everything was either broken down or twisted, while sharp metal strips were protruding everywhere. The door shielded by a panzer of more than a centre meter thick was crumbled-up like a piece of paper. Somehow I managed to crawl out through a smaller hole in the fuselage, by using one arm and a leg, this took nearly the last of my energy. But although almost overcome by pain I did not succumb to unconsciousness.

With all the speed they could muster, I was taken to the Royal Devon and Exeter Hospital. The medical staff stood awaiting me. Immediately they cut away all the clothes from my body. As they already had identified my blood-group from my identification-disk, straight away I was given a blood-transfusion. I just succeeded to pass on the address of my wife. Last but not least I remember two doctors bending over me, contemplating to amputate my right arm. My answer to his question if they were allowed to experiment with my arm, was affirmative. Then everything blotted out for me.

About nine the same evening I partly awoke out of my narcosis and noticed that my arm was still there. Nurse Lenten who kept watch at my bedside told me that she had phoned my wife and that she would take the next train from Holyhead. In fact it was going to be 7 p.m. the next night before she arrived. The staff had prepared a room for her, so my wife would be able to visit me regularly.

Next day Jan Maas and Gerard Claassen paid me a visit. It must have given them some shock to see me in this condition. The staff had concocted some structure where my arm laid in, blood transfusions where the blood dripped down my fingers. At the foot-end of my bed a heavy weight was attached to my right leg to keep it stretched all times so the muscles in the backside of my thigh could regain their strength. I confessed the following to Jan: during the flight back I could follow all conversations over the intercom. In my mind I was thoroughly convinced we would succeed in reaching England. Through one of the many holes I saw that of the steering-cables only two strands were left intact, but I didn't report this to Jan. So that's how I owed up now. Jan looked at me and his answer was *Leen we're here and alive and that's all what counts*. It took approximately 24 hrs before I regained control over my mental faculties due to the fact of tension, fatigue and loss of blood. The Canadian orthopaedic-surgeon attached to the Hospital, paid me daily a visit. He told in full what his plans were if the operation would succeed.

Also the C.O. of the airfield paid me a visit. Accompanying him were a Doctor and a man of cloth. They all immensely admired the performance of Jan Maas. Only supernatural powers must have assisted him to keep this kite, in such a terrible condition, in the air and to land safely. Beside the aforementioned big holes another 1300 smaller ones were accounted for. Jan was a Pilot of great class who proved to be self-disciplined, courageous and dutiful. Furthermore Jan personally expressed his thanks to the Spitfire-pilots who escorted us home in our heavily mutilated plane. Some time later I learned that our own losses were quite heavy. 5 members killed, 1 severely wounded, 3 wounded, 2 received shocks, one of them being our telegraphist Hans Pennock, three baled out and were captured and made prisoners of war by the Jerries.'

Mr Jonker was awarded the Flying Cross on 2 November 1943 and six days later he was transferred from Exeter. He was later visited by both the Royal Family and Winston Churchill.[106]

French

There were some French people in Exeter including two involved in the Resistance. Ray Holmes, who was a Fighter Pilot with 504 Hurricane Squadron at Exeter, met them on several occasions. He was then in his late twenties and recalled he was told 'go to Deller's and rendezvous with a lovely twenty-year-old French girl called Vivienne, who will be seated along at a table beside the dance floor. I saw this beautiful girl running a red-nailed finger lightly round the rim of her Martini glass, watching me with an amused smile when I caught her eye. This was my first-ever blind date. If they had all been like that it would have been a good war.' She and her mother had escaped from France and were living in a flat in Cathedral Close. It was his mission to be dropped into France in order to bring back a German pilot but orders changed and instead he delivered fighters to Russia. Mr Holmes thought that the two women were killed in the blitz.[107] Other French who are remembered include soldiers who came with the British Expeditionary Force from Dunkirk in the spring of 1940 (see page 26).

PART TWO

DESTRUCTION

CHAPTER

SHELTERS AND AIR RAIDS

ONE

Across the country an estimated 60,000 people died from German bombing raids. This nearly equalled the entire population of Exeter in 1939. In Exeter 265 were killed in the blitz and some two dozen more died in the rest of the war. This is dwarfed by the 1,172 deaths in Plymouth. Just over 1% of the country died through German bombing while Exeter lost 0.5% of its population and Plymouth 5%.[108] It may seem that Exeter escaped lightly compared to many cities but the suddenness and intensity of the blitz greatly shocked those who lived through it. Moreover, most of the deaths occurred in only a few nights.

The destruction was severe on the night of the blitz – it was estimated at the time that 1,734 buildings were destroyed and another 18,849 damaged. The city centre was mainly hit with a number of churches, the General Post Office, the City Hospital, Bedford Circus, the City Library, the Lower Market and many business premises lost. The cathedral had some damage but survived. Most of the destruction in the centre came from fire caused by the incendiaries. Fire swept along South Street, Sidwell Street, Southernhay West and High Street long after the bombers left.[109]

The blitz is remembered most vividly of all wartime experiences. It is not just the sights of the bombing that are keenly recalled by many but also particular sounds and smells. Christine Caldwell distinctly remembers the whistle of the bombs falling and then the loud explosions. She had an overwhelming biblical sense of fear: knees trembling, the hair rising on her head and her tongue cleaving to the roof of her mouth. For others it was an unforgettable smell of burning, others the dust in the air. What one woman remembers most clearly is seeing remnants of burnt paper littering the air and falling slowly to the ground. Likewise, Helen Mann remembers when her family left their shelter in Countess Wear after the blitz 'everything was covered in ash and we were 3 miles out.' Some bomb victims, who were still in

On the front line: an Exeter fire crew, outside the New North Road station, c.1941.

shock, surprised themselves with the random thoughts that occurred to them once they realised the destruction. Fifteen-year-old Joy Hawkins thought of the pile of homework completed that day she need not have done. She also remembers the ten shilling note left on her dressing table and wished she had spent it at a recent fair. When she saw the ruins of her family's piano she reflected upon the lessons she had grudgingly been taking; she recalled 'I saw it was wrecked and thought to myself *at least something good has come from this'*. I hated playing that piano.'[110]

One woman summed up her experiences of air raids. Mrs D. Thomas wrote 'we frequently could hear the raiders and even an occasional bomb, not aimed at us but jettisoned to lighten their load as the planes passed over the estuary back to their continental base. One raider was brought down in the sea and Paul – Martin's father, head of the local Observer Corps – joined us in our walk one afternoon to show the three boys where another had crashed in open country. Adrian, Martin and Philip excitedly followed Paul's pointing finger and thought they could see a distant smoke rising though I could see nothing but the woods and the fields. Two men had baled out to safety, one had perished in the plane, and as we stood just below Paul's look-out post – the peaceful countryside now veiled in spring's soft green – it seemed an unbelievable business. But it could be real enough at night when doors and windows rattled, and especially on the two occasions when I had actually seen the flash of an explosion. I had then roused my household and taken them to sit close to our shelter in the wine cellars until the 'All Clear' signal. The boys usually slept well and rarely heard the sirens and to me my times of listening and watching seemed next morning like a bad dream of the night.'[111]

The city authorities anticipated Exeter would be bombed but not all residents had. Pamela Taylor, then a seventeen-year old living in St Leonards, remembers it not being suspected. 'I'm sure they hadn't because it was regarded as a non-military target. Plymouth of course had been very badly bombed but we thought Exeter was fairly safe. My parents of course had experienced a lot of bombing in the London area and it was the last thing they expected was to be bombed out of Exeter.'

For some, it was the ludicrous aspects they remember. Olive Wakeham recollects 'in 1942 I had my appendix out and afterwards

I came to in an air raid warning with a washing up bowl over my head. The nurses would normally put you under the bed but I was knocked out. The poor nurses couldn't bring you out – where could they put you? There were no places to put patients.' Pamela Taylor also remembers of the destruction of her family home that 'our bathroom was completely wrecked. The only thing that remained intact was a glass shelf with a glass of water and my father's dentures in it.' Others recall finding humour during extreme danger. Sister Edward Mary remembers she and the rest of the convent went into the garden and two of them picked up a large bin of sand to cover incendiary bombs. Sister St Patrick threw on earth but Sister St Columba used a stirrup pump. Instead of using it the proper way on one occasion she tipped the entire bucket of water onto it. This created a mass of flames which shot into the air and considerably startled and alarmed her. Her fellow nuns however found this hilarious and were incapacitated with laughter. Their Mother Superior vainly urged them to come in because of flying shrapnel but Sister Edward Mary remembers 'it is possible to see the funny side in the midst of tragedy.'

Others have odd disjointed memories. Nicholas Toyne was a young boy during the war and recalls 'walking past Exeter prison and looking across to Northernhay Gardens across the railway, and seeing a crashed plane hung up in the trees. I cannot remember whether it was German or English, just that it was there.'

There are also strong memories of destruction. Ivy Facey, who was living with her family at 22 Beaufort Road in St Thomas, remembers that just before the blitz 'a friend of ours came in, they used to call my mother Duchess, and asked *Duchess, how many windows have you got in your house?* It was a big one, it had a flat in it – the next morning we didn't have one window. Even the big shop window went. They didn't put glass back in it – only a wooden board – for some four years.' One woman who lived in Tudor Street and was then in her twenties recalls she did not have damage during the blitz but on another occasion 'it was so strange. I had a sideboard – across from the window. I think we went into the reinforced cupboard. When we came out we found the sideboard had moved across the room and windows were broke. We had wartime glass for the rest of the war. It wasn't clear – you could get the light through but you couldn't look through it.'

Many remember the loss of life. Bette Simmonds recollects the bombing of Prospect Park in April 1942. She was living in Albion Place and 'these two old ladies were great friends of ours. I went up to see whose house was hit. There was nothing there. It was all crushed and I thought *Oh my goodness me*. I couldn't see hide nor hair of them. I wondered where they took their bodies. I went to Heavitree and there they were. They only had the names of them on their feet.'

Flight Lieutenant George Millington protected Exeter and remembered the German attacks in an altogether different manner. He arrived on 26 April 1943 and had some 45 patrols from the base. He later wrote 'the Germans seemed to be very lacking in imagination in planning their raids. During the whole time I was at Exeter (nearly 7 months), I cannot recollect that they made a raid after 1 a.m. We spent scores of nights in the crew room waiting for them and we knew that once midnight had passed there was very little hope of any customers. We had beds in the crew room and we always turned in between midnight and one o'clock. I am sure if the Germans had launched a heavy raid about 3 o'clock in the morning they would have done a lot of damage.' They worked two nights and then had two nights off. He wrote 'I invariably spent my first afternoon and evening off in Exeter. It was pleasant to get away from the noise of aeroplane engines, wander round the cathedral, look in a bookshop, have tea in a café, go to the pictures and finish with fish and chips in the British Restaurant. I never got accustomed to the contrast between my last night on duty and my first day off duty. The night could be quite hazardous and noisy and the next afternoon (only a few hours later) I would be in a café having afternoon tea and contemplating the ancient cathedral. Everything would seem so peaceful and secure and yet only the previous night I would have been in great danger, miles above the city with a sense of feeling that civilization was coming to an end. There were many more of them 'than there were of us' and it was doubtful if we could 'hold the fort'. In the peace of Exeter I would be seized with an insane impulse to tell the passers-by *Hell is two miles up*!'[112]

The first casualties were on September 17 1940 at Blackboy Road. There were a number of deaths.[113] Over the next few years there were raids during the day and at night. Bombs fell not only on missions intended for Exeter but also as a result of 'tip and run raids', from planes returning to the continent after attacking other parts of Britain. The destruction was the first the city had experienced from warfare for nearly three hundred years.

Many have memories of how helpful friends and neighbours were after bombings and through the war. However, there was some looting although some do not recollect it taking place while others recall even

The bombing at Blackboy Road.

garden plants being taken from bombed houses. One woman recalls 'there was some looting, some things that could be picked up easily and taken like a watch' while one man remembers 'there were stories of it happening more in the poorer parts of the city.' Another resident even said 'there was quite a lot of looting I think. As far as my family was concerned, we had a cleaner who used to come once a week and after the house was bombed and we left, my mother met this woman wearing one of her dresses. So she had obviously come in and helped herself to various things.' Her mother said something along the lines of *oh, how nice you look* and her former cleaner looked overcome with embarrassment. The Thomas family lost their home in Pennsylvania and returned to find that not only had their spare linen been stolen but every rose bush had been taken from the flower bed.[114]

The High Street was of particular concern. George Barnes reflected 'I suppose that's why there were so many police and wardens on duty. But so much of the stuff was so heavily damaged there wasn't much to loot.' One former constable said of looting 'oh yes, there was a lot of that. After the bombing if shopkeepers were away and the premises were smashed up a bit then the petty thieves got in, they were mainly after cigarettes. There was a warehouse in St Thomas

Burnthouse Lane.

that was broken into and everything taken.' Another policeman recalls 'there was a bit, but not a great deal. Generally it was only when shops were damaged. But by and large Exeter was a respectable city and there wasn't that much to loot anyway.' Another woman recalls her father's jeweller's shop in the Arcade. She wrote 'my father was fire-watching when the Arcade had a hit. He hurriedly picked up his watch and a few sovereigns, and ran from the building as it was being bombed. He lost his shop and all its contents due to this raid. In the morning, when he returned, the safe had been broken into and everything had gone.'[115]

It was because of potential theft that Alan Fray, who was in the Queen's Own Regiment Royal Engineers and on exercises on Exmoor, was sent to Exeter. He was given the task after the blitz of guarding a bank: the bombs had blown money out of the strong room.

Sheltering

Through the war attitudes changed regarding the need to shelter from bombing. On the declaration of war some panicked and thought the Germans would bomb them that day. It was nearly a year later that the city had the first bomb and by then Exeter people had grown accustomed to hearing planes flying overhead. Many remember that they stopped getting out of bed and gradually took little or no notice of air raid warnings. The reprisal raids at the end of April 1942 changed thoughts on safety and the immediate period after the blitz concentrated many minds on having adequate protection in or close to their homes.

Sirens sounded to alert the danger of enemy planes but many remember occasions when this happened after bombs had been dropped. Sirens interrupted lives. Ethel Harris recalls a speech day at school in 1941 when 'the school orchestra was playing *Marche Militaire* as the siren went. We naughty ones said it was hard to tell which was which. We had to disperse to the lower corridors of Bishop Blackall as we had no shelters. I grin when I hear *Marche Militaire* now!'

There were several different type of shelters. One of the most common was the Anderson. These were named after the Home Secretary, Sir John Anderson, and were outdoor shelters, built over a hole some six feet long and six feet wide. Six curved sheets of steel were bolted together and formed an arch. Steel plates protected either end. Those on lower incomes were provided with them but most middle-class families had to pay. Even so, many of the poor did not have a garden large enough for a great hole. Many have memories of climbing into their shelter in the middle of the night. Peter Philips remembers his father and neighbours building their Anderson Shelter in a dry ditch in the back garden at Barley Mount in Redhills. The shelter was covered with several feet of earth, seats were placed inside and sacking hung over the entrance to block light. Many remember their Anderson Shelter filled with water and gradually their families did not want to leave their warm beds for what they considered to be a chilly and wet ordeal. It could be difficult to wake children up in time. This was particularly

A shelter being constructed in Wykes Avenue, 1940. The photograph was taken by Kenneth C. Harvey who noted 'these grown-ups can't take it! Pat Thomas, stripped to the waist, directs operations; Joey Green, an evacuee, toys with a hammer, while Mervyn Cobley (wearing glasses) puts in some useful spade-work. These Exeter children are building their own air-raid shelter.'

true for women with several children. One woman recalls 'I'd go into his room and say *Come on lovey, the sirens have gone* and then I'd get my daughter up but he'd have gone back to sleep.' Helen Mann remembers that in Countess Wear 'my dad had a brick-built air raid shelter made underground in our garden. It had bunk beds and electricity in it. My mother, my sister and I spent many a night in it. It is still there I understand.'

The second most common shelter was the Morrison. They were named after Herbert Morrison, the second Home Secretary during the war. In effect this was a steel table, six feet and six inches long and four feet wide. It stood two feet nine inches from the ground.[116] These too were intended to be free for the poor and were more popular in that families did not have to leave their house. David Melhuish, who was a young boy during the war, recalls his family's Morrison Shelter at 9 Rosewood Terrace: it 'was a strong steel table the size of a double bed with a spring built into the base to take a mattress. It could be used as a table and could be slept in if a raid occurred at night. Fortunately we didn't have to use it very often. I can remember that

Second photograph by Kenneth C. Harvey who noted 'sixteen kiddies will use this shelter, when completed. Here are most of them, getting in the way, while Pat Thomas vainly tries to wield a pick'.

one day I was walking home from school when the air-raid siren went off. Mum was wondering if I was all right and made her way to the bottom of the road. I "took off" at the sound and Mum found me running at full tack down the centre of the road over the railway bridge! At first the shelter was erected in the kitchen where we used it as a dining table. Later it was moved into the front room, I can't recall why. It was in the front room when the blitz occurred.' John Tregale was only six at the time of the blitz and spent that night with his family at home. It had been suggested that they should shelter in the City Brewery but his mother felt taking four children down was too difficult. She ran a second-hand clothing business from their home at 16 Edmund Street, later to become famous as The House That Moved. They were later provided with a Morrison Shelter which was placed half in the shop and the rest in the kitchen.

The sisters at Palace Gate had a Morrison Shelter for their pupils. On the night of the blitz there were only a handful of the boarders resident. The rest were due to return the following day. Normally Sister Edward Mary did not want to leave her bed. She had been in Plymouth from 1939 until Easter 1941 and had become used to the many air raid sirens there. On one occasion she remembers a fellow sister calling to her *Aren't you coming down?* and she replied *I'm staying here until something happens. I'll come down when the Germans are sitting on our lawn and not before.* But when they heard bombs falling they gathered the children together and made for their Morrison.

Many did not like their Morrison either. Pam Coombes who lived off Longbrook Street remembers their Morrison Table as being 'hot and stuffy, and beastly, we didn't like it.' Helen Mann, who lived in Countess Wear, recalls 'I have also slept in a friend's Morrison table shelter, but they were not so popular after some people got burnt to death in them, because they got hot in fires from incendiary bombs as they were made of metal.'

There were unofficial table shelters – many used their existing kitchen or dining room table. Sidney Richards sheltered with his family under their kitchen table or part of it. During one of the April raids they had slept through the siren and he woke when the flares were going. He woke his mother and they went downstairs along with his older brother and 76 year old grandmother. Bombs were already falling so they stayed in their home in Cheeke Street. As the youngest he was half under the table and the other half was sheltered by their piano. The front and back of the house was heavily damaged but they were safe.

The third type of shelter, which many families had, was a 'refuge room'; a room which had the structure strengthened by additional wooden or steel supports. Owen Michael Mullarkey was a young boy and remembers the shelter preparations at his family's three-storey home at 3 St John's Terrace which was off Paris Street. Their living room was made 'semi-bombproof' by 'having four thick upright timbers in each corner, joined at the top by crossbeams. The idea being that this would support any collapse of the structure'. Likewise, Joyce Flack recalls her home at Pinhoe Road Post Office had the kitchen strengthened with extra beams and 'they built a blast wall outside the kitchen of brick with another inside the kitchen'. The family was given the choice of a shelter or a reinforced room.

Many were also innovative and made use of their cupboard beneath stairs. This may be one of the most common memories; many recall gathering together even with their pets. Some forget why they used it when they had a Morrison or Anderson except it was suggested to be the safest place. Elsie Wills lived near the cathedral and had various forms of shelters but used the cupboard under the stairs. She recalled 'I had an evacuee to stay and an elderly lady, Miss Baker, would also

Rescue men and the rubble.

come across to be with us at night times. She kept a tuck shop near the school, and I knew her from church. As she was frightened at night she would come across to sleep with us and shared a back room with Peggy Walker, the evacuee. Miss Baker would spend the evening knitting. If she heard a plane overhead she'd stop knitting and undo her stitches. As a result she never seemed to finish what she was knitting. She always dressed in black and wore a black hat. She carried a little case with her, but we never knew what was in it.

We had a Morrison Shelter inside the house, but we never used this. Instead, I cleared out the cupboard under the stairs, and as I always turned the gas off if there was a raid, we used a nightlight. It seemed safer under the stairs as we had observed that in most places that got bombed this was the only place left standing. There was an air raid shelter in our street and in a road of terraced houses it took up a lot of space. However, we didn't use it as we had heard stories of large groups of people all being killed together in public shelters.

One night the bombs came so quickly, before the siren had even sounded, so we got under the stairs and were there for ages, listening to the loud banging and crashing. When the all-clear sounded I came out from under the stairs to find that all our glass had been blown out and the doors thrown open by the blast. I told the others to stay in the cupboard while I looked round the house. An armchair which I had just had re-covered was embedded with glass. I noticed there were coach-loads of people outside. Their hair was all wet, and they had come from nearby streets which were burning. They were dressed in their nightclothes and were much in need of the toilet and a cup of tea, so I let them file through our house to use our toilet and then we made them all tea. Everywhere all around was lit up with burning and the shops in the city centre were all burnt out.'[117]

There were other shelters; some were built in the streets of brick. One street shelter near the cathedral was remembered by Sally Morgan. She wrote 'when the sirens went, and we had to hastily make for the nearest air raid shelter which was in one corner of Mermaid Yard, each family had their bunks and there were facilities for tea making and toilets. The ladies in Mermaid Yard were responsible for keeping it clean and ready for all emergencies. I hated going down into the claustrophobic atmosphere, and listening to the bombing but all the grownups were brilliant and made sure that the children were kept occupied. You never knew when you came up out of the shelter what you would find, would your home still be there?' One woman, in her late twenties in the war, went to a brick street shelter towards the end of the war. 'I'd always pack a bag at night and if the sirens went I'd wake the children up and join the people going to the shelter. We never thought of locking the door – we'd just pull it to – and we never lost anything. People would laugh and tell jokes. We'd do it as many as three times in a night – go home, put the children to bed and then the siren would go and we'd have to go back.'

Many public and business buildings offered shelter. Mary Reeves was a young girl at St Nicholas School in The Mint and they had two shelters she remembered as being delightful. One was the priory itself and the other was the nearby Catacombs. Likewise, Mrs V.M. Dean lived at 6 The Mint and used to go into the crypt at the priory near the stone coffin. Joyce Abery was thirteen years old and sheltering with her family at their home in Bartholomew Street West when her father decided the bombing was too intense. They ran up to the priory seeing the German planes flying low over the city. The nuns welcomed them in and they spent the night there.

Mrs E. Dolman had to shelter in several places on the night of the blitz. In 1977 she remembered the underground shelter in the Co-op on the corner of Verney Place. The building was hit and barrels of sugar were set alight which started rolling down. She wrote 'everybody got into a panic but I held my children back because I'd read so much about people racing to an exit and getting crushed. Me and my friend Nell with her two children, we stayed back. We said *Alright, let 'em go*. But a bomb dropped and I think it shut a great many in the exit. Anyway, we didn't know how to get out 'cos all these barrels of burning stuff had come down into the shelter. They were all right the other side 'cos they were able to run up the other way. Anyway, P. C. Barrett come down and he saw we were trapped both sides so he said *Now you stand there and throw the children*. And you know he caught all five of them. We had to pick 'em up and throw them over the barrels of burning stuff and he caught 'em. I could no more tell you how we got over or around that fire . . . never . . . my mind is a complete blank to that.' Their ordeal was not yet over. Mrs Dolman also remembered 'we went to run across the road to the Odeon to get in behind where they had the big pillars – it was the only place we had to run. My oldest son, he lost his shoe and running up through in all that broken glass I thought *Oh, my, his foot. It'll be cut to smithereens.* We met this young boy who lived just near us – he was worried 'cos his mother and the rest of this family were in this street shelter in the main road. And all of a sudden he fell on the three children and me and layed on top of us. I didn't know that they were flying low and machine-gunning the street and I honestly believe if it hadn't been for him we should have caught the [gun]fire: I think I should have walked right into it, not knowing what they was doing. Anyway we got in behind the Odeon. I had on a pair of black suede shoes and they were cut to smithereens and yet my Roy had one shoe on and one shoe off and he never had one mark on his foot.'[118]

Some sheltered in ditches. Maureen Smith remembers her father building houses on land along St Katherine's Road. He and the local farmer, Mr Wilson, dug a big trench off Calthorpe Road where the residents would run to when the sirens sounded. From there they watched the dog fights in the searchlights. Likewise, Pamela Morgan was a very young girl during the war and remembers the family leaving their home at 2 Exe View Cottages along the canal and sheltering in the fields and ditches. Patricia Parkinson recalls how she disliked sheltering under the stairs and on the night of the blitz her family took blankets and sheltered in a nearby field. They lived in Beacon Heath which was then a small development of houses. A bomb fell in a neighbouring field and their neighbour, an air raid warden, 'shot straight up the alley between the houses. But he survived.' Many others simply hid in nearby fields (see pages 224–6).

In one daylight raid May Balkwill of Russell Street discovered her mother had been inventive. She wrote 'the sirens went and I picked up Carol and put her in the table shelter and got my father out of bed. There was a blacksmith's at the top of our road and he was shoeing a horse and the horse went galloping down out street. And my brave, intrepid soldier husband, instead of rescuing his mother-in-law who'd gone shopping, went chasing down the road after the ruddy horse. And I looked up and this plane was over Sampson's Pit, where the sports field is, and I saw him drop a bomb over there. And I thought, *oh, it's a raid.* He turned on the Triangle and he came right up the back of our house with all his machine guns shooting right and left. Then into Belgrave Road which is on an angle to Russell Street. In the attic of one of the houses there one woman had an eiderdown drying and he shot right through this and the place was all feathers. I left my father with Carol and went up Hammett's Dairy to see where me mum was. As I was going up through Cheeke Street I turned round and I saw this pilot bailing out down over the estuary; I hoped he dropped in the sea. When I got to Hammett's Dairy, I said *Where's me mother?* A trap door opened up from the floor and my mother's little head came up, *Ooh*, she said, *Ooh, my god, May, I'n't this awful?* I think we got our two penn'orth of corn beef and our half a round of sausages.'[119]

Some families used different types of shelters at the same address. Angela Hancock was eleven when war broke out and her family moved to 5 Salutary Mount next to Eagle House. They had moved from Cornwall where their home was requisitioned and came to Heavitree to stay with her uncle, aunt and Miss Vooght, their companion house-keeper. They initially sheltered with them in the cellar of Eagle House but it caved in during a raid so an Anderson Shelter was placed in the garden. They were not the only ones: she remembered how the nuns from the nearby Catholic Church were saved from a bomb by sheltering with them.

The clearing up.

One family survived even though their shelter had not been installed. Dorothy Wynn recalled 'we lived in Lower Brunswick Place, just about where the bus station is now. My father was out on air-raid warden duty with a colleague and my brother, my mother and I took shelter under an old oak table, because our air raid shelter was still propped up against the wall outside, waiting to be put up next morning. For a long time we could feel the vibrations of bombs dropping and hear lots of aircraft about. Suddenly there was an almighty bang. The lights had gone out and there we were surrounded by choking debris. It was for just such an occasion that my mother kept her wooden rolling pin with us on raid nights. We could hear men coming around calling *is there anyone in there?* Mother kept banging on the tabletop and a few hours later we were dug out and taken to a shelter by Mr Wills, who owned the dairy in Paris Street. It was dark and I do not know how he managed to find us. Daylight came and with it the all clear. We emerged from this outdoor shelter and I was amazed, as almost everything around us was either a heap of rubble, or the buildings had no fronts to them. The dairy had almost vanished. My father had been killed, so had Girly Widiger and her father, who had kept the antique shop. We also heard of a family who lost nine children that night farther up Paris Street.'[120]

There were also sheltering agreements: the 'Help Your Neighbour Scheme' started in the autumn of 1941.[121] Donald Sheppard recalled this saying 'we had an arrangement during the war that if you got bombed, you made arrangements with another family, that if you got bombed you stayed in their house and if they got bombed they stayed with you. Well, these people did get bombed. I think he was Deputy Surveyor at Devon County Council, he was on roads and bridges. They lived on Okehampton Road. It was not a direct bombing, it was a land mine, right on the corner, they were aiming for the railway bridge. They were with us for a few days and nights.' This altered their subsequent shelter arrangements. He remembers 'one funny thing happened during the time they were with us. The mother-in-law, the wife's mother, who lived with them, her sister lived at Coaver House, called Thomas who had the silk factory. They heard a broadcast from Haw-Haw, or somebody had, that Exeter was next in line to be bombed. We all traipsed up to Coaver, and they had a cellar and they used to get all the kids from the deaf school when the siren went and they all went into the cellar. So we went up this evening about midnight. We were down the cellar for about 2 hours and the all clear went, the kids went back to the school, we all had something to eat and drink at about 3 in the morning and it was summer time and the birds were beginning to tweak and my father said *I've had enough of this, we're going home.* We hadn't had any sleep. All the other people stayed there. But we went home. That was before the blitz, in one of the other raids. We said if we had stayed where we were we would have been all right but around Coaver a number of bombs fell. St Leonard's, particularly Magdalen Road, had been badly hit and it was all a bit close.'

Sister Edward Mary remembers her convent's cock and hens made their own arrangements: they would lead themselves into their hutch to shelter when an air raid warning sounded and come out when it finished. This amazed the nuns who afterwards often collected buckets of stray bullets which had rained down and would have killed the birds had they not known to shelter.

There were problems in supplying shelters. Demand was greater than the supply. Ivy Facey remembers 'a lot of houses didn't have Andersons or Morrisons until after the bombing started – in 1941 I think they started to put in reinforced rooms. All the Londoners came

The destruction of Exeter.

down in the first place as evacuees thinking Exeter and the South West would not be bombed. When the bombing started they went back on their own. They thought London was better protected. In Exeter we had nothing.' It was not possible for schools to provide shelters for all their students. Ethel Harris recalls there was 'no shelter at school. The older pupils had to go farther away – I had to go to a house in Pennsylvania Road at first and then to one in a side road. It was quite a rush, 3 or 4 to each place & we stood in the hall or passage. On one occasion I heard that a few from a year below us had gone across the road to houses which had been a school. They thought it fun until the Head realised they had been taken over as soldiers' billets & got them a new place very quickly.'

Air Raids

Exeter was bombed at various times through the war. The main attack took place over a fortnight and was a series of four night-time reprisal raids for the Royal Air Force attack on Lubeck on 28/9 March 1942. Other cities attacked were Bath, Canterbury, Norwich and York. The Exeter raids took place on 23/4, 24/5 and 25/6 of April and finally, the blitz on 3/4 May 1942. There were also sporadic attacks both during the day and at night from 1940 to 1943.

Everyone interviewed remembers being bombed at some time. Dorrie Langdon was a schoolgirl and recalls 'one particular Wednesday I was in my bedroom at the back of the house, when a single bomb fell about a hundred yards away, I was thrown to the floor and felt really shocked. A large house on the main road had been severely damaged but no actual damage affected our house. It had been a lone plane dropping its last bomb en route back to Germany. That was something unusual to tell my surprised parents on their return from work.'

Nearly all remember a sequence of bombing raids. Sylvia Hart, who was a child during the war, recalls Exeter was a beautiful city 'but then the bombing started. My father was in the demolition squad based near the council yard in Exe Island. The depot windows at the back looked over the slaughterhouse in Tudor Street. Their first call out was to St Loyes, a landmine had been dropped killing 2 men and 2 children. I remember my father saying one of the men worked for the Admiralty and when they picked him up his watch was still going. The children were killed by blast. Then sometime later we had a daylight raid. Bombs were dropped but I cannot now given the exact location. I do remember Mr Bidgood, the undertaker in Holloway Street, having bodies of some airmen in his chapel of rest and after a bomb went off they were picked up in the street nearby. I think the airmen had been killed at Exeter Airport.' She also recalls a bomb falling in Glasshouse Lane onto some cob cottages; 'my father went down with the squad and they said one man was missing but couldn't find him. My father thought he heard a murmur and they picked away at the rubble. They finally found him and he was trapped by a beam of wood. He was taken to the hospital and once a year, for many years, he would come into Exeter to make a point of finding my father.'

Many people have memories of being bombed before and after the blitz. Douglas Newbery, for example, remembers a land mine floated past the chimney of their house at Barley Lane. The parachute carried it to Exwick Cemetery where it caused damage to graves. In April 1942 Eileen Reynolds was nearly fifteen years old and living with her family at Barley Mount in Redhills. On one evening, she later wrote, 'we looked out of the window and a parachute was heading for the back garden. The A.R.P. Warden, who lived a few doors away, came to investigate what exactly was at the end of the parachute. I thought that he was very brave to go so close – it could have been a German! The warden was a Mr Mills whose wife had just had triplets.' Mr P. Stacey recalls working in the basement of Colson's after the blitz. He was trying to repair the electrics when he heard bombing in the distance. Shoppers came racing downstairs and later they heard that Paris Street had been bombed.

Kathleen Fletcher was a young girl during the war and remembers two particular bombings. Her first experience was when a land mine fell at the bottom of Mayfield Road and Avondale Road, off St Loyes Road.' She recalls 'I was in bed although we had a shelter in the garden but had had no warning. My father was an A.R.P. warden and had gone to a meeting and then to the Royal Oak in Heavitree. When he came home he found all the damage. The wall of our house bulged out by at least two inches – when we went up the stairs you could see the bulge. The damage blew out windows, and everyone else's. They later covered the windows with this horrible black stuff.' On another occasion 'just after Christmas one year we had a daylight raid. I was told to put my presents away but was trying not to. I looked up and saw a plane was coming over and there was a black cross on it. Then the undercarriage came down, I screamed and saw one bomb come out. That demolished two houses in Atwyll Avenue.'

For many the bombings were extremely traumatic experiences. Edmund Forte was a young boy living in his family home in Dunsford Gardens. He recalls his 'most enduring memory is of one of the nightly air raids. Sirens going off in the middle of the night in the blackout, filled us all with fear or when the sirens' first warning growls slowly rose to it's howl, we knew it was a signal that we all had to quickly take cover under the stairs but sometimes we were placed in special metal cages under a table, which had been moved to the front room. Here we made our bed, and snuggled up close together. This was an adventure, although we knew it was dangerous. For some reason we would whisper during the bombing, as if we might be heard, and the Germans might arrange to have a bomb dropped on us. Air raids were for a while a nightly affair. We would hear the faint drone of the enemy bombers. This grew louder and louder, turning into an ever-increasing loud 'throbbing' noise. This noise was made by their engines, which had been set up in such a way as to produce this effect. Then came the whistling noise made by the bombs as they came down, this too had been arranged by the Germans, having strapped whistling devices to the bombs . . . And the heavy "crump" as they exploded somewhere in our lovely Exeter. I remember it all so clearly. The sound of the enemy planes, the searchlights, the "Crump" of the bombs falling around us, all mixed up with the noise of the anti-aircraft guns firing. We made little gasping noises as the bombs exploded and snuggled into each other for comfort and safety. The grown ups would say *That sounded near the gasworks* or *I hope so-and-so is all right*! I think I was brave. I remember the girls used to snivel a bit, but it cannot have been very nice for them. Especially when I wet myself. My urine was famous for it's strength, and smell, and my good old pyjamas held a lot of the stuff. We were all united in fear when we were being bombed, with the grown ups pretending to be as brave as they could for our sakes. I remember always feeling protected and safe, but the grownups seemed vulnerable at times and got a little bit crotchety and nervous. Later, the 'all clear' siren would sound, and we would emerge from the steel cage beneath the table, and hastily be put to bed. There was usually only one raid each night, although there were exceptions.'

Sally Morgan also had a traumatic experience. She recalls living in Mermaid's Yard, near the cathedral, when a child. Her grandmother was responsible for her and her sister because their father was in the Home Guard and her mother was an A.R.P. Warden. She later wrote 'Gran would never go until the last minute – and I remember when we ran to the shelter the noise was terrifying and the sky seemed alight with search lights, smoke and fire. Gran was debating whether we should go to the shelter or sit in the stairs when there was a banging on the front door, and it was the chief A.R.P. Warden shouting *you must come right* away. When we opened the front door the blast of a bomb blew all the windows out. I was blown from the front door to the back door which was quite a distance and my sister, who was in her carrycot, and placed by the fireplace, was completely covered in soot! We managed to get to the shelter, but I was in shock and had to have

The Cathedral from Bedford Street.

treatment from the doctor who told my parents that I should not be subjected to any further trauma, and it was suggested that I stay with an aunt who lived in a small village.'

Many remember their first air raid warning. Vera Jex's first one came when she was a young woman living with her parents at 116 Rifford Road: they pushed all their furniture into the middle of the room and sat with their backs to the walls with cushions on their heads. Mrs J. M. Bishop remembers her family's first experience. They came downstairs in their dressing gowns and squatted behind the sofa, away from the then still unprotected glass, and held a tabletop over their heads. The need to dress quickly could cause amusement. In Mrs Bishop's case her father once dressed in the dark and later was revealed to be wearing his black tailcoat along with a pair of old grey gardening trousers.[122] Jeremy Setter's first experience was as a small boy walking with his mother along Sidwell Street when a German plane dropped a landmine. The plane was flying so low it barely missed hitting the top of the Savoy Cinema. One woman recalls the first air raid warning came on a Sunday evening. She and her family had been out for a walk 'then the siren went. It was a false alarm but it scared the people'.

Others remember near misses. One woman who lived in Tudor Street recalls during a raid 'I was walking up Frog Street with my daughter and when we got to the top of Stepcote Hill I heard the bullets on the nearby roof. We quickly ran on and got indoors.' Peter Philips remembers a daylight attack when he was a young boy living at 23 Barley Mount. He later wrote 'I was in the back garden and mother was hanging out the washing when this plane flew over. The swastikas were clearly visible and the plane appeared to be so low that I could see the pilot's head. Mother shrieked at me to get indoors and then we heard a large explosion'. Rod Coles was a young boy during the war and remembered he 'was with some of my pals. I was having a kick-about with a tennis ball right in the middle of Homefield Road, Heavitree, just around the corner from Oakfield Street where I lived. I was about eight at the time. Suddenly I heard the sound of aircraft and knew from the engine noise that they weren't ours. Then I spotted two German fighters roaring overhead just above the rooftops. I can still picture them with the Luftwaffe crosses on their sides. I heard guns firing and pushed my cousin, Ray Seldon, down on the ground and lay down on top of him. We weren't hit, but afterwards we saw bullet holes in the wall above the front of Anne Day's local general store. The bullets must have missed us only by feet.'[123] Barbara Shute was eight years old when the war started and was living at 17 Pinces Garden in St Thomas. On one night her father felt the bombing was too severe to stay in their back garden so he brought them into the house. There were several houses nearby destroyed as well as the nearby Colour Glass Factory. From that explosion glass littered their back garden and they realised in the morning it would have severely damaged, or even killed, them had they stayed there overnight. On another occasion she was walking down Regent Street with her friend June when a German plane suddenly appeared from the direction of Ide and began machine-gunning the street. They sheltered in a coal yard. Sheila Pike recalls her mother telling her of crossing Paris Street during the summer of 1942 when a German plane suddenly appeared. Two small children began running and Sheila's mother caught them and threw them onto the ground with her on top. Bullets were sprayed all around them but not one of them was hit.

— The University College of the South West —

It appeared bombs fell indiscriminately. Sue Andrewes remembers being surprised when she was bombed in 1942. She recalled 'the air raids came at the end of April and beginning of May. We, at Exeter, were unused to the omens of a clear night sky and a shining moon. The oracle had oft warned London, Plymouth and other Channel ports; they knew the signs only too well. In any case, what on earth was there to bomb in Exeter?' She had come down as a full-time agricultural worker and was staying with a family in Streatham Drive. On the night of April 23 she was 'sleeping, tired out from a day's land work, I awoke quickly that night with the drone of aircraft overhead. In those days we all thought that we could tell the difference between 'ours' and 'theirs', so I turned over as it was obviously ours who were flying rather low. Not for long though as the crump of the explosions in the distance was the signal for us all to get downstairs with the sleepy children & quick. We all knew that the place to stay was in the hallway with its fewer windows and the under-the-space hid the little ones wrapped in eiderdowns. The crumps we heard came interestingly in fives – you counted them with baited breath. Then it was our stick – one, two, three, and just outside, 'us' & number five the distant neighbours perhaps.

The noise and blast were hugely physical, like a knock-out punch in boxing. The front door and glass crashed in on us and then came that never-to-be-forgotten smell of acrid vile cordite. Mr Short, by the flattened door, found that, amazingly, none of us had suffered physical injuries and said, masterfully, *it's all right, there will be no more bombs here now*! The children stopped their crying & somehow we were indeed all right. I don't remember any A.R.P. wardens coming round but they must have had much more urgent calls with which to deal that night, one thinks. Later, inspecting my room, climbing up the much-damaged stairs I found the bed covered with broken roof tiles, glass & dirt. How lucky we had all been. The roof had been blasted off & there was a deep crater in the garden. Dear Mrs Short said sweetly *I'm afraid that you won't want to stay with us ever again*! How all of us needed to laugh at that moment and so we did.

I had news that my sister Christine, very pregnant at the time, & my brother-in-law had mercifully escaped. A great relief, of course. John arranged for me to be housed in a room at the back of Mardon Hall (the building unharmed). I was hugely grateful to have a bath as soon as I got there & well needed it. I was conscious, incidentally, that I was possibly looking quite respectable for once considering the night's events. This was because, early on that fateful night, I had washed my hair & put in the usual metal curlers. So, if not quite Deanna Durbin, I thought that I was a near offer for the Saanen Goat's consideration in their milking stables.'

– Culverland Road –

James Whiteside, the city's Information Officer, visited Culverland Road to see bomb damage from an April raid in 1942. He saw an unexploded bomb there which was 'an ugly thing – as big as a man. It had fallen in the side garden of a small house. The householder had an aviary and the bomb was buried in the ground within inches of a cage

(Opposite) Culverland Road in the 1930s showing Culverlands.

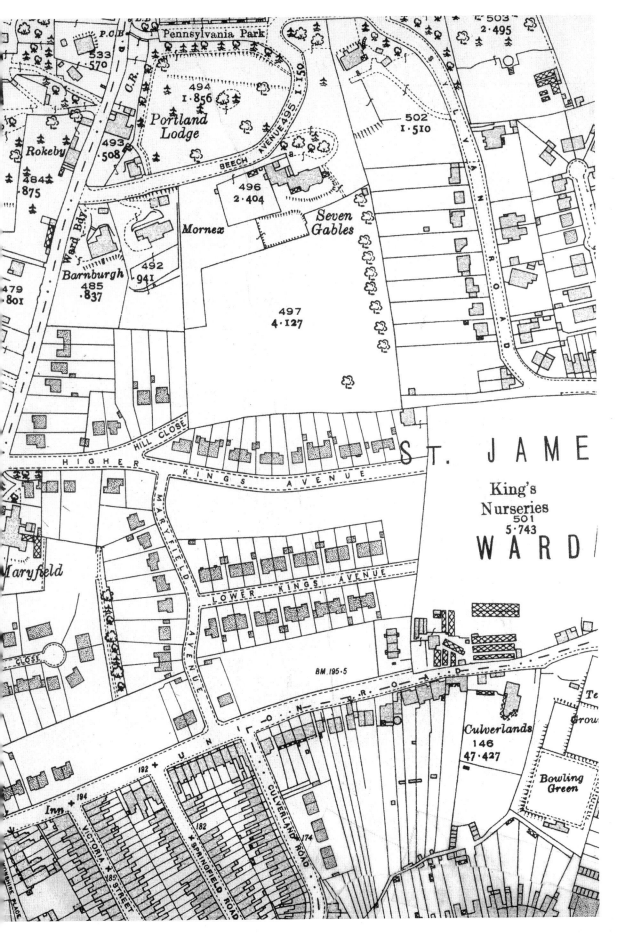

of Indian pheasants and other birds of bright plumage. The police had been feeding them with corn. Lucky birds, I thought. They did not like strangers, but seemed not to mind the bomb.'[124] David Melhuish remembers 'the unexploded bomb in Culverland Road has a family connection. Uncle Buller Melhuish was walking down Culverland Road after we had a raid, and came across a guy who was filling in a hole in his garden. Buller asked him what it was and the guy said he didn't know what had dropped there. Buller told him he better get it checked and this set a sequence of events in place which eventually led to the finding of the bomb. The police closed the road off, and the news went round the neighbourhood, so a crowd gathered to watch from behind a barrier. The bomb was in the last house on the right side before the block of flats. They must have rated the bomb as quite low power because we were less than 100 yards from the disposal team as they worked. They used a tripod and pulley blocks to lift it out.' Caroline Cornish, who lived at Culverlands in Union Road, also recalls that bomb. She later wrote she and her brother went to investigate the damage and 'peered into the substantial crater in Culverland Road where there usually was an aviary. We were most concerned as to the fate of the birds. Noticing a metal object poking out of the ground I cautioned my more intrepid brother not to get any closer and said I thought we should report this to our father. Father was Chief Warden for the Pennsylvania District. This we duly did. Later . . . was it that day or the next? . . . Father set about recommending immediate evacuation of the houses in the area up to and including Culverlands. *Nonsense Les*, said my mother. *You know I can't possibly leave the house at the moment. I have a hen sitting and the eggs are due to hatch any day soon.* She was adamant. No unexploded bomb would cause her to abandon a hen so imminently to embrace motherhood. So that was that!' Caroline and her brother were sent away to Drewsteignton but later heard their family's 'hen house had been blown right over by the blast, but the hen had hatched her entire clutch of eggs successfully so we also had a much larger family of adorable chicks to take care of.' The birds in their neighbour's aviary were not so lucky on the night of the blitz: James Whiteside wrote that he passed Culverland Road the following morning 'and I saw with regret that the house with the aviary that I had visited so long ago on the previous day had fallen with its neighbours: a direct hit from a high explosive bomb. The luck of the Indian pheasants had been short-lived.'

Another person in Culverland Road also remembers the bombing. She was then twenty-two years ago and recalls for her family fortunately 'not much happened. There was an unexploded bomb further up the road and they came hammering on the door and said we must come out. I didn't shelter, I slept in the attic. I think I preferred to be bombed out than buried. Everyone rushed to get into the cupboard under the stairs, which wasn't for me at all. It used to worry my mother a bit but I didn't use to come down. Still, the wallpaper came off the wall, it peeled off perhaps with all the vibrations. A lot of tiles gone and bits inside missing. They didn't let you stay in two minutes – they stand outside and let you go in but they weren't keen, they weren't going to let you repack. It was just the odd two or three bombs that went off. We were evacuated to Ottery for not long, perhaps a few weeks until they patched it up and we went back.'

Mrs C. Jewell was living with her young son and sheltering in her Morrison Shelter on the night of the blitz. Their roof was damaged and the windows were blown in. It was thought an unexploded bomb was in the drain so the family was evacuated. It later turned out that a paving stone had been blown from Culverland Road. Her father-in-law took them away but when they got as far as Lion's Holt she remembered having left behind not only Pongo the goldfish but also six precious eggs. She went back for both.

– Paris Street –

Paris Street suffered badly on April 24/5 1942, possibly the fourteenth raid on the city. After an earlier raid Sidney Richards, then aged twelve, went to nearby Paris Street where the Salvation Army was handing out corn beef sandwiches. He stayed in the van and continued eating when the siren sounded again despite his mother being desperate for his safety. After the raid of April 24/5 he and his family came out of their grandmother's home in Cheeke Street to find great devastation around them. He remembers his grandmother calling up to a neighbour who was still sitting on his bed on the third floor – the front of the house had been blown off as well as the stairs. He sat there unable to

The centre of Exeter in 1932 showing Paris Street and the dense housing.

leave his bed, having slept through the bombing. The family left for Silverton and intended to return to Exeter on May 3 but decided to stay for another week. They missed the blitz.

John Pickard was sixteen years old and his parents ran The Cosy Café in Paris Street. He recalled 'the café was on one side of the shop front in Paris Street and there was an ice cream parlour on the other side. We had two soldiers from the Royal Army Pay Corps billeted with us at the time, one called Reed and the other called Giddy. Mr Reed was a good pianist and we used to enjoy getting round the piano for a sing-song in the evenings. After leaving Episcopal School I was working as a store-man in Woolworth's in the High Street. I had also joined Dad's Army which had a depot in Bedford Circus . . . on the night of the Paris Street air raid, about a week before the big Exeter Blitz of May 4, I had been to the Odeon. My dad was on fire watching duty at Woolworth's. When the air raid sirens sounded I took shelter under a very strongly built table in the kitchen with my mother and a married sister. Paris Street was hit by a number of high explosive and firebombs and it was terrifying to hear the explosions and the sound of the building crashing in over our heads. I thought we had been buried alive but we managed to crawl out to safety. Our two boarders also escaped. They were sheltering in the passageway between the café and the ice cream parlour.' The business was destroyed and the building was not rebuilt.[125]

In 1977 May Balkwill remembered the raid. She recalled 'about that time there was a bomb dropped in Cowick Street and one in Okehampton Street. Everyone was going out of the city into church halls but my husband's mother was sleeping in the fields under a hedge. This worried me so I wrote to my husband: *I'm a bit concerned about your mother; she's sleeping in the fields: she shouldn't do this but she wouldn't listen to me.* Anyway, he was given 24 hours compassionate leave; it was known as passion leave in the army'. She also remembered 'we'd had a raid in Paris Street the beginning of the week and he arrived at half past nine in the evening, had a meal and before he could get to bed the sirens went. We had to get the kids up: there was my baby, my sister's baby, my mother and my father. So we get them into the table shelter which was a big steel affair like a rabbit hutch with wiring on the side. Inside we had a mattress, a blanket and some pillows, hoping the kids would sleep. Mine never did: she always used to sit up and say *Whee, bang*! My mother used to say *Stop her, May, do stop her. You can't hear what's going on*! And when she said you can't hear what's going on you must imagine all hell breaking loose outside the house: bang, crash, wallop – and the bullets hitting the kitchen.

My husband said *I've got to go out*. Neither of us could get under the shelter: I suffered with claustrophobia and would never get under. When he got outside the front door he came back, called me out and said *We've got to get out: we're the last in the street. If we don't get out now, you know, we're going to be burnt*. By this time the planes were still overhead. So we go back and say we've got to get out. He took the two babies and my sister and sent back a little air raid warden: he was only a little short man and he picked my mother up and put her over his shoulder and she kept shouting and screaming *Put me down, put me down, I haven't got my teeth in*. I dunno who she thought was going to look at her with no teeth in 'cos by this time it was what, 12 o'clock, one o'clock in the morning, possibly.

Anyway I was left to take my father down to the shelter. We got my mother's teeth and sent her off on the back of this little air raid warden. My father and I set out to try to go to the shelter; my father had arthritis and walked with two sticks. Outside the front door the incend-

Paris Street after the bombing.

The ruined Palladium in Paris Street.

iary bombs were still burning in the gutter; it was a pure white flame, possibly two foot long and we had to step over these things. It looked as if every house in the street was on fire except ours and next door. As we went down the street the bedroom floors were falling in and crashing everywhere. Right opposite was poor old Mrs Hitchcock's house; through the window – course there was no glass, all blown out – there was her poor old piano, her pride and joy. I'd taken her to the shelter about seven o'clock the night before with all her worldly goods in the pushchair. We always used to laugh and say *Let's take the crown jewels to the shelter.* A lot of 'em wouldn't sleep in the street; they were nervous. We used to stay in – if you're going to get bombed you might as well get bombed.

Going down the street with my father there was nobody else in sight. The planes went away, I think, unless I didn't take any notice of them. At the bottom of the road . . . a telegraph pole snapped in half where it'd been burning. My father got tangled up in the red-hot wire; I had to untangle him. We had to make a little detour round the telegraph pole which almost took us into the burning building the other side. We eventually reached the swimming baths and went in under the Denmark Road entrance to the shelter.'

She found her sister and children there but not her mother. 'Eventually I got out of the shelter, possibly about nine o'clock next morning and the Salvation Army were there with cups of tea in big white china mugs and their corn beef sandwiches, about three inches thick – went down lovely. I was worried about my mother 'cos I didn't know where she was. Eventually I found her in a shelter in the Triangle with neighbours. And all the neighbours kept saying to me, *May, is my house alright? May, is my place o.k.?* And what could I say? You can't say, *No, yours is gone, yours is gone, yours is gone, but ours is all right.* How the hell could you? You just said *well, you know, we can't really tell 'cos of all the smoke and fire.*'

The family's house was saved although there was only the ground floor. They then left Exeter for Rugby at what was the end of the 24 hour compassionate leave. Mrs Balkwill later reflected 'we never had any passion out of that 24 hours.'[126]

– Okehampton Street –

Four bombs fell in Okehampton Street and Road on 23 April 1942. Joy-Hawkins Smith was living with her parents at the Exe Bridge end of Okehampton Street and sheltering with her mother in their Morrison Shelter when the bombs began to fall. Her father ran a butcher shop

The Okehampton Street bomb damage.

at 9 Okehampton Street and was outside talking to a neighbour, Henrietta Baxter, who owned a nearby sweet shop. She remembered 'the first bomb dropped in the road beside them outside No. 8., the blast sucked Mrs Baxter, still holding her pet dog, into the bomb crater, and she and her dog were killed. My father was lifted by the blast and blown into the surface air raid shelter on the opposite side of the road.' Her family were not seriously injured although the house was completely destroyed. She and her mother were trapped under their shelter and 'could hear father shouting our names. The part I remember most is the feeling of choking on the dust of broken plaster as the other three bombs went off, shaking more of the building down around us. Father came digging at the rubble with his bare hands as he tried to reach us. He was later aided by rescue workers who broke through to us about 7 a.m. We had been trapped since 11.30 p.m. the previous night. We owed our lives to that Morrison shelter'.[127]

Five people were killed in that attack and eight houses and business premises demolished. There were 36 other buildings damaged.[128]

— Holloway Street, the bouncing bomb and the laughing pilot —

More than six months after the blitz on the 30th of December 1942 another raid took place. It might have been the seventeenth on the city. In the early 1970s Mr E.S. Pope remembered this daylight raid. He wrote 'it was a Monday between 9 o'clock and 10 o'clock. I was a security man on the gate entering the gas works. I saw three planes come up the canal and they opened out like the Prince of Wales' feathers: one went straight on, one went and bombed Holloway Street and the other went around St Thomas. They did a lot of damage'.[129] Ken Triggs recalled 'I was on leave and visiting the home of my wife Winifred in Hazel Road, Burnthouse Lane, when I heard the terrific noise of low flying aircraft. I ran to a window and saw two FW 190s flying to the city centre in a line parallel with Topsham Road. They were only 200 to 300 feet up. From the noise I judged that two other FW 190s had already gone over ahead of them. One of the two I saw released its bomb, which hit the wall of a house in Briar Crescent, went right through the house and out through a rear wall, hit the garden and ricocheted up into the air again, but never went off. I understand that the second FW 190 dropped its bomb on Holloway Street. That one did detonate at Holloway Buildings, where my grandmother lived, at the approaches to the Home of the Good

Shepherd, and I believe that a young man in his 20s was killed.'[130]

The enemy planes had flown low over the city. One bomb was probably intended for the gas works along the river. It missed, bounced and hit a house in Isca Road. The occupant was killed. Doreen Louchex remembered she was a young schoolgirl and 'my grandmother, Clara May, was standing in our garden and she told me that the plane was so low that she could see the face of the pilot and was amazed to notice that he was laughing.'[131] H.J. Frost was ten years old and recalled 'my friend John Goodies and I were making our weekly trip to the gasworks to buy two bags of coke for our mothers. We were pushing a heavy wooden barrow with two large cast-iron wheels. We reached the path outside St Thomas Church when we heard a loud explosion, then machine gun fire. We looked up to find a German aircraft flying low over Cowick Street in the direction of the pleasure grounds. It was so low I could see the pilot. It was followed by an R.A.F. aircraft which was trying to shoot it down. All this happened in a few seconds. Then we heard the air raid warning siren. I pulled the barrow over me for protection while John ran towards Robson's cooked meat shop. The end house of Isca Road was hit and there was a search going on in the rubble for survivors. There was a small dog digging away. On the piece of ground opposite were the remains of a static water tank, just a heap of tangled steel. While all this was happening, my mother, walking down Locarno Road, saw the German aircraft flying low up the road and belting out flames followed by our plane still firing its guns. She leapt over a garden hedge and hid underneath. I think the German plane finally crashed in Farmer Towell's field at Barley Lane.'[132]

Bob Vanstone was thirty-one and 'was a blacksmith at the Gas Works, which was then run by the Exeter Gaslight and Coke Company, and we used to make gas from coal. Suddenly on that morning we heard aircraft overhead and someone shouted *Gerry*! I had been overhauling a boiler and I dived right inside it to use it as a kind of air raid shelter. We heard one of the planes machine-gunning the railway lines alongside Willey's Avenue. We could hear the bullets hitting the rails. After it was all over we discovered that the bomb which was dropped had gouged a groove in the concrete about a yard long and a foot wide, and going down around a foot into the soil underneath. It had struck near the purifier plant, a structure with no walls, only a roof. When it took off again it smashed up through the roof of the purifier and over rooftops adjacent to Willey's Avenue before blowing up the house in Isca Road. One of the fins of the bomb broke off and a colleague of mine picked it up, but quickly dropped it again. It was almost red hot.'[133]

Peter Newman recalled 'four of us lads – who all lived in Cotfield Street at the back of the gas works – had been out on some errands to local shops for our mums, and we were on our way back when the bomb landed. The three with me were Ray Hatley, Les Jones and Ron Hemmings. I was probably around nine years old at that time. Around 10 a.m., just after the air raid warning sirens had sounded, we were walking alongside the high wall which was the boundary of the gas works site when we heard the noise of aero engines. Then we saw three German planes going overhead – low enough for us to be able to see the pilots. They came across from the Holloway Street area and flew off towards Haldon. Next came a big explosion and we saw debris flying up into the air. It turned out that the bombs had blown up houses in Isca Road. We didn't discover until later that the bomb had first of all come down in the grounds of the gas works . . . if it had gone off where it first landed we wouldn't be telling the story today. It would have blown the gas works wall apart and we would almost certainly have been crushed under it.'[134] Ray Hatley was one of the lads. He remembered he was on an errand to collect his family's meat ration from the butcher in Wardrew Street. He recalled 'the meat was tied with string and I had my finger through the string to carry it – just as well because I probably would have lost it in all the excitement. As it was, the string nearly tore my finger off. We suddenly saw these three planes with big black German crosses marked on them. We saw something dropping from one of them and heard a screeching noise followed by a big thump, then silence broken by a huge bang. The thump must have been the noise of the bomb bouncing off the gas works yard. The blast threw us face down and we could hear stones and bits of debris showering down. We took to our heels down Water Lane and it was only then I realised that I still had hold of the meat ration, which I was able to take safely home.'[135]

The place where the bomb first fell was marked. Ray Hatley recalled 'when I went to work at the gas plant as a maintenance engineer later in life the foreman fitter, Dennis Hellier, showed me the spot in the yard where someone had chiselled the shape of a swastika into the concrete . . . The swastika vanished from view when a new city council car park was constructed on the site.' Bob Vanstone was the man who did it. He remembered 'the gasworks manager decided that we should permanently mark the spot where it bounced and I was given the job of making a three-eighths-of-an-inch-thick steel frame to set into the ground around the edges of the gouge mark it had left – a frame around a yard long and a foot wide. One of the bricklayers then cemented it neatly into place. The marking was there for many years and was still there when coal gas production ended 30 years ago on the change-over to North Sea gas – and my job ended.'[136]

One anonymous resident recalled 'my wife was employed by Woolwich Arsenal testing anti-aircraft shell cases which had been refurbished by the Vulcan Stove Company. When the warning siren went, the girls left the building to disperse, in accordance with company policy. My wife looked up and saw the bomb coming away from the plane as it was right over the large gasholder. But by the time it hit the ground it was right by the Gas Works boundary wall. It then ricocheted right over Willey's works, Hodges engineers, Chamberlain Road and Fords Road before exploding in Isca Road. I was still in Willey's and didn't evacuate because there had already been several false starts. A plane went over which we thought was one of ours from the airport. Then there was a big thud followed by a loud explosion. When I looked out of the Pattern Shop window I saw a crater about 20 feet across near the Gas Works boundary wall, from which I discovered the bomb had flown up into the air again over to Isca Road. It was all kept rather quiet at the time, so as not to damage local morale and to keep the Germans in the dark about the results of that raid.'[137]

Beryl Currey was eight years old and living with her parents in Isca Road. The house opposite was destroyed. She recalled 'I was still in bed and telling my five-year-old brother Bob a story when we heard the plane swoop overhead just as the warning sirens were sounding. I pulled Bob under the covers. The windows were shattered by the blast and our front door ended half way up the stairs. There was debris everywhere. The wooden footboard of the bed was peppered with shards of glass from the window. I was unscathed but my brother had a slight cut on his ear caused when the bedside clock was blown at him. My mother had just received a letter from my father who was abroad on active service. She was standing at the window reading it when she was knocked over by the blast and never found the letter again to finish reading father's news. She had a piece of glass embedded in her calf and it didn't come out until VE Day, several years later, when she was dancing in the street. The glass had turned pink.' She added 'a strange thing which impressed us all was that a picture entitled The Guardian Angel right above my bed was still intact. It was one of a pair and the one in my grandfather's room was shattered and all the drawers beneath it were pushed open.' Afterwards she remembers a stray dog coming into their house and eating the remains of their Christmas cake which had been blasted out of its storage. Another young girl was Hilda Ogg who happened to be with her aunt at No. 8 Isca Road. She recalled 'my aunt told me to stay put but I wanted to get home to my mother at No. 23 so I ran out along the road as fast as I could. There were bombers overhead, just above the rooftops, it seemed. My mum was glad to see me but told me off for not staying at my aunt's. She said I could have been machine-gunned.'[138]

Barbara Clark's grandfather was killed. She recalled 'he worked at Willey's and was at home that morning because he had just finished a night shift. I believe Willey's was a munitions factory at that time. My mother and the younger daughter of a neighbour had a very luck escape. Just before the bomb struck they had gone to see if there was anything he needed. He asked them to get some sugar and they were on their way to the shop when he was killed. I was just a schoolgirl then. A friend and I were on our way back from the shops when the air raid warning sirens sounded and this German plane appeared overhead with its guns firing. Then we saw the explosion which killed my grandfather at the other end of the road.'[139]

Irene Lyne was then 22 years old and a member of the congregation of St Andrew's Church in Willey's Avenue. She remembered 'I was working in the meter department at Willey's. It was late morning on December 30th 1942 and most of us at Willey's had gone to the air raid shelter . . . The church was destroyed by the blast of the bomb. The green building which remains on the site today was our church hall. St Andrew's was known as the 'Tin Church' because it was constructed of corrugated iron, rather like St Philip's Church in Buddle Lane which was recently closed . . . After our old Tin Church had been demolished we held some services at St Edmunds-on-the-bridge which was still in use then and some in our church hall which survived the bomb.'[140] Peter Newman recalled that 'blast from the explosion in Isca Road pushed the church sideways and it was so badly damaged it had to be pulled down.'[141]

Len Hales was a young lad working in Willey's Avenue – he was delivering logs from a horse-drawn cart. He recalled 'I distinctly saw the man who dropped the Exeter bomb. As at Exmouth [see below] he had pulled back the cockpit canopy and was wearing a leather helmet and goggles. He handled the *Focke Wulfe* 190 fighter bomber very well. He flew right under the high voltage power cables and I could see him laughing his head off. He seemed to be a young chap just enjoying himself. He machine-gunned along the Willey's Avenue embankment and, if he had gone a few hundred yards further, would have hit a trainload of children who had just left St Thomas Station for Dawlish Warren. I think he may have been aiming at the goods train which was approaching the station on the 'up' line. He might have been shot down the same day because I saw our planes in a dog fight with some German ones later over the city.'[142]

Dorothy Coke was also attacked by a laughing pilot. She remembers when she was eighteen she was at Exmouth: 'it happened in daylight as I was walking on the beach with a solider who was a boyfriend at

The Tin Church.

that time. This German plane had been machine-gunning a train at Starcross and came screaming low across the water to Exmouth, where the pilot was laughing as he started firing his guns at us. We threw ourselves down and the bullets thudded into the sand just above our heads. If we had taken another step we would both have been dead. We literally escaped death by inches. The pilot in a leather helmet had the cockpit canopy pulled back, and I could see him laughing. I remember it as clearly as if it were only yesterday.'[143]

Altogether there were nineteen deaths from the six different incidents at Holloway Street and Holloway Buildings, Isca Road, Polsloe Road, Topsham Road, Attwyll Avenue and Laburnam Road. Ten buildings were demolished and a considerable number of others were damaged from the six 500 kg high explosive bombs.[144]

– Stepcote Hill and King Street –

On the night of 24 April 1942 Mary Reeves was nine years old and living on the top floor of a block of flats in King Street. During air raids they sat in the hallway of an older woman on the ground floor. They heard bombs fall, a deafening noise and 'all I remember was the thick dust, the eerie light of torches and the cries of the injured.' The bomb had fallen nearby in what was called 'The Cut'. Her paternal grandmother lived there and her father went out to check on her only to find all six houses were destroyed. Fortunately 'Nan' had sheltered in Preston Street where the houses were merely damaged. 'All Nan could say was that she had left her handbag on her chair and demanded that Dad should go and find it. No one wanted to tell her that her house had gone. It was the end of an era. All six houses were tenanted by elderly people – people who scrubbed their steps and sat outside on a kitchen chair and watched the world go by.' The family stayed downstairs and could hear the cries of people in the streets. One neighbour was killed by a falling slab of masonry. Three families survived and there was a search for one missing woman. Many years later Mrs Philips, as she came to be, remembered 'my childish horror to hear that she had been sucked up the chimney by the blast'.

Colin Hopkins was sixteen years old and living with his family in Stepcote Hill. He recalls 'I had been to work that night at the Chevalier and as usual my father collected me and brought me home. The sirens went and we all went underneath the stairs as we were taught to do. My father was an A.R.P. Warden and his post was down the bottom on King and Preston Streets in a building called the Norman House. I don't know why they called it that. A bomb actually dropped on the houses which were opposite and my father was fifteen feet away from this bomb and yet all he had was burst eardrums. My brother was home on leave from the army and went out to keep my father company and they both had burst eardrums. I know they staggered into the house with blood coming from their ears. After about ten minutes they composed themselves and went out of the house because my father said there were people trapped down there, with quite a lot dead. So eventually they went on out and the raid seems to have stopped. I don't remember how long it went on for but I can remember seeing Haldon, with the Belvedere, with a blanket of light come across the top. It was from the Germans dropping incendiaries, then they came along the river. The nearest bomb to our house was seventy or eighty feet and brought our ceiling down. That was the only damage we had.

Before they went my mother poured out a brandy to give to my father, after his eardrums were burst. At the same time my brother wanted a drink – because the plaster had come down and the air was full of dust. So he saw this glass and poured it out not thinking what it was. My poor father was waiting and it turned out it was the only brandy my mother had – there wasn't another drop.

I went outside and saw a plane coming along all lit up flying low. I thought he was one of ours. Then he started machine-gunning the gas works and I realised it was a German plane. There was a lovely sight of all the coloured flame going right up into the sky. After that we came out down to Norman House. At the top of the street we could see flames coming out of the vaults in the Lower Market – where there was wine kept. I can still see the flames coming right out.

I can remember going out of the house with my mother and two brothers and my sister, we were going down to the spot were the bomb had dropped. I suppose to see if we could help, or we were being nosy? I don't know. My mother was in the front and she fell down into a manhole. I suppose a blast had blown it off and she grazed her leg. We went down there and they were trying to get people out of the debris from the row of six houses. They had had a direct hit. We waited until the bodies were brought out of the houses because we knew the people. In the corner house was a man who used to drive around Exeter with a horse and cart. He used to keep dogs – cocker spaniels they were. They were rummaging through trying to find them and they were all under the stairs, dogs and all, all dead. Then there were people called Blunt, their son luckily enough wasn't in the house but his mom and dad were killed. So we stayed there until they were found and taken away.

Luckily my father and brother had been standing in the doorway of Norman House otherwise they would have been killed. Up along on King Street were two men on fire-watching duties for Brocks and both of them were dead – the blast had caught them and their stomachs were wide open. I can see them now. Just lying on the floor, the whole of their insides were out. They had worked in Brocks. They had been stood outside in the road.

People were coming out from the houses opposite, all cut with glass in their faces. There was a furniture van into which they put the bodies. They were going to drive it to the hospital. Father Browne, vicar of St Mary Steps, he sent us lads down to the church hall because they had stretchers there. We brought them up. There was one person in particular and he got cut up badly about his face. He was told to get into the back of the van to hospital. He went in there, I'm laughing about it now but it wasn't funny then, he went in and saw these dead bodies and came out quick saying *I'll walk.'*

That former boy also recalls that night. He remembers 'we were home. We had gone to bed 11 or half past ten. Father used to always wait up until 12 o'clock. He said if they don't come before 12 o'clock, they won't be here. He had that in his head, and that was that. It was true enough, as soon as you heard the 12 o'clock news, Father would come on up to bed. So that night the news went and he said *Oh come on maid, time to go to bed.* Half past one the next thing we woke up to was not the sirens – it was the bombs. The bombs came down before the sirens went, they never picked them up. The planes come up the river before they realised they were coming in for Exeter. We got up, being in the dead centre – what they was aiming for – the bombs were dropping all around us. And all of a sudden, my mother said *quick get downstairs.* At that time I was not fourteen. I run down there with my brother's shorts on. Right, you don't stop to worry about that. Poor old Father was in the first world war and he was a prisoner. He said *put these lights out*. My mother said *you can't put the lights out Frank, you can't see nothing*. He said *then when old Gerry sees these lights, they'll be after us*. And there's mother arguing about the lights and then all of a sudden a bomb dropped. At one time it wasn't too bad, we would have run into the shelter. *Oh no*, father says, *quick under the table*, an old ordinary table, under we went. Except my brother Leonard, he worked for Calloways, the tailor. He was stood there – putting his tie on. He stood there, and I'm under the table with me facing the window. Next thing, my father is saying to my brother, *come under here*. My brother says *I won't be but a minute, I'm putting on my tie*. Then bang. They said later *what did it sound like?* I can't explain it really. You didn't know what was happening. It only happened in seconds. Father had the roll call. He thought us was buried. We couldn't see nothing. *Don't move*, he said *I think we're buried. Mother are you alright? Yes, something bumped me on the head*. That was blast. *Leonard?*, well he mumbled. *He ain't right*. The next thing he was on his hands and knees. And then, *Cyril? Yeah, I think I'm alright. Raymond? Yeah, I'm alright*. Though I didn't feel this part of my face from then. Never felt it. Glass or blast, or something whatever, I don't know what it was. *And Peter and David?* There were eight of us. And they was all right. The next thing the dust went up. Because all the front was gone. My face was down here under the table. The next thing the hall bit the dust. We could see three houses completely flattened. That was the first shock that we had. So anyhow, no sooner had the bombs dropped then the sirens stopped.

And we were wide open to the lot. We had no guns, no barrage balloons, nothing in Exeter. Well, they weren't going to bomb Exeter. And we could see the planes coming down. The flares coming right down to the door. After a while we could hear old Mrs Mortimer's daughter crying out for help. Somebody rushed over, next thing there was a lull, and someone came over and said *we found your front door out in the street, with our name on it, Sidwell*. So Mother said *there's no point in having a front door if you don't have anything else. Help yourself*. They put Mrs Mortimer on it and said *she's dead*. And I was feeling a little bit giddy and I didn't realise the blood was pouring down. I kept on saying to my mother and father *is it raining?* So I went outside and sat on a gravel heap. And said *oh look, that's poor old Mrs Mortimer, she wouldn't harm a fly. Are you sure she's dead?* So I walks over and she starts to moan. So I run back to my back to my mother and father and say *What's wrong with Mrs Mortimer?* and they say *She's dead, you fool. She isn't* I say, *she's moaning. What?* They rush over to the poor old maid and she was lying there, and she died at four o'clock in the morning.

Now my father said my brother was a stretcher case. He had about 12 or 14 pieces of glass in him, he was covered. They were all going to get into an ambulance. Well, we waited about twenty minutes and my father said this is no good. *I'm going to get this boy over.* As I understand he carried him. My father was a great big bloke. Eventually he did come home. Father came home and said he'll be all right but he's knocked about pretty bad. He had put on my brother David's coat, who was the smallest of us, and we don't know to this day how he did it. My father was about 18 stone. He was complaining about the arms fitting. So anyhow, we eventually walked out to my Gran's. She said *none of you lot have checked up on me once, with all my windows smashed.* Mother said, *Now, you wait to you see our house – not only are our windows gone but the whole house.* Ah, nonsense, she said. After a while we saw the police sergeant. And he said *oh what a night, how are you boy?* and I said *oh well I'm all right.* So he said *all right boy, wash your face out and I'll get an ambulance.* So my mother washed my face out, trying to get the dirt. So the policeman come back and he put me in the van, in there was a chap whose Christian name was Horace and he worked for Turner's, the fruit wholesalers, and he was cursing. And I said *what's going on?* The policeman said *half of his back is off and his legs hanging off.* They kept him there with the pile of dead bodies instead of rushing he off. And they put me in there. I said *what about them?* And he said, *don't worry boy, they gone.* I hadn't seen a dead body yet. And sat me on the splasher. He said *the driver will be back, he won't be long.* I jumped out then and run. My mother saw me and said *what are you doing back here then?* So I says *Horace has asked me to kill him and the rest of them are dead. Oh my God* she said. Then my brother Cyril said *come on boy, us'n better walk over.* On our street there were five bodies waiting there and I went over to the hospital.'

He recalls that on the night after 'the bomb dropped we could hear

Mrs Mortimer's daughter screaming out *Help, help, help*. At eight or nine o'clock the next morning all the neighbours were down there. They had it cordoned off. The next thing they said *my god, look, there is Mr Mortimer sat up in bed*. They rushed him off to hospital and about three hours he was out. Nothing wrong with him. And his future son-in-law was courting their daughter and just was going to come out to rush home the bombs were dropping so close that he went back in. No sooner did he go in and shut the door then the bomb fell. All he had for injuries was the top of his finger off. Mr Mortimer didn't wake up till eight o'clock, with all the noise. But the neighbours all wondered how he could sleep through it.'

They almost found everyone in the street. He recalls 'there was only one person missing on our street, unaccounted for. He was called Darkie Bright, had black hair and features but not skin – a dark-looking chap. He had a pair of the old sand shoes. He was the only one. His stepdaughter who was about twenty-five or thirty, had to go down, every time they found a body, to the mortuary. And no, she couldn't find him. Some said, look at that, and all the years she knew him and can't identify her own stepfather. One day all our mothers were out looking at the damage and thinking it would never have happened to King Street and they were about to start clearing the back streets. And they started at our blast wall. They knocked off two bricks and there was this hand sticking out. They sent for the police and looked for his identity card. He said *here is poor old Darkie Bright, he is the only one missing. No, it isn't Darkie Bright*. He said *its William Hole*. My mother said, *you twerp, they buried him last week*. The widow had identified the wrong husband. They had to exhume him and identify him and then bury him again.'

Arthur Blunt remembers part of that night. He was seventeen years old and lived with his parents at 25 King Street. He recalls 'on Friday the 25th of April I was serving in the Home Guard. Previous to that I used to fireguard at Webber's. It was nearly all woodworking there and we used to go down there after work. Two of us, myself and a chap called Bill Rowlandson. There was also a permanent firewatcher employed by Webbers, and we did one night a week. The actual

(On following page) Beacon Downe in Pinhoe, the home of the Hull family, destroyed through bombing in April 1942.

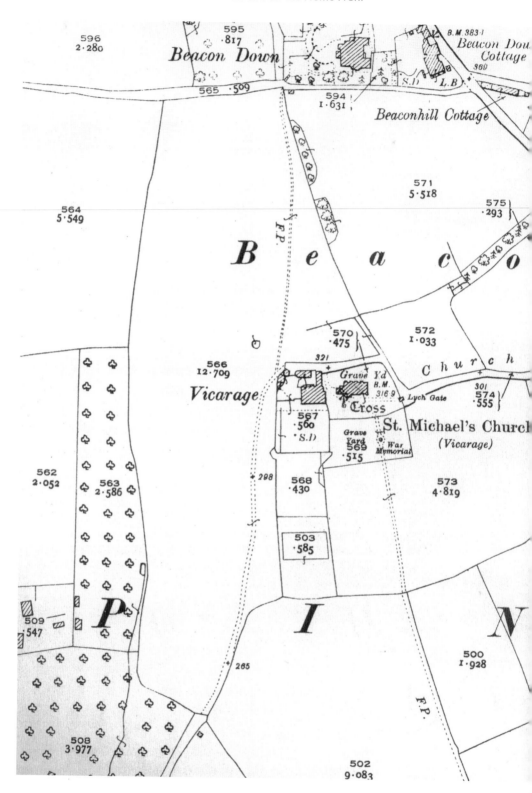

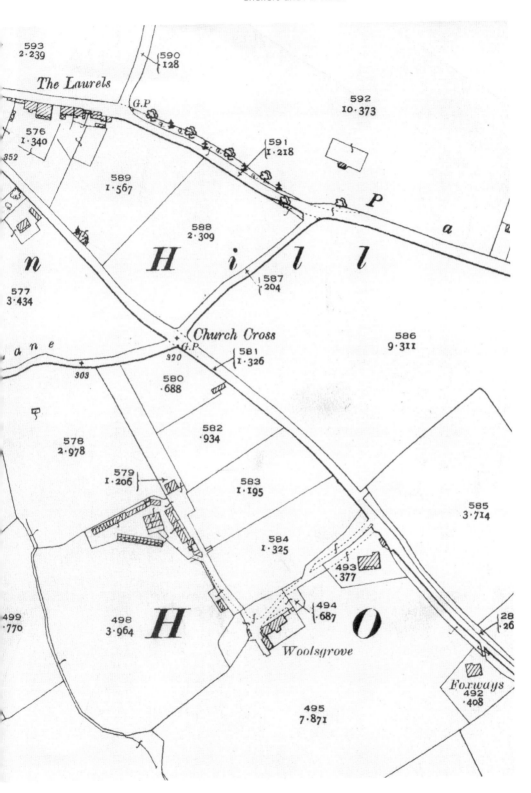

firewatcher was employed to stay awake and we went to sleep. If there was an air raid we would have to deal with incendiary bombs. On the night of April 25th I was on duty with the Home Guard and went home, still in uniform, it must have been about quarter to twelve when the sirens went. I went outside to see what was going on. On the previous night planes had come up the river Exe and dropped bombs, the first lot that dropped on Buddle Lane and Okehampton Street. Opposite our house we had the Norman House near us and I went around the corner and down the bomb came. I was pretty lucky that night. On the opposite side to it was an air raid shelter. After that I'm not sure what happened – I just knew that when the bomb came down it was my house that got hit. It was a direct hit. This is strange because I can't remember much about it and what happened after then. My mind went blank. I found myself in the firewatcher's bed down at Webber's on Bonhay Road. The landlady in the Alexander pub was giving me a brandy. I walked all that way. I used to go down there Friday nights and instinctively I ended up down there. Then the firewatcher that night took me up through Preston Street and there was nothing left of my house. That's when both my parents died – one died a few minutes before twelve and the other a few minutes after. I didn't then have a home. I walked up the road and was still standing in my uniform. Captain Knight of the Home Guard was marvellous. He saw me and asked what was the matter. I told him and that was it – he took me in. He let me lie down and gave me a cup of tea. After that a friend of my brother's she saw me and took me out to Dunchideock. This was my brother's fiancée at the time – she was called Irene Coombes. When I came home after three nights friends of my mother and father saw me and gave me lodgings in their house in Preston Street. A house owned by the Church Army. I went back to work and after that I thought I had to do something – and decided to break out on my own and went up to the recruiting office and explained my situation to them. And they took me in. I volunteered, had the King's Shilling and later went across to North Africa.'

— Beacon Downe, Pinhoe —

Frank Potter was a teenager in the war and remembers a bomb falling on Beacon Downe, the home of Lady Hull, in Pinhoe; a baby dropped through a hole in the first floor and landed unharmed on the ground floor. Two 1,000 pound bombs fell on the building but all twelve people in the house escaped. Lady Hull recalled 'our bomb at Beacon Downe did not frighten us at all. None of us heard a single sound. All I was conscious of was a tremendous rushing wind and the curtains rushed up to the ceiling. The floor went down and my elder daughter, tucked up beautifully in a camp bed, went down with it like a package. I tumbled down and next I knew I was looking out on the lawn where there was a beautiful oak tree which I could see silhouetted against the sky. I was buried to my armpits in bricks and things. Baby was buried under a pile of bricks, rubble and carpets. I could hear her calling out. When the gardener arrived he lifted the carpet and this little face looked out. The bed, carpets and stuff had protected her. My sisters-in-law were both in the dining room when the bombs fell and the two little boys were in the bedroom above. When the floor came in, the elder boy slid out of bed and landed in his aunt's lap. The other little was still safe in his cot. The main staircase had vanished, and fortunately, my mother-in-law in the darkness came down a back staircase which had survived. Had she tried to use the main stairs she would probably have been killed. One must thank God for this most wonderful thing that nobody was killed, and not a single animal injured. My sister-in-law, Mrs Swinburn, had a red cocker spaniel called Copper which was still missing at dawn, but when my sister-in-law picked her way through the rubble that had been the dining room she found Copper pinned against the wall by a picture which had fallen down. The dog was all right, but was so terrified it would not move.' Lady Hull was sent to the Royal Devon & Exeter Hospital and was a patient there a week later when it was bombed during the blitz.[145]

The death and destruction in that single night dwarfed the suffering from every other raid.

CHAPTER

THE BLITZ, 3–4 MAY 1942

EIGHT

As destructive as these raids were, particularly the reprisals of late April 1942, most memories centre on the events of early Monday morning, the fourth of May 1942. The deaths and level of destruction in those few hours were greater than anything Exeter had seen in the war or would experience later.

Ernst von Kugel, one of the German pilots, said of it the following week 'it was a night of terror for the Exeter people. When I approached this town the bright reflection of fires on the horizon guided me. Over the town itself I saw whole streets of houses on fire; flames burst out of windows and doors, devouring the roofs. People were running every-where, and firemen were frantically trying to deal with the fires. It was a fantastic fascinating sight. No one who saw it will forget the greatness of this disaster. We thought of the thousands of men, women and children, the victims of our deadly visit. But we thought of our *Fuhrer* and the word of command he gave – Revenge. With cold calculation we carried out our orders.' Another said 'we were glad when we saw our bombs fall on Exeter, as we were conscious we were fulfilling the *Fuhrer's* promise to retaliate, blow for blow, for attacks on German towns. In the centre of Exeter there was not a house whose roof was not burning brightly. New suffering and misery have come to Exeter. Terror raged in the rows of streets. Bombs of the heaviest weight caused enormous explosions.'[146] Those on the ground viewed the destruction with less glee.

The previous Sunday had been a fine spring day. Marion Daw, then thirteen years old, recalled 'on the beautiful Sunday afternoon before the night of the blitz there was a big youth parade at the Salvation Army and every youth group in the city sent representatives. I was there with a friend called Jean Down, whose father was a doctor, and afterwards we walked home together and I stopped for a while at her parents' house in Polsloe Road.' The next morning she heard 'a bomb had hit the house and that her brother and mother had been killed, though she and her father were saved. It was probably because her mother had taken the brother out of the air raid shelter to go to the toilet when the bomb fell.'[147]

She, along with the rest of the city, woke up at 1.30 a.m. the following morning to find Exeter was being bombed. Some 30 bombers dropped 10,000 incendiary bombs and 75 tons of high explosive bombs causing the loss of nearly two thousand buildings and many more others were damaged.[148] Some residents may not have expected it but George Barnes remembers the city was 'not really surprised, there had already been raids on places like Bath and we knew they weren't really concerned with military targets but at hitting civilian morale.'

Sue Andrewes was recovering from being bombed out in April from her digs in Streatham Drive. She remembers 'life was, for Exeter, then a great clearing up and an assessment of the considerable damage & unhappy loss of life. The German wireless, with the demonic voice of Lord Haw Haw, was taunting us: *and Exeter, don't think that we cannot visit you again when ever we choose to do so* or chilling words to that effect! Fear of the unknown is bad but fear of the <u>known</u> I have always said is much, much worse. We now knew what a big air raid was like, and it was very frightening indeed! Fight or Flight is the known human reaction to danger but if you are being bombed what then do you do?

So it was that only ten brief days later, when again I had curiously washed and set my hair in night curlers, that the city was subjected to an even bigger air raid from Hell. This time the main assault was with incendiary bombs as well as the land mines & bombs. It was a night one's memory can never be rid of. The opening sound of that dreaded siren no one of my age ever forgets. From the elevated site of the University grounds we were looking over the city and seemingly totally on fire. As the smoke drifted over us it made it all the worse as a drama. Mardon Hall had a land mine which exploded at its back wall, so, once again I had a bed showered with debris, but escaped again. We all crowded together in the long basement corridor & later on we tried to drink some tea and chat.

Other than admittedly being contracted with my own special fears, I now was convinced that my sister & brother-in-law must be in the heart of that all-consuming furnace, and be in immense danger if not worse. All one could possibly do was to wait for the daylight & somehow get some sense of the importance of simply waiting & not trying to walk down to the town to find out how they possibly were. The relief of seeing a very haggard and near-exhausted John coming up the drive with his news of their terrible night but safety, was like an amazing moment of deliverance for me. It so nearly needn't have been so, and how well one knew that other homes and families were lost that sad terrifying night of that raid.'

People were frantically concerned for friends and family. Joan Bedford was a child when her family home was damaged by a bomb in Tarbet Avenue off Pinhoe Road. When the all clear sounded they went to check on her grandmother in Monks Road. She later wrote 'I distinctly remember the bodies being brought out of bombed houses but fortunately my grandmother was unhurt.' One woman, then in her twenties with a young family, sheltered with her mother in Stepcote Hill and after the bombing her husband came to see if they were safe. She recalls 'I was so pleased to see him. One of the first visitors was my mother-in-law who had walked in from Whipton to see how we were. She was shocked at the state of Exeter. But we were all right – frightened, but all right.'

Some regarded themselves as having been lucky. Margaret Ball was twenty years old and living with her family. She along with her mother and two sisters climbed under the Morrison Shelter 'like sardines' when they heard the sirens. She wrote that as the bombs fell 'we were all terrified. My youngest sister, who was thirteen, began to say the Lord's Prayer. We could hear the planes overhead and the thump as the bombs fell. Suddenly there was an almighty crash and I was sure the roof had fallen in. But it was the back door, which had been blown off its hinges and landed on top of the shelter. After what seemed like hours the sound of the planes faded away. We got out of the shelter, still barefoot and in our nightclothes. There was broken glass every-where. My mother and I went outside and looked towards Exeter. The sky was red. The city was on fire.' She notes 'we had a miraculous escape – only 50 yards away on the other side of the road two houses were demolished and the occupants all killed. It had been a terrible experience, to lie there helpless and in fear, none of us ever forgot it.' Likewise, Pamela Taylor felt she and her brother were fortunate. She recalls she was then seventeen years old and living at her family's home at 6 Marlborough Road. They had bicycled out of the city for a picnic and returned 'home very tired. We had had several raids on the preceding nights. My brother and I had bedrooms at the top of the house. It was an old-fashioned Victorian house with a lot of floors. And he came into my room and said *come on, get up, there's a raid.* And I said *Oh, I can't be bothered. I'm fed up with having my sleep disturbed.* So I did agree to go downstairs. And I am sure that he saved my life for after the raids we found the beds were full of tracer bullets.'

Betty Govier's father jotted down notes of his work as a carriage and wagon examiner at St David's Station. She recalls 'soon after midnight the train from Plymouth left Exeter for London when German planes appeared. They seemed to be making for the city centre, passing close to the church spire on St David's Hill. A parachute mine came down and hit the main air raid shelter at Riverside Yard killing railwaymen who were inside. The blast also killed an engine driver, a fireman and a very young lad who was a greaser. Dad said he and two mates were thrown to the ground by the blast. He pulled himself together and made for the platform as he had the presence of mind to turn off the gas mains, for which he received a commendation. They then went to the sidings to find most of the rolling stock was badly damaged by machine gun fire.' Ethel Harris' father was also a railwayman and remembers 'when Dad went to work, I think it was after the blitz, his first job was to bring out the bodies of some long-time railway friends from a shelter in the goods yard which had a direct hit'.

Some helped save the lives of strangers they never saw again. One woman recalls coming into Exeter on a fire engine 'down Pinhoe Road and there was a little boy, not much more than a toddler, three or four, wandering up and down the road with the street being bombed all about him. The firebombs were still coming down. His mother was frantically looking for him, they must have been in an ambulance or in a car. And there weren't many people with private cars so they must have been doing something and wouldn't have had a child with them. He was not perturbed at all and surprised when I snatched him up and sheltered him in the ambulance. The ambulance driver said *well, what are we going to do with him?* and I said *well, we can't leave him there in the middle of the street.*' Then mum arrived.

Many small boys found the bombing fascinating. Nicholas Toyne was eight years old and living in his family home in Argyll Road. He recalls 'one late evening there was the sound of many, many planes flying above us. They dropped masses of flares and incendiary devices and completely missed Exeter with all the ordnance falling on the Haldon Hills and lighting up the forest. The next night they came back and unfortunately lit up the city centre, then dropped their bombs. As far as we were concerned, to my small eyes at the age of eight it was most exciting. It looked as if the whole town was ablaze. The most grand firework display which seemed to go on forever. My parents were terrified, though they managed at the time to cushion me from any sort of fright. The Labrador just carried on chewing his bone with me under the table. The house in Marlborough Road that we had left the year previously was flattened by a bomb at this time! The only thing that happened to our house was the thick metal bolts on the bottom of the French glass doors breaking off. All the glass was not even cracked. Oh yes, some shrapnel scattered over the garden, being continually dug up by my father's fork over the next few years. My music teacher in York Road, had an incendiary bomb fall through her roof and land in the header tank which put it out. She had this bomb on her mantle shelf for years afterwards!'

'Trekkers'

The bombing at the end of April had alerted people to the possibility of further attacks. Many left the city for the night for the safety of neighbouring villages or to sleep beneath the hedges. They then returned the following morning. Local officials called them 'trekkers' and tried to discourage the practice. One woman remembers being on a bus passing local people walking with their possessions in prams. The conductress said loudly they were 'like a lot of rats leaving a sinking ship'. Many other families left when the sirens sounded, including that of Norman Watts who lived in Blackboy Road. They went up to Stoke Hill to sleep. Peter Philips was six years old and living at 23 Barley Mount in Redhills. His parents carried him in a blanket up to Higher Barley Mount where they sheltered under a hedge. They watched the flares dropping on the city as it burned. At one point a parachute flare dropped nearby and his father forbad his mother to get the parachute. The silk was a useful commodity. Although N. Gill's family had a Morrison Shelter they became accustomed to leaving their home in Bowhay Lane and walked up Farmer Towel's lane so they could sit under a hedge for safety. Some neighbours routinely went as far as Ide. Douglas Newbery was only nine years old and walked up Redhills night after night and slept under the hedges and trees. His family preferred the open countryside to their Anderson Shelter. Eileen Reynolds had a similar experience. She later wrote that after one of the April raids 'the next night all the local people took

Scenes of devastation.

some, not all, of their belongings on prams and carts and walked up Redhills in droves, towards the village of Nadderwater. We went into a field and stayed the night in a huge cowshed, with a galvanised roof. Needless to say I never slept a wink. I was terrified that Germans were going to drop from parachutes. The very next day Mum packed up everything and we went to stay with another brother of my Dad's in Topsham.' Arthur Powell was a young boy and remembers 'one particular time when all the families in Merrivale Road, because of the closeness of the raids, we all decided to go up to the quarries together. People were sheltering under the trees and a bomb dropped right near them in a field.' Likewise, Val Eaves remembers how as a five year old she was taken out of the city at night. She later wrote that each night 'we went each night to a farmer's field outside, where the farmer had cleared the field of cows for the night, where we slept in a barn. I remember on our way we could see the whole of Exeter alight, and there must have been a pub on the way where children were crying, having lost their families.' Some went a considerable distance. Elsie Wills recalls 'most nights during the 1942 Baedeker Raids we went out of Exeter to my sister Renee's in the countryside. This was a three to four mile walk for us all. One evening when the bombing was bad we sat under a hedge at the edge of a field as this felt safer than being indoors.'[149]

Even out in the countryside it was dangerous. Joyce Stabb was nineteen years old and remembers groups of residents leaving the city for the countryside to stay in barns and other outbuildings which farmers let people use. On one occasion a group was climbing Dunsford Hill when her uncle was killed by German machine-gunning. Trevor Searle was then thirteen years old and recalls 'all the people went up the fields, old Gerry came along and machine-gunned them. My father was a lorry driver and acting like a warden. He was at 100 Newman Road and jumped right over a wall and into a great rose bush'.

Seeing the city burn

After the sirens stopped many in Exeter went outside and saw the city burn. Pat Salter, for instance, was only eleven years old and she sheltered with her mother in the cupboard under the stairs in their family home in Pinhoe. When the noise finally ended they got out to find that there was no damage but the water, gas and electricity had stopped. Her father took her to Church Hill where they could see Exeter burning – the cathedral was the only building they could recognise among the flames. Ten-year-old Audrey Hammett stood on the garden wall of their home in Sweetbrier Lane and watched the city burn. Nancy Mead was a teenager sheltering with her family in their Morrison Shelter on the corner of Newman and Merrivale Roads in St Thomas. The closest bomb to hit was an U.X.B on the Buddle Lane Ladies Convenience. She looked up from Newman Road and could see the West Front of the cathedral and the red flames around it. Many others saw it from a distance: Mrs D.E. Skinner was seven years old and saw the red sky from a farm in Mohuns Ottery near Luppitt while Angela Hancock watched it from Copplestone.

Many had left Exeter before the blitz. Caroline Cornish, then ten years old, and her younger brother Nick were sent to stay with their aunt in Drewsteignton, who was in the Timber Corps, because of an unexploded bomb in Culverland Road. They travelled by bus and she recalls they 'were installed in the cottage where our aunt lodged. It was owned by a Mrs White and she gave us a tiny bedroom almost completely occupied by a huge bed . . . I remember vividly, looking out of the window with him at the huge red glow in the sky, hearing the strange noises, and Aunt Norah coming and telling us that it was some large fire at Moretonhampstead. She was a good liar. We believed her, and it was many years later that the full impact of what she must have been thinking and feeling during those hours really struck me. She was watching the city where her sister and family might be burning to death before her very eyes. She must have wondered if she was clutching a couple of orphans to her ample bosom, as we rather enjoyed the spectacle. Would she have to bring us up and when would she know the awful truth? In fact it was two or three days before she had those answers, days which were pure enjoyment to us as we danced down to the mill to watch the wood being sawn, and visited the post office where (miraculously) freshly cooked doughnuts, still warm, would appear from behind the counter. Then, I think it was the Tuesday afternoon, we were in the mill office when we saw a uniformed figure, in air force blue, coming down the path. Lee Walker, a one-time dancing pupil of my mother's, had arrived in Exeter on leave (she was a W.A.A.F.) on the evening of the Blitz. She and Mother and the dog, had spent the night in the cellar as bombs rained down everywhere. My father, of course, was on duty doing whatever was possible. When it was over they emerged to find every single pane of glass in the house shattered but mercifully no serious damage to the house.'

Drewsteignton was to some extent cut off from Exeter. She recalled 'there was no telephone communication and out at Drewsteignton people eventually came bearing rumours from the city. They came on foot or on bikes with stories my aunt was to hear about how the whole of this and that district had been destroyed and no building left standing etc. so what mighty relief it must have been to her to hear from Lee's own lips that all was pretty well, and that she had come to take the children home'.

Firemen

John Langdon remembers 'fire brigades came to help from all over the South of England, one on an old fashioned fire appliance came all the way overnight from Reading with the crew sitting outside in the cold. They asked where the fire station was. That must have been quite a journey as all the signposts had been removed and car lights and street lights were very dim because of the blackout. In those days of course there were no motorways.' There was some disquiet in the city over fires not being prevented from spreading widely. John Drodge remembers his mother telling him about a procession of firemen which paraded through Exeter after the bombing. Firemen from other parts of the country were coincidentally in Exeter resting at the time of the blitz and it was said that their equipment did not fit that of the city. Some local people booed the fire brigade as they paraded because of the belief that the ineffectiveness had contributed to the city burning.

Lionel Gould recalled his fire fighting at Colson's Store (now Dingles). The former fireman remembered 'we had a fire hose running right

The High Street with Colson's on the left.

through the Mol's Coffee House building to reach the store. As we were on our way from our Polsloe Road station to the Cathedral Close the incendiary bombs were raining down on us. We felt the blast of the high-explosive bomb which hit the Singer Sewing Machine Shop in the High Street. It almost lifted our vehicle. In the end we were completely surrounded by buildings on fire and it was impossible to tackle them all. What could one pump with five or six men do against so many fires?'[150]

In 1982 a second fireman recorded his memories. Ralph Alford left his home in Netherexe and was driving 'past the cricket ground in Prince of Wales Road [when] a bomber dropped some flares which lit everything up like daylight. The anti-aircraft guns in the cricket ground had shot down one bomber, but then a following bomber scored a direct hit on one of the gun emplacements, killing all its crew. You could see our own fighters chasing the bombers around. You could see the tracer bullets. I saw two of the bombers shot down, but there may have been more. Certainly one enemy pilot surrendered to some of my fire service colleagues, and they took him back prisoner to the Elms Station in Wonford. I believe his aircraft had crashed near Wonford.

In the city centre one of our crews saved Colson's from burning down. Others were at fires in Polsloe Road, Clifton Hill and Blackboy Road. We had no more pumps left. At the Blackboy Road fire a piece of flying debris gashed my hand badly and I had to go back to the station in Polsloe Road to have it bandaged. Then I went back to the fire again. We were lucky to have plenty of water, but in many parts of

High Street with cleared sites.

the city the crews did not, because bombs had shattered the water mains. Where the pumps were working, though, they were run so long and so hard that in the shadows you could see their exhaust manifolds glowing hot. Running the pumps was the most dangerous job. You couldn't hear the bombs falling, so you did not know when to duck. In the end there were too many fires, and not enough of us, nor enough water to fight them all, and the tragedy was that when a relief column arrived it could not get through the city centre to report to the fire headquarters at Danes Castle and had to wait in Heavitree Road until its officers could get their orders. As to the rapid spread of fire in places like South Street, it was almost impossible to stop. I have seen fire burn along a street as fast as you can walk.'[151]

The events of the blitz

There are personal accounts of bombings across the city. For instance, Graham Hessé was fifteen years old when his family heard the sirens sound at their home in Bagshot Avenue. They huddled in the Morrison Shelter in their front room, together with a neighbour and her two children. A parachute bomb detonated between their road and that just below. It destroyed four houses. The Hessé's home had the tiles blown off their roof, the window glass shattered and the front door was blown in. It took six weeks to repair the house during which most the family stayed with friends in St Thomas.

David Melhuish was only six years old and remembers his father 'was on fire duty at work that night so I was at home with Mum. I was settled in the shelter and Mum went outside into the street. I can remember getting bored and going outside to join her. She was talking to Mr Lethbridge and trying to work out where the damage was occurring from the glow in the sky from the fires. She packed me right off back into the shelter. Mum showed no fear at all although she must have felt quite worried about Dad. Of course Paris Street, where the bus depot was located, actually took a massive pasting. I can just remember Dad turning up the next day. As I recall he had taken quite a while to negotiate his way back across the city. When I next ventured out after the blitz there was some odd sights as I recall. A street had been hit along Well Street and one of the houses had one wall still standing, a toilet pan was attached to the wall with no floor for it to rest on. There were bombsites all over the place in our area, Sidwell Street, Sunderland Road, High Street, Clifton Road and Paris Street. These streets were quickly cleared for traffic, and soon after the sites were levelled and tidied up. This had to be done, as it was hazardous for kids to play in. Later of course the bombsites were to become recreation areas and car parks. In Southerland Road a cycle speedway track was built for example. I remember that the bricks Dad used to build the kitchen extension in Rosewood Terrace came from the Well Street bombsite'.

Pam Southen was seventeen at the time. She recalled 'my father was an A.R.P. warden and he was based at St James Football Ground and their headquarters was beneath the grandstand. During the blitz Dad went off and left us, and we were sat underneath the stairs. It wouldn't have done us any good. We used to crouch under there with pillows on top of our heads.' Bombs blew out the glass of their house when 'two houses behind us at Mowbray Avenue went completely, we knew the people who lived there. The railway line was right next to them. One family was called Bartlett, I've forget the name of the other family. I can still hear the whistle of that bomb. And there was also an unexploded bomb and we had to get out. My mother took my brother and myself and we went to Topsham. We came back after a couple of days. It was so stupid – after the blitz we were given a Morrison Table.'

Christine Caldwell and her husband were lodging at 21 St Leonard's Road and remembers they cowered, still in their nightclothes, in the hall. When the All Clear sounded she went into the back garden, still in her slippers and nightie, and began putting out some of the incendiary bombs that had fallen in the neighbourhood. She gradually became aware that not only was the house in front and behind them in flames but that all of nearby St Luke's College was ablaze. She realised her own efforts in the shrubbery was futile. At some point she felt the wind suddenly changed and years afterwards read Samuel Pepys' account of the Great Fire of London in 1666 when the force of the heat had caused the air to change.

David Smith was eight years old and under the Morrison Shelter with his mother and brother in the kitchen of their home in Clifton

Road. His father, Emlyn, was an A.R.P. Warden and discovered a house about to catch fire from adjacent properties. His father told him the door was answered by a young girl whose mother was still upstairs. He told her to 'get her mother and he would escort them to the nearest Air Raid Shelter. She went in and came back out by herself. My father asked her where her mother was and she told him she was upstairs in her bedroom putting on her best hat because she said if she was going to meet her maker that night she was going to meet him wearing her best hat.'

Mr H. Agget remembered arriving at St Sidwell Avenue after the bomb which killed six men. He later wrote 'I went down there a few minutes after the bomb had pitched. You know when children play with cards they stack them all up and then they touch one and they all go down, well that blast was so terrific that all the houses had gone down like that, right down to the bottom of the Avenue each side. You could see them with their bay windows still intact in a sense but all leaning down. There was a terrific crater there in the centre of the road.' He also remembered the nearby fire in York Road. In 1977 he wrote 'there's only two or three now but there was a whole crescent of

A ruined site with an automobile caught in the debris.

them which ran right up to St Sidwell's School. Well, soldiers had been billeted in these houses and they had ammunition in there, small arms ammunition. There were a lot of incendiaries dropped and they caught these houses afire and this small arms ammunition was exploding but it sounded like machine gun fire. We'd been warned that after a raid there might be parachute troops dropped and at that time there was a scare that he was going to invade. Course they heard this small ammunition going off and everyone thought it was street fighting – they all thought Gerry was here, see.'[152]

Bill Hole was only fourteen and living at his family home at 213 Monks Road. Bombs had created a crater in the road by Pinhoe Road. He recalls 'when my father and I walked to the top of the back lane between Pinhoe Road and Monks Road, coming out into Cloister Road, we came upon a huge crater. To my surprise, being very young, I stood amazed to see a great column of water shooting some thirty feet into the air. Up through the centre of the column of water shot a huge jet of fire. I could not understand how a column of fire could burn through a huge jet of water. I was mesmerised by this spectacle. The bomb had fractured the water main and the gas main, creating this effect.'

– Cowick Street –

Donald Shepherd's shelter was unusual. He was only eleven at the time and lived in St Thomas with his family. He recalled 'we didn't have an air raid shelter at the time and the people next door had a Morrison Shelter which is one of those table-type shelters. It was a pub next door, the Prince Albert, they have changed the name. We went in there. If I remember correctly the bombs started dropping before the siren went. But we got very complacent because we didn't always get up in the end because the planes used to pass over to bomb South Wales – Newport, Cardiff and Swansea. And then the all clear used to go and then about three quarters of an hour later the sirens would go again when they came back. So very often we never used to bother. But that night we did, so we were in their Morrison Shelter, in what they called their beer cellar. It wasn't an actual cellar, because it was the ground floor. There were six of us, the landlord and his wife, my mother and father, and my sister and myself.

Well, the planes seemed to come in and fly straight up Cowick Street, they were circling over Dunsford Hill way somewhere and coming in and flying straight up the town up Cowick Street and Fore Street and started dropping their bombs. I can't remember how long it went on for. Quite a while. We were afraid because the church was next door that they would hit that church and the thing would collapse on top of us. But it didn't of course. A funny thing happened that night. It was a pub you see. After the raid had finished the landlord said to my father *I suppose you want a drop of whiskey* and so my father said *yes I would, thank you very much*. And my father said *I wouldn't mind another one*. He charged him for it. We always thought it was a bit mean.'

– The City Hospital –

The City Hospital was destroyed. Lady Hull had been bombed out of her own home in Pinhoe in April and sent to the City Hospital. She was still there on the night of the blitz and recalled 'it really was an absolute nightmare for everybody. Quite early on the hospital was hit by incendiaries and bombs were still falling. Whenever a bomb dropped broken glass rose up from the floor and crashed down again, and we thought we had been hit again.'[153] One woman who was nineteen at the time remembers 'I was a nursing auxiliary then but had only been at the hospital for a few weeks. I was in Ottery when the sky was all lit up. But there were fire engines and things going to Exeter and thought I might be able to help. They were quite happy to take me though I suppose they weren't really allowed to. But with petrol rationing it was difficult and no one was going to drive me into Exeter with the bombing. It was quite funny one part of it – when we got to Livery Dole an air raid warden came out looking very harassed indeed. He said *when you see an ambulance could you divert it up here? Somebody's having a baby*. Well, I have never forget the fireman's face grinning from ear to ear who said *I have a person in the back*, as if he had brought me on purpose. I wasn't a midwife then and they only gave you sketchy emergency procedures to do if you were ever confronted with a birth. So I nearly had kittens but luckily she had had it when I got there. I was very thankful even if she wasn't. When we

Heavitree Road and the City Hospital (shown as Public Assistance Institution), 1932.

got to the hospital it was still blazing and they got most of the people out that they were able to. Nurse Emily Knee was wonderful. She was a permanent night nurse and she treated them all as if they were her mother and father. I then followed on where they were still trying to get people out. It was the old workhouse and a lot of the patients were old inmates. It was sheer murder really because we couldn't get them out. We didn't have a fire escape. On the ward where I had been nursing, and where I went, they had put in emergency boxes inside the windows, where you put the patients in a canvas chute and hoped that someone was at the bottom to catch them. Some of these old patients had been bedridden for years and they couldn't help themselves. They dropped down the chutes. We couldn't get the beds to the windows so we had to carry the patients. It wasn't any distance but it didn't help. To begin with there weren't people there waiting at the bottom but it was working by the time I got there. But not everyone was saved. There was one ward with old inmates with nowhere to go, they died probably of smoke. There was one old man we had who had sat in exactly the same position for years, we used to put cushions all around him to make him comfortable. He was one of the ones that the bed went down through the floor before we could move him – with the flames. It was an old building where they had just polished it and polished it for years – not much to it and you only had to strike a match and the whole place would have gone.'

Then 'the next day they evacuated them as best as we could, mostly to North Devon. They had old Devon buses with stretchers all ready. They were prepared for that. There was no comfort in it. It took us over an hour to get from Heavitree Road to the Barnstaple road because every road was blocked with something. They weren't really injured, mostly suffered from smoke or they went down into the flames. It was pretty awful. Nurse Knee was devastated. She tried not to show it but she was. We were too busy to think about it at the time, to worry about it.'

The deaths were investigated and she recalls 'I remember when the inquest came, which seemed to be weeks afterwards, some of us were asked to identify them – they were only skeletons. And we said this was so-and-so and this was so-and-so. And he said to me, *I don't know how you could know that – you said his bed was here and he was found there in the ward beneath*. Well, I said, that was the shape of his skeleton, he had sat like that for years. What had happened was he was one of them that was moved to the window but they decided he was already dead then so we got somebody who wasn't to put down the chute. It was awful.'

One resident remembered at the time 'the majority of the inmates were very sick or chronic patients. Others were bedridden or elderly. We set to work to get them out. Our aim was first to rescue them from the hospital building and lay them in the courtyard in front. Many were transferred by means of the shute which had been installed for fire escape purposes.

We could not move all the patients at one time, and our method was to take them down in relays and shift them on periodically, working them gradually farther and farther away from the building. Eventually we got them down near the front lodge, which is a considerable distance from the hospital, and not far from the road. As this operation proceeded 20 or 30 yards at a time, there was no respite. In some cases the night clothing of the patients began to catch alight. The patients bore their ordeal very well considering the circumstances.

The only casualty from the evacuation – a fractured leg – occurred to an inmate during the use of the shute. We were all too busy on this job to notice much else, but it seems certain that the hospital was machine-gunned by an enemy raider and one man received a slight bullet wound.

When we had worked down to the lodge I went out into the street towards the children's annexe of the hospital and I was shocked to see that this was also apparently blazing. However, it proved to be some villas alight a little further on. The annexe was apparently intact, and we all tackled the final stage of getting the patients safely to this building, along the public street, carrying many, helping others till finally they were made as comfortable as possible inside. They had now been evacuated to other institutions.'[154]

Another Exeter man recalled at the time 'I went over to the hospital. There were patients lying on the grass, and others walking towards a nearby building. It was a pathetic sight. The door of one building fronting the road must have been partly blown open by blast. One or two of the patients were being carried in. We cleared some debris at the bottom, and the students managed to lever the door completely open. I carried over a couple of patients and dashed into a playing field and asked for volunteers. A crowd of students came over with me. We used doors as stretchers and managed to fill the building except for three beds upstairs. These patients were evacuated on the following afternoon.[155]

Retired Inspector Stanley Cole was on the beat. He recalled 'I was on the main street on duty – working from the police station on Waterbeer Street – for 23 hours. I didn't know what happened to my wife and she didn't know what happened to me. When I did eventually get home she was two doors away in Avondale Road – taken in by people – because our house had got damaged in the bombing. I was at the hospital – helping to bring old folks out of the City Hospital – I think I was in there for at least four hours getting bodies out. You were on your own, it was impossible to have supervision. You were you own boss and just had to help out. I was at the city hospital with the building in flames and just trying to get the poor old souls out. There was no form of communication so you just had to do what you thought was best keeping an eye out and then going on to the next thing that had to be done.'

– Royal Devon & Exeter Hospital, Southernhay –

Vivian Bussell was on guard duty. He recalls 'a young solider (R.U.R. I think) went A.W.O.L. stealing an Army truck which he eventually crashed in the Haldon area, sustaining very bad injuries to his face and head. He was moved to the R.D. & E. but the hospital, being a civilian one, could not keep him there unless he had a military escort & he was too ill to be moved on. I was the only person available at such short notice so I joined that evening. He was delirious and kept calling *I want my breakfast* – several times I threatened him that I would give him his breakfast – the fist type if he didn't quiet down but the poor chap didn't even know I was there. Anyhow some time during the evening the doctor performed a Lumbard Punch on him – one of several tests I suppose. Eventually around about elevenish he calmed down and I was able to relax a bit. About midnight a young nurse – I don't think she was much older than 17 to 18 years old – came into the room, handed me a blanket and told me to try to get some sleep in the chair – seeing that our friend had quieted they would keep an

Royal Devon and Exeter Hospital, Southernhay, 1932.

eye on him. Well, that didn't last long because around about one-ish the sirens sounded & Exeter endured that terrible bombing during which patients in the hospital were being taken down to the cellars etc. for safety. Our R.U.R. friend & I seemed to have been left to last & when eventually we were taken down no sooner had the stretcher, bearing our friend, been put on the floor the all-clear sounded and we were put back into our room . . . I stood in the doorway and saw the casualties brought in. There was nothing I could do. I remember one quite clearly. We were very near to the lift. I remember the doors coming open and the trolley came out. There was an individual laying there and all I could see was a black face looking to me – and a white line. I had the impression it was a woman. And I took it that whoever the victim was [she] was smiling at me. And that was that. I think they must have had a tough time in that hospital.'

He was woken in his chair by a young nurse who was off to fire watch on the roof. One of the nurses he saw might have been Margaret Scott who was part of a group of sixteen trained to fight fires. She recalled in the early 1980s 'the roar of the fire coming down Southern-hay was really terrifying. I still cannot understand why it stopped short of the hospital. We knew every inch of the hospital building and became adept at clambering over roofs and through the insides of the roof spaces. Our order of priority was nursing first and fire-fighting second so that on the night of the raid our first duty was to look after the patients. We really enjoyed it, although we realised the seriousness underlying what we were doing. Now I think about it, it was hair-raising the way we would run across one particular roof, but in those days we just did not seem to have any nerves at all'. Edward Greenwood was a member of the maintenance staff and was deserted by the rest of the team of firewatchers. He recalled at the same time 'I remember going in rather a panic to the night sister to tell her we were on our own and that incendiaries were being dropped. Within a few minutes there were a number of young nurses climbing over the roof of the old centre block, which was a mass of valleys and gutters, and they literally threw incendiaries off the roof out into Southernhay. Next day those girls were back on duty as usual in the wards. If it had not been for them, there would have been a major tragedy that night.'[156]

– The First Aid Centre at Wrentham Hall –

Ann Adams was ten years old and lived with her family at the top of Sidwell Street. She later wrote 'my father was the doctor in charge of the first aid centre at Wrentham Hall in Prospect Park. When the sirens sounded he walked up Old Tiverton Road and left my mother and me with my two younger brothers and the mothers' help under the Morrison Shelter . . . my mother was also a doctor and she went to assist my father with the many casualties at the first aid centre.' Her father, Dr Charles Marshall, also wrote an account of his experiences at No. 2 First Aid Post. He recorded 'on the night of 4th May 1942 we were awakened by sirens about 2 a.m. and hardly had I got out of the house when bombs began to fall, and three times I lay in the roadway when I heard them drop. This was the accepted procedure as you could not then be blown over. The first one fell outside the Odeon when I had reached the cut into Toronto Road, another 50 yards and down came another where Sanderson's now is in the Blackboy Road, the third time one fell a little further off. When passing Yeo & Davey's, then Seamarks, I saw chandelier flares dropped round the city making it like day and we realised that we were in for serious trouble. Sure enough hardly were we at the post when a very loud whistle was heard (a falling bomb has a sound all its own) and, the explosion sounding near, a party of us ran out to see the result. Our firewatcher on the roof was all right but a house at the top of Prospect Park (now replaced by a new one) was completely demolished. All the occupants were killed but out of the damaged house next door came the family in their night attire, having escaped by sheltering under the stairs. The only other casualty was a warden with a broken leg. Windows were blown in and the trees which then lined the street were festooned with debris such as window curtains. There was an uncanny silence for the moment and the smell of cordite lying in the air, the only time in the war I can claim to have 'smelt powder' as they used to say in earlier wars.

Many incendiary bombs were dropped in this raid and various first aiders had left their homes burning, having just helped the occupants out. The fire fighting possible was limited, there were a certain number of static water tanks about including one opposite our front door, but firemen were few in proportion to the trouble, and their orders were to give priority to the preservation of food and petrol. When the shop next to St Anne's Chapel, then a grocers, began to catch fire from flying debris from St James Church (which then stood where the school playground now is) the fireman at the water tank could no nothing until told by my wife that it was a food shop, when one jet along the eaves put it out.

When the raid was over my wife took stock of the situation. The right-hand side of Belmont Road was ablaze, nearby a shop was on fire – where Howard's now is, all down the street there were fires including a burning block of flats in Verney Place opposite the Odeon. Not knowing which of her friends were free from damage, she consulted a police inspector who she knew and met outside. He told her that he had just come from his home in Mount Pleasant where all was well and invited her up there, telling her at the same time that the house which had all its main services would be wanted for an incident post. So all set off up the Old Tiverton Road, receiving many invitations to come in as they went up, carrying wet towels to deal with sparks from the burning church. Peter picked up his mother's 'calls' bag and brought it along as well as his own evacuation bag, thinking his mother had forgotten it. She had in fact transferred essentials to her other bag but we gave our seven-year-old a good mark for his thoughtfulness in the circumstances. Incidentally, when there was a daylight raid in surgery hours the patients commented with approval on the orderly way in which all three, aged 10, 7 and 5 came down to the shelter.

This done, she came on to the post and was soon joined by my partner Dr Watson, who had been seeing to the evacuation of some neighbours in the proximity of an unexploded bomb. An R.A.F. medical orderly on leave had come to volunteer, his services and his help was invaluable. Once again I set off with Wilfred Selley to see what I could do outside. A heavy bomb near the brickworks in Monks Road had demolished a row of terrace houses. Bodies had been brought out and laid on the pavement of one of the little cul-de-sac side-roads, all were dead from the effects of blast. Nearby in the Pinhoe Road another terrace had been hit. On the rubble of one house at first floor level lay a Morrison Shelter lifted bodily from next door. The occupants were alive and not obviously injured, but I gave some morphine to one in a lot of pain.

After this I returned to the post where the cases were being dealt with smoothly. The patients sat round the hall waiting their turn and each anxious to be sure that there was not someone more seriously hurt who should be given priority. The more severely injured were on rows of stretchers in the middle of the hall.

The picture was now getting clearer, looking down past the blazing St James Church to the many fires in the city we had difficulty at first in seeing what was happening. It appeared that an early fire bomb had set light to the City Library in Castle Street in whose basement was the control centre with all the service chiefs. The exit for their cars through Castle Street was blocked, so they had when evacuating the centre to make their way on foot through the Rougemont Gardens to Queen Street and thence still on foot to the reserve centre in the Topsham Road down opposite where the Municipal Golf Course now is. This was not manned by their deputies for the first time for ten days, so that for twenty minutes or more the system by which the wardens reported incidents and resources were allocated to deal with them broke down completely. There was telephone circuit round the City so that communications with the reserve centre were assured if there was damage in the centre.

As far as hospitals were concerned the City Hospital was on fire and out of action: access to the Royal Devon & Exeter Hospital in Southernhay was difficult and ultimately we had to send our hospital cases out to Exminster.

I had attended two *primigravida* during the day: the first had lost a lot of blood and in the evening Dr Robb, the pathologist, came out and we gave her a transfusion and finally left her about 10 p.m. well satisfied with her condition. She was in a basement flat at Verney Place and when the block caught fire burning debris fell into the area and blocked the exit as it did the staircase. The husband tried frantically to tunnel out through the back wall, but it was too thick and at great personal risk the warden got the exit clear and the people out. He later got the George Medal for this effort. When I arrived at about 6 a.m. they were just getting my patient out: the stress had been too much for her and she was dead. The baby survived and was adopted.

The other case I had left at midnight, a tired but happy mother at Grosvenor Place. A bomb sliced off the back of the house, and I next saw her safe and sound with her baby in the basement of the Devon General Garage nearby. She and her baby did well but her milk never came in.

At about 8 a.m. things were quietening down at the Post and rein-forcements were starting to come in from Sidmouth and round about so that our staff could have a breather. My wife and I decided to go home and get some breakfast, the Post was well off for tea but did not keep rations, and we were very relieved to see it still there though the front windows had been blown out. I say out, as the suction effect after the blast wave passed took the debris outwards.

The police post [in front of his home] was in full swing organising special constables, wardens, firemen and dealing with enquiries. They used what was later Dr Edwards' surgery. I continued my normal surgery hours and looked up such patients as I could. It was a lovely sunny May morning and we and all the neighbours were very pleased to see each other alive and all had a word for each one though normally we never spoke! Dr Lowy, the Polish assistant, turned up rather gloomily, his hotel, the Globe in Cathedral Yard, having been burnt down.

Looking back, we were very pleased with the organisation the Home Office had set up: the reporting of casualties went smoothly and the lists of the patients and their disposal was put up outside the Health Office. A symposium held at Bristol the previous summer had been a

Destruction.

great help: they had experienced some heavy raids and told us in helpful detail the sort of problems that had arisen and how they had been dealt with, such as dust in wardens' eyes.'

— Southernhay West —

While the staff of the Royal Devon & Exeter were struggling in the south-east corner of Southernhay there were worse problems in the north-west part of this Georgian development. Dr Charles Wroth lived at 45 Southernhay West and on the 19th he wrote to his uncle Jack. He explained 'I hope you won't mind a typewritten letter, if I do it this way it will be much more legible, and I can do a copy for each of you. I thought you might like to have an up-to-date report of the recent events in this ancient city. In brief we have caught a packet and it would be a waste of time and bombs to bother to do much more. As regards the city the material damage is appalling. Most of this was caused by fire although we had in addition a very fair share of high explosives and from a bombing point of view I should rate it as a most efficient fifty minutes work. I don't wish to weary you with bomb stories, but as you have probably had a lot of conflicting stories, a brief but incomplete account may help you. As regards the deaths, I think about 170 in the last raid with about 120 as a total for the previous three visits would be about the mark, with as usual an equal number of seriously injured. As regards material damage, the houses destroyed by high explosives are pretty evenly distributed throughout the city and the suburbs and no area of any size has escaped. Many of them were socking great bombs too! The worse areas include practically the whole of Sidwell Street from the Odeon down to Ross the tailors on the North side and from beyond this down to Colson's on the south. Paris Street had been destroyed before and the area between Paris Street and Sidwell Street is now completely gutted. You can't recognise the roads from the houses. The top half of Southernhay is completely gutted and the ruins have now been pulled down. This includes the Arcade, our house and down to Bedford Circus, the whole of Bedford Circus being burned out too. Several houses in Southernhay below the Bedford Circus entrance are no more. No. 20 is the last one left standing. On Southernhay East it is completely gutted down to and including the Congregational Church and the whole of Dix's Field. Large numbers of houses in Magdalen Road and Heavitree are burned out. The cathedral is damaged, but standing. The City Hospital is badly burned and is out of action for the moment, but mercifully the Devon & Exeter and the Orthopaedic are so far not much damaged. The Orthopaedic was surrounded by unexploded bombs which have since been dug up.

Speaking personally we had rather a rough night. The raid started with high explosives, incendiaries, cannon and machine gun fire and they fairly plastered the place to their heart's content. The incendiaries came down in thousands and a large number of buildings were burning from end to end within a quarter of an hour. I managed to kick away our own incendiaries and none fell on the roof, but I had to nip round next door to tell the Registry Office people that there was an incendiary in the roof next door to us. From then onwards for about for about an hour and a half we rushed madly on all the landings and rooms on the North side. Unfortunately the blast blew in all the windows and there was a terrific northerly gale which brought innumerable and upending embers into all the rooms setting fire to the carpets, blackout and even the window frames.

A view from Bedford Street to the cathedral with cleared areas.

Vi was downstairs trying to comfort the Poppet. Nanny, the maids, Sheila, Peter, Michael and myself threw water all around the place, ripped up the floor boards, jumped on the embers, first on one floor and then on the other. Eventually we got the lot definitely out and were thinking it was time for a cup of tea. Unfortunately they never got the fires under control next door and the fire came through the roof on both sides where it is quite un-get-at-able and we were driven out by smoke and heat. At the end the stirrup pump got fire and by then we were pretty well all in. The fire spread rapidly from above downstairs so we were able to get out safely. We were taken in by Dr Mackie who lives in Barnfield Crescent, which miraculously escaped. As a result of putting out our fires we failed to save anything except what we were wearing and what we had in a few suitcases and the whole of the contents of the house, furniture, clothing, food, plant equipment, records and everything is completely burned out and welded together.

Vi and the children are living at the Vicarage, Bradninch, with some great friends of ours called Woolley and I am living with Dr Fuller in Exeter. I am carrying on my practice, such as it is, in the Department in the Devon & Exeter Hospital.

I have been in a frantic state as to whether my last premium was paid for War Risk. No one could remember as our records had gone. My accountant is gone, my lawyer is gone and the bank is burned out and I could not remember the address of the firm in London; the Post Office is gone, so that we could not look it up there, and of course the hospital has been very busy so that I have not had the time. You can imagine my feelings!

However, I heard a few days ago that both policies were in order and these are £6,000 for the business scheme and £2,500 for the private chattels. This won't cover it of course, but the private chattels insurance was so very expensive and I did not visualise fire destroying everything. I thought perhaps we might be knocked down by bombs, but then you can retrieve a surprising number of things fairly intact.

I shall carry on in the hospital for the moment, as of course there are no rooms available for me and my colleagues and one can't grow an X Ray outfit overnight.

Meanwhile everyone has been extraordinarily kind and helpful. We are well equipped with clothes although some of them look a bit peculiar. Maynard has sent me a suit, but the moth has been at the trousers.

Hope to see you all some time. Don't come to Exeter unless you want your heart broken.'[157]

The site of his home was re-developed in 1974.[158]

— Willey's Avenue —

Irene Lynne remembers that as a young woman she was living in her family home in Willey's Avenue. She later wrote 'we had an indoor shelter, it was made of iron and used as a table. That night we were in it. After the All Clear we went outside and found the gasholder was on fire and it was a terrible sight. Two Watchmen who were in the Meter Shop at Willey's were in an iron bell-shaped shelter. It tipped over with the force of the bomb which fell in there. Both men were released but afterwards they were very deaf. There were also a mother and child killed in nearby Chamberlain Road. My mother, who was in the W.V.S., went across to the church hall to give help to all who needed it. There was an unexploded bomb in the railway bank so those living near had to leave our homes. So later my mother, Gran, and other members of the family all went to the Salvation Army Hall in Church Road and were taken by coach to Tiverton where they stayed for several days. My sister and I stayed at home by day and at night her husband took us to Chudleigh to friends to stay by night. Once the bomb was removed we all returned home to stay and my sister and I returned to work at Willey's which was in a terrible state. The roof was of glass, also we had rain and all the tin had to be wiped and dried which was a long job before everyone could start any real work.'

— South Street and the Palace Gate Convent: the Holy Firewatchers —

A tremendous effort was made to save the Catholic and Baptist churches on South Street. Much of the street was destroyed by fire but these buildings survived due to the efforts of a group who have been remembered as 'the holy firewatchers'. Father Phil Pedrick recorded his experiences while at the Church of the Sacred Heart. He wrote to a friend shortly afterwards 'South Street is burnt down but for our church and house and the Baptists next door. We fought hard to keep God's house and attribute our safety to the Sacred Heart and His Holy Mother. Fires came down our side of the street right to the corner house, with the wind our way. Embers showered all over us, and the old sand-bags in the tower caught fire. Our poor legs – we were up & down. We plastered our house roof with sand and also the top of the tower, then pumped water all over the front of the house and church to keep things cool. When all the houses opposite were on fire the heat was fierce and melted our paint and buckled some of the lead in the West Window. Our doors were scorched and blinds & window frames stuck hard with the heat. Early in the morning another scare came – fire was coming from behind us near the Deaconess, it broke out again in the afternoon but was put down. All South Street is down but a few houses on our little block may be repaired, but I doubt it.

Palace Gate had fire licking their wall but it stopped there. First, they ran to get all our books down from our rooms & then had to go over to see to their own home. Truly, the centre of Exeter was ablaze. Parts of High Street, Fore Street, Bedford Circus, Southernhay, are burnt as is the City Hospital & St Luke's College. Heavitree presbytery is down and Rosary House School is damaged. The church house is badly knocked and the tower unsafe. A bomb skimmed the tower before landing on the presbytery. All are safe there. They hit a chapel of Exeter Cathedral and we got all the debris – we thought we had been hit. Bombs here very close to us, even in our street. My view is lovely now, all across Haldon. We have had some meals at Palace Gate to relieve Miss Jane, so much dirt and want of gas is a bother but we have electric and a fuel stove. Father Barney stood up to the ordeal very well.'

One former policeman, who was on duty the night of the blitz, recalls of the church buildings on Heavitree Road 'I was on Heavitree Beat and coming up Fore Street when a bomb hit the Catholic Church tower and the blast blew me into the doorway of a house – maybe 100 to 200 yards away. It blew the tower down and knocked me over but I wasn't injured. People were sheltering in the underground toilets in North Street. Everything was going haywire. I didn't go down because

The centre of Exeter in 1932 showing South Street.

I wasn't that keen on being underground.' Some forty years later Ruth Hilliar recalled the fire watching at South Street. She remembered 'you could see him through the smoke on top of the tower. He had stayed there all night and I remember my father telling me how the man had thrown incendiaries off the roof as they fell.' Another woman who recalled Father Barney was Kathleen Godwin. She remembered 'he stayed there throughout the raid disposing of the incendiaries despite a heart condition, and he survived the ordeal.'[159] Don Burlestone, an A.R.P. Warden, recalled telling Father Barney, who was in charge of the church and then covered in black dust, that they had to evacuate everyone as they were in danger. He said *Hmmps. The captain does not leave a sinking ship, neither will I, as I am the Captain here.*'[160] Canon Michael Walsh was also there and remembers of Father Barney 'its just typical of the man – that's the kind of thing he'd say.' On the night he helped save the building. He recalls 'the blitz, oh what a night that was. The people disappeared out into the woods at Exwick, Cowley. But we stood our ground here. There was very little to prevent the raids and the incendiaries. They fell like hailstones – that's a bit of an exaggeration. There is a tower here in the church, with a stairway and then a ladder which takes you up to the top. We could have a good view of what was happening. Somebody went up there – I used to often go up. There were a few big bombs dropped – one of them knocked out a couple of buttresses of the cathedral and with the blast I nearly came off the tower the short way so to speak. There was a drop of flares – it was like daylight with these flares – the next thing then the planes came diving in and dropped the incendiaries, but very few bombs. The nearest one was the cathedral – showers of stones came down upon us. That was my first great experience of the effect of incendiaries. But we were fairly well drilled in how to deal with them, we had sandbags piled up against the door of the church here, others right on top of the tower, pails of water, and so on. That's more or less how we were able to deal with what came down. We put out a good number of those incendiaries. Course a lot dropped into the street and did no damage, but if they dropped there you didn't bother with them. There were very little in the way of firewatchers in other part of South Street. Whatever there was, the local people just cleared out during the bombing and the raids. This was a notable fact, the local constabulary looked into it later. Most of what might have been saved had there been any firewatchers with a pump or bucket of sand. Of the Baptists there was nobody there at all, we never saw a caretaker. The fire swept down South Street, which was very narrow actually – so much so that if you leaned out of your window and someone across leaned out of theirs' – you could shake hands, well, that's a bit of an exaggeration but it was very narrow. We watched the fire sweep down along here until it was stopped by the break of Coombe Street. And then it crossed the bottom of South Street, it was daylight by then, and went creeping up along Palace Gate towards the convent.

I went around there to the convent to see what was happening. There was a fire brigade there – exhausted, and the chaps sat down to have a cup of tea and a bite to eat. So I asked one, *would you mind if I took hold of this hose? Carry on*, he said. Well, it nearly knocked me over. I never had experience of one before. I kept spraying the approach to the convent, and the fire just stopped short there. I don't know how much I had to do with it, but the building was spared.

We spread sand all over the flat roof on the side of us where the Baptists are, doused the church with water and used stirrup pumps.

A view of the corner of South and Fore Streets showing the extensive loss of buildings.

We were responsible for saving the Baptist church although I'm not so sure they ever knew much about what happened here. We saved it directly so to save ourselves indirectly.

There was such an acrid smell, of burning embers, ashes and cinders whenever a building collapsed. The sand bags against the church – the actual canvas began to get alight, we saved those doors from getting charred by pulling away the sand bags.'

He also thinks the blitz had an effect on his appearance. He remembers how 'my hair began to go grey after the blitz and not long after went completely white. My barber said *Father you don't have a grey hair on your head – they're all white!*'

Sixty-three years later Sister Edward Mary recalled her own experiences at the nearby school at Palace Gate which was run by the Sisters of the Presentation of Mary. She remembered 'when the sirens went we got the children and sisters down to the cloak room, it was below the level of the garden and we had a big Morrison Shelter. The children knew they had to pick up a little suitcase already packed, and a pillow, and they came down. We put them in the shelter and they went to sleep. I was studying at the University College of the South West and grabbed some books, went into the shelter and realised I had forgotten to bring my matches for the candle. One dear old sister was praying and the others were trying to go to sleep. I climbed the stairs to my room which overlooked Palace Gate and I literally saw a bomb go passing by the window – I forgot the matches and bolted back to the shelter.' At the all clear the sisters found buckets and threw water from their windows onto the walls of their building because next door was on fire. A fire engine, from Oxford, later passed by South Street and helped to put out their fire. In the meanwhile the sisters had been busy throwing out of their windows items they wanted to save and during the following day they spent their time bringing these back in. They also tried to bring the children to safety at Rosary House in Heavitree but en route there they learned from a warden that the building had taken a direct hit. The sisters returned to their building having entrusted the children to the warden who took them to the Roberts Road shelter. On arriving back home they found the building in complete silence and discovered their fellow sisters were receiving communion in the chapel. On that Monday some of them spent the day serving tea and sandwiches to the civil defence workers.

— Sidwell Street —

Phyllis McGill was nineteen years old at the time and lived in Merrivale Raod. She recalls 'my aunt lived in Sidwell Street and her house was one of those burnt to the ground. She then had three sons and a baby boy. They had to grab him and fly from the burning house. My mother, her sister, was with us in the Anderson Shelter. And she had one thought and that was to get to her sister. The whole city was on fire and they cordoned off the Exe Bridge and my mum got under the cordon and went through the side streets to get to her sister who lived near the Old Coach & Horses — near St Sidwell Church. She couldn't rest until then. It was still dark. She ran around, frantic, with everything burning. She eventually found out that the family had run down along Summerland Street to Newtown where a Salvation Army family took them in for the night. I had four younger brothers and was left looking after them in the Anderson Shelter.'

Vera Budd was staying with her sister Mill and brother-in-law Walt in an end-of-terrace cottage at Strong's Court off Sidwell Street, nearly opposite the Odeon Cinema. When the sirens sounded Walt left to perform his A.R.P. duties and put the two women under the kitchen table pushed against the wall. He gave both women a kiss, said he would see them later and went out to direct people to the underground toilets which served as a shelter. Mrs Budd remembered 'Mill and I clung to each other, crying and in absolute terror as the bombs fell, we felt sick with fear and had to keep running to the toilet, which was out the front door and round to the side of the house. Outside the sight was unbelievable it was like daylight with all of Exeter on fire and the German planes so low I could see the markings on the side of them. The bombing seemed to go on forever. We came out during the morning and realised our house was the only one left intact, and because of the rubble and fires we could not get out the normal way along the passage. Then we saw a big ladder up against the high back garden wall, which some of our neighbours must have used, so we went up and over the wall where we were spotted, wrapped in blankets and taken off to an undamaged house where we were given tea and biscuits by the Red Cross and Salvation Army.'

They never saw Walt again and no trace of him was found. They heard later that he had left the shelter to check on their safety. Mrs Budd wrote 'we started looking for Walt but became more and more

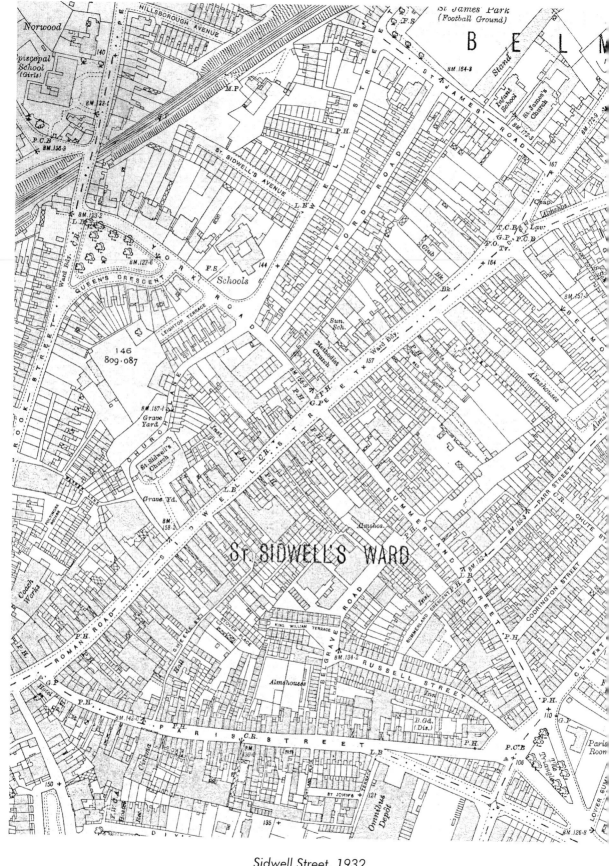

Sidwell Street, 1932.

upset as we had to look at all the bodies in the rubble that were by this time covered in sheets. We looked for days, and on one of these days as we walked near the cathedral, arms around each other and crying all the time, we came across the King and Queen talking to local people. The Queen saw Mill crying and asked us why we were so upset, we told her about Walt, so she called the King over and told him our story. The King wished us well and said that he hoped Mill would find her husband safe and well, we then shook their hands and off they went. Because of the state we were in we thought nothing of this incident at the time, but when we went home to mum and dad, dad was so excited that he rushed straight down to his local pub in Wonford to tell everyone that the King and Queen had spoken to two of his maids'.

Betty Fursman was also living at Strong's Cottages. She was then twelve years old and recalls 'my mother, father, sister and my brother were living at No. 5 Strong's Cottages, Sidwell Street, nearly opposite the Odeon Cinema. It was about 1.40 a.m., we were told to get out of bed because bombs were falling and a lot of premises were on fire. We put on a coat over our nightclothes and went to a brick air raid shelter which was in the middle of Sidwell Street, alongside the shelter was a metal water tank (for use by the fire service). This tank was hit by a bomb and it had burst. We got soaking wet. Then my father said we must find shelter in the basement of the Co-op. A neighbour was helping my mother with my brother who was 5 years old. My sister and I were with our father. As we were going down the stairs a bomb exploded and the building was on fire so we had to get out of there and we went across the road to the Methodist chapel in Sidwell Street. We stood in the area where the gates are (they are still there), we waited until things quietened down. I will always remember the fire which was all around us.

We then went to the Duke of York pub, a Mrs Clarke was the landlady at that time and she gave us a drink to warm us up. We were very frightened and still soaking wet. My father's mother, sister and brother-in-law lived in Well Street, which was not too far away, but we did not like to go there as there was fire all around us and our father did not know what he would find. We had no outside clothes and we did not know if our house was still standing because a lot of shops in Sidwell Street were burning.' She also recalls 'we did not know for some time where our neighbours had gone. My mother's father and mother and sisters lived only four days away from us but what had happened to them we did not know at that time. We learnt later that they had gone up Sidwell Street to the underground toilets (now replaced with new above ground toilets) by the fountain which has been re-located.'

— Bradninch Hall —

One unusual account is from a local woman, then 27 years old, who was on fire watching duty at Bradninch Hall with a seventeen-year-old girl. They had spent the evening making cups of tea and talking in order to keep awake. After the sirens sounded they looked out to see both High Street and the bottom of Castle Street in flames. She later wrote 'we climbed onto the rafters of Bradninch Hall and put out the incendiary bombs which were coming through the roof. We dumped them in the buckets of water. Across the road we could see the main library ablaze and the books being destroyed. My boss said we should NOT go to help as we had to protect Bradninch Hall. The night sky was alight with fires. We could hear the crashing down of buildings and much shouting and screaming. Ambulances were careering along roads taking casualties to hospital. The gas and electric failed. After some hours the All Clear sounded. I collected some sticks and paper and lit a fire in the grate and boiled water for tea. Just as the water had boiled Mr Colin Ross [her boss] appeared at the door, pale and stressed out. He had come from his house when he had heard the city was burning. He was so pleased to see my young companion, my boss and myself unharmed and the building still standing. He asked for a cup of tea and declared it was the best cup of tea he had drunk in his life, even though it tasted of smoke! In the morning I returned home and saw Bedford Square a heap of rubble, and stretcher bearers carrying injured people to hospital. Ironically, when I returned home to Magdalen Road my flat was destroyed and there was nothing left of the building.'

— Magdalen Road —

Several versions of some incidents have been recorded. In 1982 Marion

Dawes recalled when she was thirteen years old when 'at our house near the top of Magdalen Road, my grandmother who was 78, my mother and the rest of us stayed in the hall because we thought that was the safest part of the house. My father had to go out because of his job as co-ordinator for the relief services. We could hear planes coming over, and bombs screaming down. People used to say, though, that if you could hear the scream of a bomb you were safe, because it would not be coming your way. Then, we saw a light coming in from outside, and found that a lot of incendiary bombs had landed all around the house. We heard some of them bouncing off the roof. We went out and I put out about a dozen and my brother George a lot more. My worst memory, though, is of seeing that some of the bombs had set the house next door on fire. The people were away and all their daughter's wedding presents were inside. She had been married only the week before. For the first time I faced the dilemma of choosing the lesser of two evils. George said we would have to break into the house to put the fire out. I knew it was wrong to break into anybody's house, but we decided it would be right now. But we couldn't put the fire out. It was much too big for two kids. The wind was blowing the flames towards our house, and so my mother decided we should take out such furniture as we could. Some boys from Exeter School helped us and we stacked the furniture on the wide pavement outside. Fortunately our house did not catch fire, and the wind changed direction so we moved all the furniture back in. The house next door was completely burnt down, and was rebuilt after the war.

On the morning after the blitz a retired town clerk of Exeter, Mr Lloyd Parry, invited us all over to his house nearby for breakfast. When a friend and I set off on an errand to the emergency centre in Hele's School, my father told us we would not be allowed through the city centre so we had to go via Polsloe Road and Pennsylvania. Even so we kept on, having to make detours because wardens stopped us to say there was an unexploded bomb in the way.'

She also remembered 'at thirteen I didn't understand a great deal about people being in love, but I did find it touching at the time when one of the Army auxiliary girls billeted in a house near us asked me to post a letter to her fiancé for her. She told me *Don't forget to post it. When he hears about the blitz he will worry about me, and I want him to know I am still alive.*'[161]

Her father, James Whiteside, was in charge of the Information Service and also recorded those events. He wrote 'on that night I went to bed, tired and carefree. I heard no siren, but I dimly remember hearing the unmistakable urr-urr of a German aeroplane. I had heard the sound often enough before and I was not unduly worried by it. I was really awakened by my son rushing into the bedroom shouting *Incendiary Bomb!* I know that I dressed because I was in a dressed condition the next time I thought about it. I rushed outside and found incendiary bombs burning everywhere; my own I put out with sandbags (delivered free to every household by the local authority) and such others as I could see about me were in the street and in gardens and unlikely to cause much damage. My wife marshalled her mother (81) and three of our four children (13, 5, 4) into the hall of the house which had been strengthened as a refuge room (the courage of all of them was marvellous: I think that I was the only frightened member of the family). Our son (15) had disappeared: tin hat worn at an angle and stirrup pump trailing under one arm. (I learnt afterwards with pride that he had done some stout work: but this is my story, not his). By this time high explosive bombs were falling – and everything else too, as it seemed. I went out several times. People were scurrying about and I scurried about too, occasionally falling flat on our faces as planes dived low over us. Everyone seemed to be dealing adequately with his own incendiary bombs. Machine-gunning was heard from time to time; but always the crash of explosives. I remember hearing one, two, three, four, five crumps with no explosions. Five in a row and pretty near and none of them exploded, I thought, and speedily forgot about them. Ringing of fire engine bells; ambulance bells; shouting; bombs crashing; house shaking; glass breaking; machine-gunning; havoc!

Quietness! Again I went out. Fires some distance away but all seemed quiet near at hand. Then I saw that the house next door to mine was on fire. I do not know if I saw it or heard the crackling; but it was on fire. (My neighbour, unknown to me, had taken fright from the previous small air raids and had gone with his wife to sleep in the country.)

Volunteers quickly gathered and in a few moments eleven stirrup pump parties were pumping water into the burning house. The flames grew in fury and, when the blessed 'All clear' sounded, the house was burning fiercely; flames caught by a strongish wind reaching out challengingly to my house only a few feet away. Volunteers were there in plenty, notably half a company of A.T.S. girls from a neighbouring hostel. (Taking these girls as a cross-section, I would assess the taste in pyjamas of our warrior girls at approximately six pink to four pale blue) And how these amateur fire-fighters and water carriers worked – but the battle was a losing one. It seemed that my house would surely take fire and I asked a few people to remove a few easy pieces of furniture from it. With gusto the girls swarmed into the place and, as it seemed, my house was stripped of every stick and stitch of furniture in a twinkling. Good work! (the rents in the wallpaper were not caused by attempts to remove that also, but by the Herculean zeal of inexperienced furniture removers – a heavy wardrobe that took four men to take upstairs took a girl and a half to bring down, and in half the time) Fun! Of course it was! The girls loved it and I loved them for it. My wife and children were in a neighbour's house organising a running buffet. My furniture was piled up on the pavement and placed in nearby garages. And still the fire raged. And other fires roared. Fires all round us. And the sky overheard burned with a glow that could be seen for miles (in fact, over thirty miles).

The direction of the wind suddenly changed. I noticed it and many people to whom I have spoken since also noticed it. The wind changed and my home was no longer in danger. But the fire still raged and sweating blackened stirrup pump parties and water carriers were relieved by sometime furniture removers.

At length the flames subsided. The incendiary bombs had completed their dirty work. Dawn came and, with fewer helpers, my furniture was returned to the shelter of my roof – dumped (as a matter of historical record, there was missing, presumably stolen, one torch, one toothbrush, and two rugs – also missing were all the buckets my wife had owned, but this loss can be understood.).'[162]

– Marlborough Road –

Olive Wakeham was lodging with Mr & Mrs Walton at 41 Marlborough Road and recalls 'on the night of the blitz itself I was in a flat in Malborough Road and I was preparing to go to Birmingham the next day to take my exam. I had a L-shaped bedroom and all my wonderful new clothes – my best bib and tukka was all laid out – all went out the windows when the windows were blown out. I had to retrieve them from the roofs near by. The first bomb dropped before the siren went off. All our doors and windows went. We had a Morrison Shelter and they were very good. We had already had a very bad raid – that was down in Holloway Street. That was very bad, it was some months before. Then I was waiting up at the bus station in Paul Street. My petrol ration wouldn't allow me to use the car every day – only three days a week. Some days I had to use the train. I heard a terrible explosion in Holloway Street itself – five people were killed. Mr Walton had to go out with his steel helmet and with all the bombing we thought oh my, he has probably been killed. But he came in and he had a wound in his hand from a piece of shrapnel. I said to him *you have to go back out*. I couldn't go because I wasn't trained – I wasn't allowed to do anything other than my work then. It was terrible – Marlborough Road had some of the first bombs. Our neighbour Mr Cornish came out of his house and it collapsed around him. He was in his dressing gown. When the all clear went he was in a state of shock of course. They brought him down to our house at the end. We were already giving tea to the end house which had the agricultural girls. I dressed his foot. I was working with the blind people then and some of them made socks on the circular machines and I had some. He had slippers on and I gave him a pair of socks. And I can tell you to this day I have never been paid for them! And he and his wife walked to Haldon House, where they had relatives, because they had nowhere else to go. After the blitz we had to evacuate because there was an unexploded bomb. I got my car out and took my sister, the cat, dog and Mr & Mrs Walton to the country. The dog and cat had run away that night but came back in time. I then caught the train to Birmingham. I spent two hours at St David's Station just shaking.'

Monica Hoare was eighteen years old and when the sirens sounded her mother and younger brother sheltered across from their home in Marlborough Road, in St Leonard's, while she and her father picked up incendiary bombs and placed them in buckets and in their bath. An unexploded bomb fell in the back garden and went through their speedboat stored there. Afterwards they were told it probably had come with a part missing, purposely left out by factory workers who did not agree with the Nazis. Once the all-clear sounded they found 'both ends of our road had burning buildings and there was a huge crater where a landmine had demolished a large house the other side of Wonford Road. I believe two people were killed in houses at the top of Marlborough Road. A lady wanted to get into the manse but I could only see as far as the umbrella stand inside the front door. The rest was just rubble.'

— Maryfield House —

Mrs D. Irene Thomas recorded her experiences when her home, Maryfield House in Pennsylvania Road, was bombed. She lived there with FG, her husband, and their two young sons. She wrote 'we had all been asleep for some hours when I was awakened by the alert signal ululating its minor wail and I sat up on bed to listen for enemy bombers and when I recognised the pulsing reverberation of their distant engines I got out of bed without putting on the light and raised a corner of the black-out curtain. I was appalled to see hundreds of glimmering lights falling out of the sky over the sleeping town; all was strangely quiet, the planes seemingly at a great height, but the stealthy descending radiance of their flares lit up the while city, a clearly exposed target, and there was no mistaking what was about to happen. I roused FG and we instantly betook ourselves with the children down the steps below the store room into the rock-hewn wine cellars; Philip had a blanket, Richard and I had picked up a coat as we sped through the hall, but with all our haste we had barely erected the canvas chairs before the raid began. FG would not allow me to go back for the dog and cat but closed the trapdoor and we prepared to sit it out.

During the next two hours we remained like animals huddled together for safety in a hole in the ground while – unlike animals – our own kind sought to destroy us. The noise was tremendous and almost continual; sometimes we attempted to crouch deeper, heads bent, into our chairs as a dive-bomber seemed about to penetrate our fast-ness, afterwards exchanging looks of relief at near-misses; we could not attempt to talk and none of us showed fear; by the light of the bare electric bulb I mechanically read the metal labels on the old wine racks – Hock, Burgundies, Claret.

At last there came quite a pause and we hoped all was over, that we could presently hear the 'All Clear'. Richard miraculously slept in my arms, Philip was awake and calm – I suppose it was about two o'clock in the morning and as nothing seemed to be happening FG, veteran of many London air-raids, proposed to ascend the stairs to the kitchen and make tea. We sat shouting hopefully up to him as we waited for the kettle to boil, and he shouted down to us that Molto was safe in his basket, and the kettle beginning to sing.

With dreadful suddenness a dive-bomber approached with an almost unbearable increase of sound. There was a sudden burst of gunfire just as a bomb came shrieking down and hit the earth so that it shook. There ensued a long and terrible confusion. The huge rending explosion was followed by instant darkness, the house shuddered, drew in upon itself, seemed to cringe, then with a tearing of wood, shattering of glass, riving apart of masonry and metal the fabric was sucked apart by the blast and flung aloft and around to fall back again to earth in a pouring down of debris that seemed to go on forever. Eventually silence; and pitch darkness.

Before anyone had spoken I had handled both children, then as though from a long way off FG's voice called from above, *are you there?* and I said *we're all right – and you? Yes, but the trapdoor's covered with rubble – I'll have to get to you from the back drive.* I switched on my torch but could see nothing whatsoever, and had clicked the switch vainly several times when Philip said quietly *if you are testing your torch, Mummy, you'd better wait until the dust settles,* thus explaining what I was then too dazed and stupid to understand for myself. While we sat breathing the smell of powdered plaster and granite rubble in the silence of another lull I became aware of water trickling steadily down the wall behind me, probably I imagined from a fractured water main, a very disquieting thought. I said nothing, and presently tried the torch again and could now see that the cellar was intact together with the steps leading up to the kitchen. I felt it imperative to get us all above ground as quickly as possible so I laid Richard down in my chair and climbed the steps. Although I pushed at the trapdoor with all my strength it was immovable. Without hesitating Philip agreed to sit with Richard alone in pitch darkness while I went with the torch into the adjoining cellar . . . by crawling and clambering over the debris we could get outside – a tremendous relief this. To this open door now came FG from the drive, almost unrecognisable as also was I, both of us covered in a grey film, features, hair and eyelashes thick with bomb dust, coats like ashy cerements. With him came a uniformed and helmeted warden who agreed that since the worst appeared to be over we should all get above ground – he did not think the water immediately dangerous but there was a risk at any moment of further subsidence of the house. Since the falling of the bomb there had ensued a long lull so we quickly brought the boys outside – but where then were we to go? Both our courtyards were piled with rubble from the outhouses from which the dust was still rising. Across the road, behind beech hedges actually blazing and crackling, the houses stood upright with roof tiles crinkled and gaping black windows, but Maryfield had no walls standing on this side, from what had been rood there now crazily tilted and protruded laths, beams and timbers at all angles, while the water tank had been blown up into a tree. In the valley a great conflagration in the city case an intense reflected glow up into the sky by which light the grain of brickwork and even the minute veining of the young leaves on the trees appeared with floodlit distinctiveness.'[163]

Another resident recalled that 'Bishop Blackall Girls School, which I attended, used a wing of the Thomas house as an annexe. My classroom was destroyed in the bombing. Had the raid been a few hours later, in daylight, we would have been there, though we would have been in the shelter. A week after the bombing, we were taken to see the damage. We looked in through the gaping walls to see our desks mangled and laden with debris. One girl wanted her paint-box from her desk, so the teachers bravely, or foolishly, climbed inside and rescued it.'[164] Phyllis Hawkins recalls the bombing of Maryfield House and that 'I think I got back my pencil box but not much else.'

– Maynards Girl School –

Helen Harris remembers 'I was a pupil at the Maynard School for girls in Exeter during the years of the second world war, and a boarder from September 1939 to the time of the blitz. The school no longer takes boarders, but in those days there were two boarding houses: Tregear, in the grounds of the main school, and mine, Summerlands, which comprised two joined buildings – numbers 39 and 41 Heavitree Road, five minutes walk from the school. The location was immediately opposite the end of Spicer Road, a site now redeveloped into several small modern dwellings. The two houses, dating from the nineteenth century, stood back from the road with railings and gardens in front and were of similar type to some which still stand farther up the hill on that side of Heavitree Road. At the back each had also its own walled

The damage to Maynards Girl School.

garden. They were joined by a prominent iron fire escape, which was accessible from the dormitories on either side.

Exeter had suffered a more minor air raid in the latter part of April, during our school Easter holidays. Because of this we were required to delay our return to school for some days as the boarding house was without supplies of water and gas. It was therefore the evening of Sunday 3 May when my parents took me back to school for the summer term, together with all my necessary belongings – uniform school clothes, a few new items (including a particularly pretty 'mufti' dress made from material obtained with precious clothes rationing coupons) and all my school books filled with the notes I was accumulating for School Certificate exams in the following year. I was then fifteen years of age.

Since the start of the war we had had to have regular surprise air raid practices. From 1940 there was a large underground shelter in the school grounds to which we had to go. The routine was that every night we would place trousers, jumper, raincoat, outdoor shoes, and gas mask, on the bedside chair. Then, every week or so, after we were in bed the shrill and startling whistled would suddenly be sounded and out we would jump, don our clothes, run downstairs, out across Heavitree Road and along Spicer Road to the school shelter. We would of course be counted, and the exercise timed. No one appeared to consider what passers-by might be thinking on those light summer evenings at seeing thirty or so young females tearing along in motley-covered night attire. A year later, however, a shelter was built for our own use, very close to the house in the garden at the back. This avoided the nocturnal sprint, and I do not recall practices then being so frequent.

Therefore, we were all reasonably prepared as to what we should do when we were awakened by air raid sirens – and doubtless also the whistle – a short while after midnight on 4 May. We all trooped down to the shelter in the garden, to the sound of approaching aircraft.

This shelter was only half below ground, built of concrete blocks. It was long and fairly narrow, with seats along the sides, duckboards for feet, and at the far end – in case of need – an Elsan closet, discreetly screened. I can still remember the smell of damp concrete and hurricane oil lamp that pervaded. I was seated near the door, on the right hand side, and there would have been probably just over thirty of us, including housemistress and matron, filling the shelter.

Soon proceedings became decidedly noisy with increasing bangs, some of them very near. I suppose we had a feeling of fear but I do not particularly remember. I do recall one of the younger girls asking the mistress if she should pray, and as she said aloud the Lord's Prayer those of us near her I am sure joined her in our hearts.

Presently the housemistress slightly opened the door and told us that the house was alight and that there were green flares 'all over the garden'. I could see this myself from where I was sitting, and this seemed to increase potential danger. I particularly recall briefly looking up at the part of the building – on the top floor – where I had been sleeping, and seeing the flames pouring up to the sky and the roof collapsing, and thinking that that was the end of my new dress and all my school papers and other things.

Eventually the situation became quieter and soon an air raid warden came to the shelter door. He said that we must move immediately because of danger from the burning house, and he led us to a terrace house in Lower Summerlands. This would probably have been between 3 and 4 a.m. The people in the house accepted our 'invasion' with great calm and were most kind, giving us cups of tea and fruit cake, but it was not long before we had to move from there also, because a house just two or three doors away was on fire. So off we trooped for the quarter-mile to the school shelter, where we found the Tregear girls still installed. By this time the raid was long over and dawn arriving. Doubtless there had been some communication between the author-ities, and the decision was taken for us to go up to Exeter School as a staging-post. It was now daylight and so we made our way – two and two in the customary orderly 'crocodile' mode of progression – out of the school environs and up Magdalen Road. By the time of our arrival – perhaps around 6 a.m. – the boys had been instructed to vacate their dormitories, and we girls sank into their still-warm beds, two girls to each, for a 'rest'!

I don't think any of us actually slept, but I suppose it kept us out of the way until the boys could be fed, and a second breakfast kindly prepared for all of us. When this was ready and we were all downstairs and tucking in, a message came for me that my father had arrived to take me home. He and my mother, at Tiverton, had with great anxiety watched the blaze in the sky during the night. My father wasted no time in driving to Exeter, fortunately getting through before large-scale closure of roads, driving over glass, debris, and hoses in the process. As he approached the boarding house he faced with horror the gaunt, blackened, skeletal, denuded wall structures and charred, smouldering remains within. Then, as he got nearer, he saw a notice attached to the gate by the thoughtful housemistress: ALL GIRLS SAFELY EVACUATED TO EXETER SCHOOL. It was a strange drive back to Tiverton – this time without any luggage – and an emotional reunion with my mother.

School did not resume for a further week or so. Although the main school building, and Tregear, had survived, the school suffered a certain amount of damage, particularly of broken glass and some involving actual construction. Leabourne, a private house on the same 'island' between Denmark Road, Barnfield Hill and Spicer Road, was severely bombed, sadly with loss of life including that of one of our school pupils. Parts of the school were repaired fairly quickly – as the head-mistress, Miss E.M. Ryan later said *thanks to day after day of fine weather* – sufficiently for use in that summer term, while a number of us and our staff were accommodated at Bishop Blackall School, on a shift system – they did their work in prolonged mornings, we started at 1.30 p.m. and continued until 5.30. As we moved about Exeter in those days the extent to which the poor city and its people had suffered became all too apparent.

Although Tregear reopened as a boarding house for a few years I spent the remainder of my school life as a day-girl, travelling in company with a handful of others from my home area on the now non-existing Exe Valley Railway.'

– Wonford Road –

One woman, who came from London with her husband to Exeter when she was twenty-eight, recalls 'we lived in Wonford Road where we shared a house with another couple, the wife was in London because her sister was having a baby and her husband was a draughtsman who that night was fire watching, I think near Fore Street. My husband was fire watching in Wonford Road. We were in the cellar (his mother, myself, a friend who had just had an operation) and after a while my husband came down and said we had to get out because there were incendiaries on the roof. There was a dugout in St Leonard's church grounds – where they trained soldiers during the day – we went there and when it was all over we left. We returned to our house and it was still burning – stupidly we went in – my husband got his bicycle in the basement and I got some clothes for my friend from her bedroom. We went to the vicarage, told the vicar our story, and asked if we could leave our few things there. We were told about a centre we could go to as we were homeless. My husband took my friend to the station in the morning for London and we then, I suppose, phoned Taunton, and left for Taunton in the afternoon. The house burnt right down eventually. I asked a friend to look after our cat and see that he could be put down. He did come back but she kept him. All we had was the clothes we were in and my husband had a tin his father used to keep his pub takings – we kept our papers in it and he took that from the house. In Taunton we got coupons and then we had to record everything we lost – how much it cost and how much it was worth. My mother-in-law was only entitled to £50 compensation because she was our dependent. Down in the cellar she had two tea chests that had table silver in them and they were lost. But it didn't matter, she only had her £50 no matter what she lost.'

– Wykes Road –

Gerry Linnell was only seven years old and living at 57 Wykes Road with his family. He recalls 'we had just had our Morrison Shelter the previous week. So I says to Mum *Let's have a lie in the shelter to see what its like tonight*. She said *all right, we will do it then*. Dad was on fire watching in the railway in Queen Street. Granny was upstairs in the back bedroom. And then all of a sudden all hell was let loose. Bombs were dropping and guns going off. Mum rushed upstairs to get Granny. She was hanging out of the window, watching all the German bombers going across. We couldn't get her into the shelter. The Germans set fire to Ladysmith School. They dropped a land mine in the cemetery and it blew all the doors in and windows out. One dropped on Pinhoe Road and the blast blew all the windows out. And in the back we had all these bones blown into the back garden. Later we decided to walk to our uncles out to Exwick – mother and me. I carried Ginger, our pussycat, and my Gollywog which I lost in the fields because Ginger didn't stop wiggling. We walked up Pinhoe Road, down along High Street and up to my uncles. He took us up in his van and we could see Exeter burning. We went back and then saw all the old bones. I think Father just dug them into the garden – the skulls got smashed up and all – as bone meal for the garden. No sense in letting it go to waste. He later planted his vegetables on top.'

– Fore Street –

Bill Brewer later wrote of his experiences on Fore Street. He was living in St Thomas and wrote 'the wailing of sirens woke us at around 1.30 a.m. and sleepily we climbed out of bed and made our way downstairs, someone put the kettle on and we sat around, disinterested, not wanting to talk, and listening for the expected sound of enemy aircraft passing overhead . . . Eileen, a friend of mine, arrived shortly. She felt safer in my house and would quickly join us whenever the sirens went.

The unmistakeable sound of German aircraft was heard, and dad went outside to look around, calling me a few moments later to join him. There in the garden the noise and concentration of aircraft was greater than we had ever heard previously. They appeared to be circling the city, and within a short while flares were criss-crossing the night sky, slowly descending to light up the buildings below. The whistling of bombs, followed by hearty explosions galvanised us into action, and whipping up our helmets and gas masks all the family raced across the road to a dried up ditch opposite the house. It afforded little protection, a couple of feet deep, but with an orchard wall behind us, we felt more secure.

It was obvious that this was the start of a planned and heavy raid, bombs rained down on it seemed without a break onto a defenceless city. There were no searchlights or anti-aircraft guns to scatter the enemy. Apart from a few strays, the main bomb loads were falling in the city centre, flames reaching high into the night sky. Having worked in the city for a number of years, I knew many of the people living and working there, and some of those fire watching that night. I decided to do something, and called to dad to say I was going into town to see if I could help. Despite objections, I ran down the road with Eileen following, insisting she was coming along.

Passing quickly through Cowick Street we saw no visible signs of damage, until crossing over Exe Bridge, away to our right, downriver, a large gasometer was burning itself out. Running up Fore Street was a very eerie experience, with not a single other person in sight. It was almost as bright as day, so much so, that we automatically kept to the shadows cast by the sun-blinds still out across the pavement. The noise all around was deafening, although the frontages we passed appeared so far to be untouched. Ahead of us however was a blazing inferno, and on reaching the corner of Market Street we could go no further. Bombs and incendiaries were still raining down in the fires, but being so close all we noticed was the final whoosh and muffled crumps as they arrived, collapsing walls and scattering myriads of sparks into the air. There were, at this corner, perhaps five or six people, the first we had seen since leaving home, two or three being firemen directing a hose onto what I believe was the Army and Navy Stores on the corner. We tried to assist in clearing some of the stock, helping some folks move their belongings away from the area, and when extra firemen arrived, manhandle hoses and equipment up from the river. Waves of wood smoke and hot air dried our throats, and brought tears to our eye. These having to be brushed away with the back of the hand, smearing our faces, already black and streaked with sweat.

We had intended to get to the top of South Street where my manager, Mr Kinch, lived with his family over the premises, but this was impossible, every building on either side of the street burning fiercely. We could not see beyond, and imagined there could be no hope for anyone in that area. At some time in the early hours the All Clear must have sounded although we did not hear it. We felt eventually that the position was hopeless and all we could do then was to stand and watch. Around seven o'clock we decided to retrace our steps. Returning down Fore Street, hosepipes covered the road, running up from the river, with here and there auxiliary pumps attached, working away on their own, with no attendants in sight. Our clothes were crumpled and smelling of smoke, eyes burning, faces streaked, hair flattened and wet with sweat from under our helmets, we arrived home. We had accomplished little, but we were left with a feeling of achievement at having 'done something' in fighting back.'[165]

— Summerland Crescent —

Brian Pollard was working for Devon County Council. He recalls 'our house was one in a crescent of seven houses. It had railings around a basement area with stone steps and a railed stone bridge over it to the front door, a cellar under the road, basement, ground floor, first floor, second floor and attic. Father, mother, elder sister, me, and younger brother and sister made up the family. Father had a plaster cast around his body from hip to neck, having cracked a bone in his spine from a fall from a ladder. I was 18 and awaiting a call from the Fleet Air Arm to start training as a pilot.

We were asleep and were not greatly concerned to be woken by the air raid siren again, as we had a reinforced room in the basement. Hearing the sound of explosions we thought it wise to dress and go there; but we did not get that far. The explosions seemed to come very near and we had a shower of incendiary bombs. The latter were 12 to 15 inches long and 2 or 3 inches in diameter. They contained magnesium and, on contact, burned white hot and spat burning fragments. Two such bombs came through the windows of the first floor front bedroom, already shattered by the explosions. We tried dousing with water but the furnishings were soon blazing. I discovered that more incendiary bombs had come through the roof and the attic was well alight and also the buildings opposite and adjacent. There was nothing for it but to leave.

No matter how good the intentions one is never properly alert when the time comes. There were many small valuable things we could have taken with us but our only thoughts were to guard our lives. The nearest public air raid shelter was in Sidwell Street about five hundred yards away. It was hazardous and not without incident but by helping each other we reached the shelter as did many others. Sidwell Street is a wide thoroughfare. There was enough room to construct on the centre line two brick and concrete shelters and two steel static water tanks. Within the shelter was more frightening than outside it, where at least the percussion of the explosions was more dispersed and you could see how near or far was the falling masonry; and burning buildings close by made it very hot inside the shelter. The noise was coming from everywhere. Then came machine-gunning. The static tanks were perforated and several inches of water entered the shelter. The planes retired, the fires continued to burn, people began to move and dawn came.'

– Summerland and Parr Streets –

Mollie Bowden recalls the destruction of her family's home at the corner of Summerland and Parr Streets. They had lived there for some six years. She wrote 'Mum kept a shop whilst Dad had a garage and workshop. Mum's shop was at 24 Summerland Street with the entrance in Parr Street. This was also our home. Dad had a workshop which continued from our accommodation onto the first house in Parr Street where he started by repairing bicycle punctures, motor cycles and cars. Mum sold almost everything but food – baby prams, cots, doll prams, dolls . . . April 25th 1942 a raid on Exeter damaged the shop and roof which needed immediate attention as rain was on the way. Then on May 4th the blitz when everything was lost. What a calamity!

The Harris family at the corner of Parr and Summerland Streets.

All we had was the nightclothes we were wearing . . . A Morrison Shelter had been brought in for us to sleep in. It had a steel top which was used as a table, so dark and claustrophobic, if we did not have this shelter we would all have perished, due to the incendiary bombs which were exploding all around us . . . Dad managed to save a car. We made for the Triangle (not a car park then). So many people in our situation, we got in the car and arrived at my grandmother's house, 1 Exwick Road, we stayed until daylight. Next morning continued to our Aunt & Uncle's farm in Hittisleigh, who were shocked to see us but pleased we were alive.'

All over Exeter the following day similar arrangements were desperately being made.

CHAPTER

THE AFTERMATH
OF THE BLITZ

THREE

On the morning of Monday, the fourth of May, Exeter woke up to unparalleled destruction with many lives and buildings lost. Yet across the city the population tried to continue with their lives. Some were involved in putting out fires, others in rescue operations and still more in supporting them, some tried to cope with having lost all that they owned, many left the city and others simply tried to go back to work. A city of many thousands of people struggled after the worst disaster in its history.

Each experience was different. Vivien Dietz was a young student at University College and volunteered as a student assistant air raid warden. She recalled that she took charge of a baby found at a bombed house in Sidwell Street and was escorted to the hospital by two firemen. Afterwards she, along with another student, cut mountains of sandwiches at a centre in Countess Wear for the fire fighters. She later joined a group of students at the deanery helping to pick up pieces of broken stained glass.[166] Hers is just one of many stories of Exeter people caught up in the bombing.

The bombing ended before dawn, at about 2.50 a.m. Many came out of shelters to find they did not have a home and their immediate problem was to find somewhere to sleep. For instance, Mrs E. Dolman discovered her flat in Verney Place was destroyed. In 1977 she remembered the upset, and humour, in it. She wrote 'now just before all this, we'd queued up to watch Laurel and Hardy down where the old Hippodrome used to be. In the film they were supposed to be dying and 'e was trying to get this drink up to his mouth, sort of holding onto the end of his tie and trying to get the drink up. Well, after the all clear went Mr Hicks, the butcher, and all they put us in the church where they had camp beds laid down where we could lay the children. Our homes were gone; we never had nothing; they destroyed the lot. I suppose after it all I was shaking, so Mr Hicks gave me a drink of water. And could I get that cup up? Course Laurel and Hardy came back to me, and I just stood there and I roared. Course he thought I was hysterical really. Then I said *Don't worry, Mr Hicks, its just a funny film that us have seen. He shook so much that he couldn't get the drink up and now me.* It was so funny.' Mrs Dolman and her children left for Barnstaple to be with her husband and later returned to Exeter.[167]

The following morning

Many in Exeter tried to continue their lives as usual. Danny La Rue, as he later was to call himself, came to work at Walton's, at the corner of Queen and High Streets, where he was employed as a window-dresser, only to find that every glass window had been shattered.[168] Nancy Mead was a teenager and attempted to go to Colson's in High Street. She crossed Lower Bridge Street and found hosepipes bringing water from the river to fight fires in Fore Street. She had to cross through via The Mint and then met up with other employees who all went to the Civic Hall for instructions.

One local woman, then fifteen years old, worked at the City Education Office in Southernhay and recalls she reported for duty. Along with the other women on the staff she was not allowed into the building because its top floor was burning. The men rescued files, typewriters and other office items while the girls cried on the grass outside. When Mr G. Tue, Exeter's Secretary for Education, arrived he reproached them for being inactive and sent them on their bicycles to Hele's

School, where the Information Centre was based. For several days they delivered messages, many regarding the Emergency Feeding Centres. The Education office staff subsequently moved to temporary offices at the corner of Queen Street and Northernhay Park.

Eileen Reynolds had just fled to Topsham to escape the April bombings. She was then a teenager and had spent the night with her family under their Morrison Shelter. She had not realised how serious the bombing had been so, as she later wrote, 'I got up next morning to go to catch the bus for work. I went to the bus stop for the 7.30 a.m. bus to be in work for 8 o'clock. The road seemed deserted. There was just one other person waiting at the bus stop – a lady going to see her husband, who was a doctor at the Royal Devon & Exeter Hospital in Southernhay. It seemed that we were standing there for ages but I never once thought to go home. Then round the corner came a Greenslades' coach. The driver stopped and told us that there were no buses running. He said that he could take us the long way round to the city via Alphington to Exe Bridge. I looked up Fore Street Hill to see burning buildings. It was horrific. As we walked up Fore Street nobody stopped us. We trod over large hosepipes the firemen were using to hose down the buildings. People were being brought out on stretchers, some of whom were dead.

I just can't remember how we got to the Hospital, but we did eventually, and we were both obviously in shock. The lady did see her husband, he came out of the hospital dressed in what was a white coat, with a stethoscope round his neck. His coat had blood and yellow stains all over it.

I then left them both and walked to Magdalen Street, turned right to the Valiant Soldier pub where I looked up to where I should be going to work and saw complete devastation. South Street was flattened except for the Sacred Heart Catholic Church, another church [Holy Trinity], the White Hart Hotel and a few small buildings. I don't know how long I stood there in disbelief. Quite a lot to take in for a small 14 year old. I just turned on my heels and ran, walked, ran, walked all the way back to Topsham some 4½ miles to tell my mum what I had seen. But when I arrived I couldn't utter a word I was sobbing and shaking so much. It's strange but on that journey home I cannot recall anyone passing me, either on foot or in a car. I suppose they did, but I must have been in a daze'.

Some buildings were destroyed hours after the bombers had left. Walter Daw, then an air raid warden, recalled in 1982 'after being on duty all night I decided to go and see if my elderly parents were all right. They lived at Richmond Road in St David's. Usually I would have gone straight through Holloway Street and South Street but I was unable to get through. Most of the right-hand side of South Street was still burning fiercely. It was while going through Cathedral Yard that I saw the Globe Hotel seemed to be still intact, and I didn't even know then that a bomb had hit one side of the Cathedral. After going to Richmond Road, and seeing my parents were all right, I came back to Cathedral Yard and saw to my horror that the Globe was completely destroyed. It was, I suppose, a lath and plaster building and it went up like a match.'[169]

Patricia Stacey was then fourteen years old and remembers she walked down High Street with her older brother. The Co-Operative Building and the Savoy Cinema still stood at East Gate 'like two sore thumbs'. On the entrance door of the ruined Plaza there hung the advertisement poster for *The Egg and I*, starring Claudette Colbert, which Mrs Stacey had just seen. As they passed the Devon & Somerset Stores they discovered that the heat had burst open tins of fruit. There was a 'sea of juice' in the street as well as a smell of burning fat in the air. Soldiers were trying to clear the rubble and fire hose lay across the street.

Another person who went through Exeter was Rita Webb who recalled 'my sister and I walked down to Exeter centre and what a shock we had on seeing so many fine buildings in rubble. A bus had been overturned and a huge crater filled the road. It was a scary time when I was alone with 2 young children and a sick mum. What I shall always remember was the sight of dead bodies in the road. One woman showed a foot from under a grey blanket and her stocking was full of holes. Her shoes were still fixed to her heels. Another sight was a woman's hand poking out with her wedding ring still on and someone saying her husband was overseas.'[170]

Life was also disrupted outside of the city centre. Bill Hole was only fourteen and recalls the bombing at Monks Road. He later wrote 'in the morning a big squad of marines came looking for clothing, sashes and medals, etc., belonging to Staff Sergeant Gale. Sgt Gale and his family were all killed.' Joyce Flack, who lived at Polsloe Road Post

Office, remembers her father had been called out as a member of the Home Guard. She recalls 'everything was in chaos – everyone was looking dazed. People were wandering about in dirty clothing coming from houses that were bombed, others were looking for relatives. I saw my father sitting on the wall just below the post office on the wall with another member of the Home Guard, both grey and ashen, talking to one another and looking like they were at the end of their tethers. He didn't tell me until years afterwards what he had been doing. He told me he had to get everyone out of the Air Raid Shelter outside the Odeon which had taken a direct hit. At the age of thirteen I didn't think much about what he was doing – thinking he was just helping. I don't think he could bear to talk about it.'

Surprisingly, not everyone in the city noticed the blitz. Liz Edworthy remembers how her mother, then twenty-two years old, managed to miss it even though she was in Exeter that night. She has written 'my mother, Mary Edworthy, worked for the first half of the war as a bus conductress in Exeter. She lodged with a family, the Langdons, in Ladysmith Road and told me many stories of her days with Exeter City Transport. Sixty years after those days she could still recall all the fares on every route! In May 1942 Mr Langdon was in the R.A.F. somewhere in England and Mrs Langdon took her daughter to Teignmouth to stay with relatives for a few days. My mother was alone in the house. On Sunday 3rd May the weather was very hot as it had been for several days. My mother had to start work at 6:00 a.m. the following day, so she decided to have an early night. Around 9:00 p.m. the air-raid warden called at the house to say that they had a warning of possible attacks that night. My mother refused to go to the shelter because she said that she couldn't sleep in the shelter. There had been some false alarms in the previous week and she wanted a good night's sleep before her early start.

Having set her alarm clock, my mother fell fast asleep. During the night she thought she heard thunder, which, considering the hot weather, was not surprising.

When she got up the following morning, my mother was upset to find that the water was off (a frequent occurrence) and set off to walk to the bus station. Her usual route was up Sampson's Lane and then down Clifton Hill. However there was a sign saying that Clifton Hill was closed, so she headed for Gladstone Road instead. As she walked along this road she noticed that St Luke's College was on fire and wondered why this should be!

As she turned into Heavitree Road, the main road into the centre of Exeter, a policeman barred her way, asking her the reason for her journey. When she explained that she needed to be at work to take the first bus out he told her that there would be no buses that day since there were no roads! For the first time that day my mother realised that Exeter had been heavily bombed during the night. The policeman did let her through and she arrived at the bus station. An inspector told her to go home which she did.'

Emergency measures

James Whiteside, who was in charge of disseminating information in Exeter, was the only local official in civil defence to record his experiences. He wrote 'I was appointed emergency officer in the early months of 1941: my sole qualification being that I was already honorary secretary to the local committee of the Ministry of Information. I was also at that time adjutant of the Exeter Battalion of the Home Guard. I gave this up. At the time of my taking over the work of the Emergency Information Officer the period of intense air attacks on England was at its height and it seemed certain that Exeter sooner or later would be singled out for a heavy raid. My large duties were defined for me very simply: my task was to sustain public morale in what was described as 'blitz aftermath' — just that!

I prepared what I dubbed 'The Emergency Information Service Operational Scheme': I enlisted a few friends, members of an organisation of which I was President, and together we rehearsed the scheme. The difficulty with which we were faced in rehearsal was, of course, the sheer impossibility of reproducing artificially anything like the conditions under which we would be likely to work, even if we had known, otherwise than in imagination, what these conditions would be. The scheme was designed so as to give every man a *key* job — something of his own which he would engage himself upon without seeking instruction or advice.

The scheme and the team then went into cold storage, to emerge from time to time for further discussion and for further recruitment of volunteers. In October 1941, with Mr Haley (Deputy City Treasurer), I prepared an eighty-page Handbook of Emergency Information. Publication was held up due to difficulties in getting paper supplies, but in March 1942, the handbook went to press and 3,000 copies were produced. These were distributed among police, civil defence workers, doctors, clergymen and all people who could be regarded as leaders of any group within the city, with the exhortation in the preface that *each would become an information officer in the moment of need and, before that moment arrived, would be a fountain of accurate knowledge within his own circle.*

And the scheme and the team remained in cold storage. I had looked at the scheme; talked about it; added to it; subtracted from it; even, at the request of the Ministry of Information, addressed conferences upon it; forced, against my inclination, into the limelight as an expert upon a subject of which I knew exactly nothing that was not born of imagination. As the months went by, and as my expectation that Exeter's turn was fast approaching was sharpened, I ceased to be fearful of life or limb in an air raid: but I began to be haunted by fears for my reputation in an aftermath. Would the scheme work? I did not know. By this time I had come to have grave doubts about it. With my team I went through the scheme again on the afternoon of Sunday, 20th April 1942.

In the following week there were three nasty raids. The scheme was not brought into operation, but some members of the team gained a little experience in loud-speaker announcing in areas that had been affected.'

Mr Whiteside went to see the damage in the city and his home was subsequently damaged on the night of the blitz (see page 260–1). Then almost immediately he found 'rumour carriers were abroad: I heard that the cathedral had been destroyed; the Guildhall burnt out; High Street and Fore Street a mass of flames from one end to the other (Later in the day several people informed me that they had heard that I had been seriously injured and was in hospital).

Eureka! The scheme was beginning to work.

The point from which the Service was to operate was Hele's School. I cannot remember the devious route we followed to get there. Unexploded bombs and debris were everywhere. Shocks galore! But no foot-weary wandering by the homeless in search of rest. No panic. No tears – yet. The city was excited and astir . . .

And so to Hele's School with banner already flying – 'Information Centre' – in the bright morning sunshine. Some of the team had already assembled. One member informed me that since seven o'clock he had been giving impromptu announcements from a loud-speaker van in districts which had suffered no damage: warning people not to rush into the bombed areas and advising them to make ready to receive in their homes their friends who had been bombed out; telling the people that the fires had died down and that work of demolition and clearance and rescue was already in hand.

The paper scheme was taking practical shape.

One point in the scheme which we had thought a year ago to be rather elaborately far-sighted related to the production of 15,000 circulars of changed addresses and other items of information which we hoped to have printed for distribution on the first day of our operations. We had had the circular set up in type in skeleton form and the type left with a printer. We contemplated the possibility that this printer's works should be destroyed so we had a separate set of type set up and deposited it in the house of a member of the team who lived in a nearby village. We thought of the possibility that the circular would need to be printed out of Exeter. And it was so. The printing works where our type had been set up was demolished and all other printing works were out of action because of the cutting off of electricity. We speedily filled in such blanks in the skeleton circular as we could and our member rushed it off to Crediton – thence to Tiverton where he placed his order.

The Regional Information Officer, who attended at the Information Centre, informed me that he had arranged for six loud-speaker vans to be sent into Exeter in accordance with the scheme and we set about the preparation of a bulletin. We gathered such information as we could from the representatives of the many departments assembled at Hele's School and at 10.30 a.m., by which time the loudspeaker vans had arrived, our earliest *official* messages were *on the air*. The messages called attention to the existence and purpose of the Information Centre at Hele's School; the situation of the Emergency Feeding Centres and Food Office, traffic and post office arrangements. These announcements were made in every quarter of the city; they were rather scrappy, but more important than what they were was the fact of them. The people of Exeter were made to know that somebody was concerned to bring the news to them.

The scheme was working; but not without difficulty in running it. Decidedly more volunteers had been enrolled than were needed to conduct operations. The wisdom of this was seen during the morning. One *key* man had been killed. Another came in pyjamas and overcoat, ready to work but preferring not to do so: to his relief he was told that we could do without him – he was led gently by the hand to a spot a few yards away where he was given immediately some coupons wherewith to provide himself with some new clothes. Another had lost home and business; others, more elderly, were hardly fit physically or mentally for the strain that the work would put upon them. For most pressing business reasons, our typist was unable to come and the typewriting job fell to me. Several girls were roped in to do the job but all of them asserted that they would not type much. In each case the girl's estimate of her capacity erred on the side of over-praise.

At 2.30 p.m. a second and fuller bulletin was similarly broadcast; and at 7 p.m. a third and more full broadcast was made throughout the city. By 7 p.m. the 15,000 circulars had been delivered and were distributed in parcels to the many wardens' posts and by hand-to-hand from the loudspeaker vans – they were eagerly seized upon by the crowds. By any standard of criticism this circular was not a good one: but the fact of its issue in such short time was important. Three loudspeaker tours and a circular on the first day; the people were beginning to have confidence that efforts were being made to interpret to them what was being done. The scheme was working.

A word about the Information Centre at Hele's School – risen like a Phoenix from the ashes. Here were established representatives of 53 government, local authority and public utility departments: the idea being that every enquiry from the public would be dealt with under the one roof. This was truly 'Enquire within about Everything'. Thousands of people visited the Centre: thousands of enquiries were dealt with and thousands of pounds in immediate relief paid out by the Assistance Board, the Public Assistance Committee and the Mayor's Air Raid Relief Fund. Many volunteers offered their help and few were turned away. At the peak period no less than 510 people were fully employed in the Centre. A shuttle service of meals was instituted and everyone who worked in the place was fed in the place. There was no panic: no fuss: no officialdom: no delay: no scenes: no displays of bad temper. Queen's Messenger Food Convoy Vans were serving cups of tea and light meals in the adjacent Bury Meadow, and with the bright sunshine, the banners signifying the different departments (some of them operating from mobile vans in the grounds), the crowds, and the scurrying arm-banded messengers, a stranger would have been excused for thinking that he had encountered a gala occasion. The perfect running of the Centre cannot be over-praised. The co-ordinating officer was Mr Haley, the deputy city treasurer.

On the next day three more bulletins were issued – morning, afternoon and evening – and were broadcast in every part of the city from six loudspeaker vans. Again was the material for these bulletins collected from the representatives of the many departments at the Information Centre. The bulletins generally became more full and informative as I acquired a greater skill in preparing them and the announcers in uttering them – there is a technique in producing and announcing a bulletin by loudspeaker.

On this second day and thereafter about 200 copies of each bulletin were stencilled and circulated among Government and local government departments, public utility undertakings, police and wardens' services. In addition to the settled bulletins, further 'rush' announcements were made from time to time about matters of urgency not contained in the bulletins, or to allay particular rumours, or matter applicable only in certain districts. By this time our typist difficulty had been solved in a rather humorous way. I found two girls who had come into the Centre to look round but who were quite prepared to do a job. They were employed by the National War Savings Association (of the local Committee of which I was a member). They were expert typists and, *mirabile dictu* [wonderful to relate], were both expert in the use of the very complicated duplicating machines that had been delivered on that day. It appeared that their office had been bombed, but was in course of being removed to other premises and they had been given the day off while the removal was completed. The Emergency Information Officer set them to work with one hand and reached for his hat with the other. He went to see the Regional War Savings Organizer and by flattery, cajolery and scripture (*What are two among so many?*) he secured them to him for the duration of the 'aftermath', subject to a day's notice to terminate the arrangement. The notice was not given and the girls did a grand job.

On this day I assembled all the skeleton placards which had been supplied to me by the Ministry of Information and which had been dispersed in five lots in different parts of the city. The poster 'For Help and Information go to . . .' was overprinted 'Information Centre at Hele's School'; 'Boil your Water and Milk' was used, and additional posters about Rest Centres were produced. Billposters were found and 600 posters exhibited. No owners of poster sites have yet made any complaints or commenced any action for trespass.

Even at the risk of breaking the continuity of the story it must be said that I refused an offer to announce for payment that a furnished flat was to let in an neighbouring town at a reasonable rent.

Another event of note occurred on the second day of our operations. Mr Cotton, of the National Council of Social Service, reported to me with a converted horse-box equipped as an office and with a loud-speaker attached. He had a team with him. He wanted work. At this time the city was almost cut in two – there were no bridges across High Street and for people on the east side of the city to get to Hele's School was a Sabbath day's journey. I gave Mr Cotton many copies of the Handbook of Emergency Information (by now come to be known as the 'blitz bible' and – joy to an author's heart! – to be seen in many strangers' hands in many unexpected places), many forms for many purposes, and told him to establish himself at a spot in the Heavitree District. I kept him regularly supplied with bulletins. He did hard and very useful work for four days.

Our scheme was now sparking on all its cylinders: no longer was it merely a paper scheme.

It now seemed to be unnecessary to issue more than one bulletin a day and I thought it to be more scientific in my collection of information for announcements.

On the third day (Wednesday) I attended the meeting of the Emergency Committee held at 10 a.m. at Southbrook House on the eastern outskirt of the city. Here the executive officers attended and made their reports to the Emergency Committee and the Deputy Regional Commissioner. It was my practice to listen to these reports and, with my mind attuned to my particular job, to ask when I thought fit *Would you like an announcement made about that?* Invariably I had the answer *Yes*, and the information I thus obtained, combined with what I received from the departments at the Centre and what I thought fit to include in the exercise of my editorial prerogative, made the bulletins more interpretive of what was being done: more helpful to the public and in every respect more satisfactory.

On the night succeeding the third day, at about 3 a.m. (exactly 72 hours after the raid) my house was shaken by five explosions although no aircraft were about. I thought this to be the Bombs Disposal Squad at work and I left for the meeting of the Emergency Committee the next morning prepared to be really angry. On my way down I discovered the cause: the five unexploded bombs which I had heard to *crump* during the raid were now exploded bombs. I had forgotten about them.

One unsought job came to me at the meetings of the Emergency Committee. I became a sort of printer's agent. When any printing needed to be done – even down to *Clearance* labels for motor vehicles – I took the order and placed it out. As every job was urgent and few printers were working and telephones were out of order, this duty placed no little strain on my powers of peaceful persuasion and ingenuity, and entailed the detachment of one member of the team, almost to sit on the printer's doorstep until the job was completed.

On the fifth day (Friday) with seven loudspeaker vans, we had the joy of announcing the coming that afternoon of Their Majesties the King and Queen and giving particulars of the route they would follow. This in addition to our usual bulletin at 2 p.m.

And so the Service went on for eleven days, gradually diminishing in volume until on the last day we were reduced to three loud-speaker vans. The Information Centre closed down. I prepared and distributed 15,000 circulars of the evacuation addresses of the many departments that had used the Centre.

The morale of the people was wonderful. I mentioned in the early part of this history that my duty was described.'

Whiteside had lost his final page and it is unknown how he finished his account.[171]

Walter Daw, then an air raid warden, recalled in 1982 that Mr Whiteside's system worked well. He recollected 'with hundreds of people left homeless and penniless, it was to the credit of the authorities that overnight they set up an information centre at Hele's School, with 53 government, local council or public utility departments represented there. It worked very well. People bombed out of their homes could obtain cash grants and emergency ration documents there. Thousands of inquiries were dealt with and thousands of pounds paid out immediately. At that time I was working at the gas company's offices which were blitzed and we had to set up temporary offices in Topsham. It was that same month that I was elected to Exeter City Council and the young woman at the gas company offices wrote to a younger colleague in the Army to tell him *Nothing much has happened in Exeter except the city has been blitzed and Daw has got on the council.* My first council meeting was devoted to reports about the number of people killed or injured in the bombing and about the numbers of houses lost or damaged. I think the councillors were shocked by the number of houses which had been damaged.'[172]

Welfare measures

There was a tremendous task in catering for those who were homeless or without cooking facilities. One of the many hundreds who needed help was Betty Fursman who recalls that 'after a while, when things was a little quieter, I remember going down to Bury Meadow at the end of Queen Street where we were given food and drinks, the next thing was to get clothes. Don't remember how we got dry shoes and clothes (that's a blank), I can only think that we must of got them at Bury Meadow as we did the food and drink. On the way home we passed the Guildhall in the High Street. On the notice board there were names of people who were listed as missing. Our names were among them. It was quite a shock. We made our way back to St James Institute where all our neighbours and my mother's family were. It was a great relief seeing I was only 12 years old, my sister was only 9 and my brother 5 years old.'

Many recall food was easier immediately after the blitz. One woman remembers that 'the day after the blitz you never saw so much food being poured into Exeter. You could pretty much get what you wanted.

It was in the shops and wasn't rationed so tightly.' John Langdon recollects 'one good thing came out of all this – those sweet shops which survived were full of things like *Crunchie Bars* which we hadn't seen for years. There must have been a secret store somewhere for sending to bombed-out cities.' Marion Daw, then thirteen years old, had two fried eggs and bacon at an emergency canteen at Henleigh House in Magdalen Road. She recalled 'with wartime rationing you were lucky to get two eggs in a whole week, so to be served with two with one breakfast was the height of luxury. But many shops were wrecked, people had lost money and ration books, many homes were without gas or electricity for cooking and so this canteen was provided for you to go and obtain food when you needed it. All the same I was aghast at being served two eggs. It was unheard of in wartime.'[173]

Many have fond memories of those that looked after them. Sally Morgan remembers with gratitude the work of the Salvation Army. She later wrote 'they were always the first ones into Mermaid Yard after each raid, with clothing, bedding, tea, words of comfort. A wonderful body of people who were very brave'. Jean Cooke was twenty at the time and living with her family at 1 Blackall Road. They sheltered under a table along with a neighbour who had very white hair but by morning it had turned black with all the soot which came down through the bombing. They had to move to another house because of an unexploded bomb and then in the morning to Lopes Hall where they had breakfast. Sue Andewes had accommodation at Mardon Hall, also on the college campus, after she was bombed out the first time. She remembered 'during the night time our staff & students crowded in the bottom corridors & I remember how thirsty we became as the water system had fractured pipes. Between Mardon and Reed, outside the stable blocks, we had always had a big static wartime tank of water and later this became our vital supply though it was actually meant for fire-fighting first & foremost. By incredibly early a mobile cooking unit, a kind of soup kitchen really, was in place in the yard. Tea, oh! blessed tea, became available for us all. Looking back the local wartime authorities certainly had their emergency plans in place and our student population was being cared for and not forgotten over the city's priorities of that morning.'

One former fireman, Ralph Alford, remembered 'while fighting the fires we might have gone without food, but thanks to the W.V.S. canteen women we did not. Somehow or other they always seemed to get their canteen vehicles through the debris to keep us fed. The ambulance girls were heroines too. They drove on through the raids to take injured people to hospital and fortunately the hospital itself was not hit'.[174] Ruth Hitchings recalled turning into Cathedral Close and seeing a mobile canteen had been set up where 'women were serving mugs of tea to a few fire fighters, so tired that they could hardly stand, the lines in their faces emphasised by ash, wet, dirty and dispirited. It was opposite what had once been a shop which sold antique jewellery. On the pavement were scattered broken brooches and trinkets which were being crushed underfoot. No one could be bothered to pick them up'.[175]

Margaret Metcalfe was one of those who provided food and drink. She was then a young women working at the Post Office in Victoria Park Road and along with her friend, Gladys Hole, was called to man a mobile canteen. They operated it around the city, distributing refreshments to men working on rescue and salvage operations.

Another woman who helped was Lee Mitchell. She was born in London but had moved to Somerset during the war. She was thirty-two years old when she wrote in her diary at Chudleigh 'long procession of weary firemen coming back from Exeter, it was burning all last night. One told me things were terrible down there, & there'll be a lot of work for us tomorrow. Feel so heavy-hearted over it all.' On the next day she was in the thick of things. She wrote 'early start to Exeter & chattering mob of women on the station waiting for the train – 26 of us! Long pause outside Exeter & watched men mending the line – bomb craters everywhere. Queen's Messengers were perched on Bury Meadow & we took over from the Taunton team, but to our disgust Mrs Mills remained in charge, bellowing & roaring at us like a mad bull. Mrs Waller (an O.C.) got quieter, a calming contrast. She's a joy to work for. In no time we were hard at it, cutting sandwiches and serving tea in a van down by the gate, where an endless of queue of people waited for it. It was fearfully hot & I was in charge of a squad there for an hour or more, we worked flat out, just serving teas, dripping with sweat. Then I was sent out with a team in a van, & drove around Exeter. It all seemed fantastic & like a dream – ruins everywhere. The High Street just a goat's track between shattered walls, heaps of debris, choking white dust under the hot sun & sweating soldiers everywhere clearing a broader path. Impossible to believe it was Exeter – I kept thinking I was back in Plymouth a year ago & so in a way it was all hideously familiar. In one way things were better – our organisation. We had a good night back at a hotel, & didn't have to look after the fires & Dixie[?] soldiers & A.R.P. men did all that, & carried the heavy urns for us. About 8 o'clock we loaded up & drove out to Chudleigh.' She returned to Exeter the following day and wrote 'toiled all day and went out twice into the town, much amusement when a soldier said *you ain't stopped in a very good place Mrs* and I looked up and saw a tottering wall slanting far above us! Babs was asked by a Bobby to feed some men digging up an unexploded bomb. She asked them when it would go off & they said *Due about now Mrs* at which Mrs Hill called out from the back *Now then boys, drink up, we must be off.'* She returned the following day and noted 'last day in Exeter, was sent out with 5 others, & parked by the cathedral where we served tea & soup. What a contrast to last time I parked there with Mrs Zorab! Now the old Deanery is in ruins, & the South Transept of the Cathedral (south end) shattered. The close covered with broken glass & long stretches of hosepipes. The cathedral looked incredibly lovely with the sun streaming through the broken side. The Bridgwater posse arrived at 1 & immediately took charge, so we were off duty & strolled about the town. Everywhere among the ruins flags had appeared, as the King & Queen were expected at any moment. We waited in a shattered shop window for ages, much interested by the crowd also waiting & in watching soldiers pulling out huge steel girders with a tractor. Then it was time for our train so we had to leave, but the royal train was leaving at the same time, & their Majesties got to the station soon after us, & came over the bridge & down the steps past us, to stand & chat on the platform. We (all filthy & incredibly tired) got a kindly smile & how we longed to travel up on that fast train! Ours crawled along, packed with refugees & us.'[176]

Olive Girt was another of the many women who helped serve food. She worked at the Emergency Feeding Centre on Exe Island and was staying at 15 Cordery Road in St Thomas. Two letters written by her in the days immediately following the blitz show the conditions they lived in and how they persevered. On the day of the blitz she wrote 'my dear Gladys & Bertha, what a time it has been, we have had such a busy time at Exe Island that I have not had a chance to write before.

I am wondering if you have written me as our G.P.O. was burnt out Sunday night, of course all letters were lost. We hardly realise yet what is left of Exeter. The High Street is burnt out from Queen Street right through to the end & then right on through St Sidwell. Colson's & Bobby's are gone. Southernhay that runs at the back of the High Street is practically gone. The Y.M.C.A. & the G.F.S. hostels are burnt out & consequently Carter, Britten & Jelliss have lost practically everything & are homeless for the time being. I brought Carter & Britten home with me last night – they had my bed & I slept with Mrs Sleeman as Pop is on night work this week. They are staying tonight but Britten has found somewhere else to go to tomorrow where several of the G.F.S. people are. Carter will stay on indefinitely.

Maxted couldn't stay in her house as all the windows were out & glass everywhere & doors all gone but she found somewhere to go last night – she just knocked at doors until someone took her in. Wilson's house is not safe to be in so she has gone to Field tonight – she went out to Cowley last night. We are very fortunate in not having any damage.

There seems to be an awful lot of damage everywhere, not only in the city but all round Heavitree & the outskirts but I am glad to say the

The cathedral after the bombing where Mrs Mitchell served tea from her canteen.

casualties considering all things are not as bad. I hear that Exeter has suffered worse than Bath but the death roll is less.

Poor Mr Sleeman came home very upset – he had a dreadful night & as the only man left out of his gang of nine men that went on at 10 o'c Sunday night. They were all in a shelter but he stayed out as he said he ought to be fire watching. The shelter had a direct hit.

When I wrote Sunday I mentioned that I had been to Stanley & Joyce's new home – I feel very anxious about them, they live at St Sidwell a bad part, but last night I didn't finish at Exe Island till 8 o'c, had been on since 7 so couldn't go. I think anyway it was impossible to get through the streets, what with ruins, unexploded bombs, fires & fire engines & hoses everywhere. This evening I wanted to go but was too done up by the time I got home. It's the heat of the cookhouse that does me – it's terrible & I was in it all yesterday morning & this morning. I will see if I can get to them tomorrow. I hear that all that part is roped off but perhaps I can find out something about them. I will let you know if I do – I was supposed to go to tea with Joyce tomorrow.

I must get to bed now as I have to be up at 6 & we haven't had many nights without warnings lately. I hope you are all well & Mum feeling brighter. With this emergency feeding we do not know whether we shall get away at Whitsun but we must wait and see. We fed nearly 600 people at dinnertime today! I made the stew but I think that only did about 200 & then the rest had cold meat & vegetables (lovely tinned tongue) & I helped with the rice puddings – about 200 had jam tart. Will you please send this on to Peggy as I have so little time for writing but I will try to write her in a day or two. Bye bye, much love.'

A few days later she sent a letter to Peggy, presumably a friend or relation. She wrote 'I hope by now you have had the post card I scribbled first thing Monday morning – I posted it about 6.30 on my way down to the feeding centre but everything has been so disorganised in fact all commerce has come to a standstill for the time being – the city was still blazing when I wrote that card. The smoke and fumes were thick, it was really awful.

I managed to write a letter home one day this week – I lose count of the days & I asked them to send it on to you. Our G.P.O. was burnt right out & today is the first day I have had any letters through. Miss Jelliss had a prepaid telegram from her father today which he sent on

Monday. Bertha said in her letter that she kept phoning the Poly: but they couldn't get through.

Well dearie, I am so very sorry to hear about Alf – your last letter was much more hopeful, I thought he would pull through – poor Maha, it is said for her such a short time, what a blessing she has dear little Sheila. It is an anxious time for you all.

You will be surprised to hear I have Miss Carter living with me, sharing my bed for the time being. Miss Britten was with me as well until yesterday – there are so many homeless people. Britten was burnt out at the G.F.S. hostel & Jelliss & Carter at the Y.W.C.A. hostel, they had a terrible time fighting fire bombs all night; they thought up to the last they would save the house; if they had realised it was hopeless they might have salvaged more of their things – they have very few clothes. I took Britten & Carter home with me Monday night, let them have my bed & slept with Mrs Sleeman – Mr S. was on night work. Maxted & Wilson & Chamberlain have had to get temporary shelters as their houses have been blasted & time bombs are near. We have been very fortunate – neither very near this time; we are also among the lucky people who have water & as we cook by electricity we are alright for that also. There is no gas anywhere in the city. At the school – Exe Island – we have to cook on the coal stoves & carry the food to the mission hall where it is served – we walk miles in a day. We served 650 diners today, I don't know how many breakfasts, lunches & teas – my poor feet & legs – I am lying on the bed to write this & rest them. I made the stew today – I think it did about 400 people – we had 80 lbs of beef to start with, tinned carrots as we hadn't any fresh ones 40 tons, & I made the thickening! 6 lbs flour about 6 tablespoons of oxo, 3 packets of gravy salt mixed with the water saved from yesterday's carrots. Everyone said it was lovely, anyway they didn't leave any for us to taste, they never do. We have tongue every day until we are tired of it. There was baked raisin pudding & custard afterwards. As they had to pay today we thought we shouldn't get so many people but it didn't stop them. The heat of our cookhouse is terrible, it gets me down more than anything.

Mr Sleeman had a nasty experience Sunday night – all the men he was on duty with went into the shelter & were all killed by a direct hit. He stayed out to do fire watching. There were 9 killed. I shall never forget Sunday night.

I tried to get to Stan & Joyce yesterday & had to go all round the back turnings – the damage is ghastly & still such a lot of smoke & smouldering going on. They had been evacuated because of a time bomb & I had a card from Joyce today to say all the back of the house was burnt & they had gone to Torquay – Stan's mother & father are living there. Joyce is expecting in September.

On my way to see them I met Elsie Anna Wood the artist friend I have told you about – she is burnt out – her father is paralysed, they managed to drag him out of the house & eventually he was taken to the hospital. Her mother does not get about very well owing to rheumatism – they were bombed out of London. She is now trying to get somewhere for them to go – it isn't easy to get invalids in anywhere – at the hospital they wanted her to take him out last night, I suppose they are needing the bed.

Do you remember me speaking of a Mrs Roberts who was evacuated from Westcliff at the war & stayed with Mrs Arman for over a year? All her family eventually came to Exeter & they managed to get rooms over a shop in a most congested part of Exeter – when I passed there last night it was burnt right out, so I went on to Mrs Arman's & found her there. They had just managed to get out but hadn't salvaged a thing. The place was blazing almost before the last siren had finished the warning – they all seemed like that, no warning at all. Only last week they had had the rest of their furniture sent here – it cost them £20 to get it here.

Will Lorr – the one who had a new baby a short time ago was at the Arman's – his mother and father have lost their home in the previous raid & his wife's mother has lost hers. Of course all the time keep hearing of different ones that have suffered – I ought not to bore you with all this, it is when you know the people personally that it seems so awful.

Bertha wrote today all about her birthday & Whitsun Holiday but it just depends on the feeding centre what will happen to us – if it is still being carried on we shall have to stay. Naturally we are working Saturday & Sunday – as people need food just as much at the weekend. I shall have to let you know later on when I know myself.

Bob is still at home, doctor says another month. He says that every time, he seems to be much better I am glad to say. I don't think I have any more news dear – I would love to see you again. I do hope I shall get home at Whitsun. Of course I have lost more of my girls again – I shan't have anyone to do any orders. One senior went home to London Monday morning in her pyjamas & coat they had borrowed from someone – she hadn't a thing & the place gutted to the ground.

My love to Olive & to Maha – I am so sorry dear about Alf. Lots of Love to you' She added 'concerning the terrific damage there was in proportion small loss of life. Have you heard if Normy is all right?'[177]

Others helped out unofficially. Mrs V.M. Dean was eighteen years old and living with her father at 6 The Mint. Their old fashioned black range came into its own and supplied hot water for neighbours who were, like the rest of the city, without gas or electricity. Firemen also built a brick oven in their garden for local people to boil water. Joyce Flack remembers how after the blitz she carried their Sunday joint to Hunt's Bakery where there was a coal-fired oven. It was the only way they could bake and other families would bring their meat with instructions on how long it was to be cooked.

Many have also reflected many years later on how their mothers coped with feeding their families with primitive cooking facilities. Caroline Cornish and her brother, then young children, returned home after being sent to Drewsteignton for safety. She recalled 'Father had rigged up an outdoor stove for us to cook on, there being no services, and the water undrinkable. For us, at the ages we were, this was all highly exciting. No school, obliged to drink Corona (fizzy coloured stuff), to cook and eat 'alfresco' and we were alive'. Sally Morgan wrote 'I've often thought since how we coped. We had no gas or electric, Mum cooked over an open fire, did the washing and all the normal household chores, as everywhere was covered in thick layers of dust and we had broken windows, and you had to pick your way very carefully over debris and rubble. Life seemed to go on, even though perhaps you had been awake all night, you were still expected to go to work, and school and to be on time! There was a wonderful feeling of togetherness, everyone helped one another, and had a cheerful disposition, after all we were all in the same boat'.

Trying to return to normal

Throughout the city people turned up for work. George Barnes was one of them. He recalls he 'went down through the wreckage down the high street, past the constables and told them where I worked, they probably thought I was somebody important and let me through. I spent a lot of that day running messages from Castle Street to the back of the University College buildings in Gandy Street. A lot of us were engaged as runners.' Monica Hoare was only eighteen years old and worked at the post office in High Street. She later wrote 'we had been told that should the main post office be damaged at any time we should meet up at the Barnfield Hall. Three of us plus a supervisor went there. Not even a telephone there we could use. But there were a few telegrams and we were told to go to the telephone exchange in Castle Street to see if we could send them on. With difficulty we walked there. Buildings were still burning and explosions around. Deller's Café was a burnt-out shell as were the buildings in Bedford Circus. When we got to the telephone we had to climb many stairs and use large switchboards. No luck with the telegrams as most phone lines were out of order. We later heard there was an unexploded bomb at rear of building.'

Tony Westell was working as an apprentice reporter at the *Express & Echo*. He was allowed through the damaged High Street and arrived to find the offices had 'been severely shaken and ceilings, in the reporters' room and elsewhere, were later propped up with two-by-fours which were still in place when I returned from my time in the Royal Navy from 1943 to 1946. The presses were out of action, and until the end of the war production was shifted to a sister paper, *The Torbay Herald Express*. The editors went down by bus everyday, taking overnight copy with them, and we reporters remaining in Exeter phoned them any urgent local news.'

George Sandy was seventeen at the time and remembers walking to work at a bakery in Clifton Street the next morning. He and a friend were on Wonford Road opposite where he had seen a Junkers 88 crash on the previous night. It was pitch black and he felt himself step on something. He discovered later it was part of a leather flying jacket which the two boys divided into half. When he arrived at work he discovered the glass roof had collapsed. They then walked along Summerland Street where the houses were on fire, down Sidwell Street and then were stopped at Paris Street where a warden warned them a wall was about to collapse. The bakery's horses were moved to the top of Pennsylvania for weekends and, as it turned out, they would have died in the stables in Summerland Street.

Bette Simmonds was living in Albion Place and had to cross the city to get to work in the munitions factory in St Thomas. Along with other women they 'had to find our way down to Alphington Road. We passed Bedford Street and there was an unexploded bomb which we didn't know about. Later we saw a sign, after we gang of workers had gone by.'

Just after Christmas 1941 Dorrie Langdon's father had come down from Edinburgh to be Transport Officer for the South West. He was living in New North Road opposite the railway sidings near Queen Street Station in a guesthouse run by a retired farmer and his wife. She remembers her father telling her that 'he walked out into the street several times to see what the immediate situation was and then back to calm the other residents. He reported fires blazing in all directions, the sounds of explosions and buildings crashing. The railway sidings just opposite the house were burning furiously, there was a series of gunfire nearby for some time, all very alarming.' Eventually 'after a hasty early breakfast my father intended to walk and see if his office on St David's Hill still existed. A Miss Mitchell, also a resident in the house asked to go with my father. She was the manageress of the famous Deller's Cafe in Bedford Street. He agreed of course. Walking down Queen Street, the Rougemont Hotel was all right, the Museum seemed unscathed, but turning into the High Street past streets and properties which were still burning and damaged, they had to pick their way through a mass of smoking ruins and debris. It was evident that there was an enormous amount of damage in the centre of Exeter. On reaching Deller's corner site that morning there was nothing! Just a heap of smoking twisted ruins. The cafe had been a renowned building with a small dance floor with two galleries for guests to have coffee or afternoon tea or a meal while enjoying the elegant surroundings and listening to a small string orchestra. Poor Miss Mitchell fainted clean away, quite a problem for my father as he recalled *she was a large, well upholstered lady*. The roads were covered with rubble, hosepipes, broken water mains gushing, policemen, firemen and wardens exhausted and bewildered, with quite a lot of people just wandering about trying to make sense of what they were seeing. He returned to the guesthouse with Miss Mitchell and continued down the hill towards St. David's to find his office intact, and two or three members of his staff who had managed to travel in somehow.' Interestingly, he also told her that he 'found out that the 'near gunfire' in the goods yard was due to a consignment of tinned fruit exploding in the burning Fyffes railway vans.'

School life was interrupted. Tom Reardon remembers that as a twelve-year old he did not have to go to school for more than a week. Jeremy Setter had only just started at St Sidwell's Infants and Primary School but due to bomb damage he had to temporarily go to St James' School. Trevor Morgan, then twelve years old, tried to walk to Mount Radford School from his home at 10 Richmond Road. He and his brothers got as far as the top of Queen Street before being turned away by the police and A.R.P. wardens. Miss J. Woodcock, then nine years old, also tried to get to school from Exmouth: she and her two sisters took the train as far as Polsloe Bridge and then followed from girls from Bishop Blackall School to get to their own school in York Road. They kept being turned away from various roads and passed buildings still on fire. They finally reached St Hilda's School only to find it too had been partially bombed and was still on fire. A teacher found them and told them to return home. Her eldest sister was working in Queen Street and helped her to take the bus back to Exmouth. Through a circuitous route she returned home to find that the news of Exeter's bombing had not yet reached the town.

The city lost thousands of books when the City Library burned down. Marion Daw, then thirteen years old, remembered that on the Sunday afternoon 'in the weeks before the Exeter Blitz there was a tremendous appeal in the city for books to help the people of Plymouth, which had already been badly blitzed, and had lost its library. The Girl Guides, of which I was a member, were asked to help and three of us, Pam Randall-Vining, Jean Churchley and I spent hours collecting books and parcelling them up. Ironically, St Luke's College, where we had them ready for transit, was blitzed, and so was the Exeter library, so neither Plymouth nor Exeter had any books.'

Leaving the city

Many left Exeter that morning. Mrs J.M. Bishop was taken as a girl to stay with her godmother. Her family had lost their home and most of the possessions and she had spent the night besides her blind grandfather who had calmly held her hand throughout. She remembered the thick pall of smoke and a 'foul, sickening stench of burning foodstuffs'. They journeyed across the city and were turned back by A.R.P. wardens because of unexploded bombs and rubble in the roads. They, like many others, later discovered they had travelled over undiscovered bombs.[178]

Christine Caldwell was living with her husband at 21 St Leonard's Road and expecting their first child. They decided it was best for her to leave and set off with her suitcases for Central Station. By then it was late morning and still impossible to cross High Street. Firemen were trying to put out fires and they happened upon Henry Hall, an Exeter magistrate and imposing local figure. His response to their request for assistance was a magisterial 'Follow Me' and he led them through Parliament Street. Mrs Caldwell remembers it being a tight fit in her condition. While waiting on the train she observed an interlude she later described as being worthy of Buster Keaton. The wooden sidings along Blackall Road had caught fire and had been completely destroyed leaving only a door standing, still in its frame. Mrs Caldwell watched as a passenger solemnly climbed the long stairs up to the redundant door, carefully open it, walk through, and then closed it behind him.

Ruth Hitchings, then 21 years old, tried to return to Windsor, in her V.A.D. uniform, from Budleigh Salterton via Exeter. She and her mother, who wanted some wool to finish a jumper, boarded a bus but at Woodbury a complicated journey began: they travelled twelve miles through a circuitous route and only got as far as Cowley Bridge. At St David's Station they found that trains were not running and that others had priority. She remembered seeing 'the platform covered with bundles of humanity such as we'd already seen on the Pathe newsreels of civilians escaping before the advancing forces on the other side of the Channel. Not much in the way of suitcases but bags and greatcoats, clothes tied into counterpanes, headscarves hiding their misery or faces staring blankly into an uncertain future. No one standing, little groups sitting on the ground not talking, utterly exhausted.' The two women walked up to Queen Street and passed a lamppost which had a list pinned to it of identified casualties. They entered into the devastation of the centre and were on their way back near Deller's Café when they spotted a heap of knitting wool which was 'tangled, dirty, soaked and grey' but the very wool that was wanted. Miss Hitchings encouraged her mother to take it, given it was thrown away, but her mother said *I couldn't – it would be looting'*.[179]

Exeter people went to villages and towns around the area. Patricia Purchese was only a small child when the family was evacuated to Crediton. She remembers watching the city burning but her main memory is of waking up in Crediton the following morning having slept on a desk. Trevor Selley recalls that for several days Crediton housed several dozen older people at Queen Elizabeth School. The men slept in the gymnasium and the women in the assembly room. The dayboys were sent home and the boarders stayed on to help serve food and clean up. Joan Bedford was a child living with her family at 7 Tarbet Avenue when a bomb hit Number 11. Their house was badly damaged and for some four weeks they stayed at a boarding house in Bradninch while it was being repaired. George Barnes recalls 'just after the blitz most of us went out to Broadclyst, to Victory Hall, where we would stay the night. Buses would take us out and then we would come back the next morning. We didn't know it was over, we thought it might just be the beginning.'

The Thomas family found themselves homeless after Maryfield House in Pennsylvania was hit by a bomb. Mrs Thomas later wrote along 'with thousands of families all over Europe during those years of wastage, we had endured the experience of going to bed in a well-ordered, seemingly permanent establishment, to find ourselves next morning possessed of little beyond our night attire, not knowing where we should live in the future, not knowing indeed where we should find a bed for the night. The men had discovered that a thousand pound bomb had exploded outside the high brick wall at the rear and that only two yards difference would have meant a direct hit on the house and the end of us all. The blast had caused havoc – the house was almost a shell with our broken possessions scattered all over the floors. They had found the Sealyham asleep and well on the pile of smashed granite and plaster but no calling or searching had revealed trace of the cat.' That day they 'went down to the city there owing to the destruction of the Post Office it was not possible to wire friends and relatives the news of our safety; the whole of the centre was gutted, reduced to huge piles of rubble, and elsewhere whole areas were cordoned off while delayed action bombs were exploded; over the ashed and skeleton houses hung the terrible smell of powdered rubble and smouldering timbers, dust hung in the air and made the eyes water. Vans were patrolling the shattered streets distributing food and drinking water; money and coupons for petrol and clothing were handed out at Relief Centres, casualty lists were posted with anxious queues lined up for news. The whole of High Street from the Guildhall to St Sidwell's being a wilderness of rubble, it was in unfamiliar shops in little side streets that we used our new clothes coupons.' They then drove out to Crediton where 'on either side of the road we saw many little groups preparing to sleep in the woods and fields, either homeless or unwilling to sleep in the burned city'.[180]

Revd John Benton turned fifteen two days after the blitz. He recalls how 'we had some bombing before and my parents thought it would be advisable for me to go out to the country, so I wasn't in Exeter on the night of the blitz though I did see the redness of the sky. My mother had a sister in Bampton, which is 29 miles away, so I went out there. Just to sleep at night. It was after one of the particularly nasty raids, in St Thomas I think, that my parents made the decision it would be a good thing for me to go to Bampton. On that night I could see the red sky in the distance. The funny thing was my uncle was a builder and immediately after the blitz all local builders were called in to repair houses in Exeter. And our house in Thornton Hill in Exeter had been damaged and it just so happened that the area to which my uncle was allocated included Thornton Hill. So I used to come in on the lorry with the men in the morning, have breakfast at home, then cycle to Exeter School, do my prep and then go on the lorry back to Bampton where I slept.'

Many also came into Exeter because of concerns about the bombing. Bill Boam recalls 'I can remember my sister turning up the next day from Yeovil and she must have had a terrible shock up Sidwell Street with everything in rubble and then found our house intact.' Elizabeth Burley's mother was so distressed at hearing that Exeter was bombed that she took the bus from Newton Abbot to see if the cathedral was still standing. They arrived to find a great deal of hustle and bustle about the building and gave their thanks on finding the building was largely unhurt. Bertha Glynn came back with her family after sheltering in Trusham. She recalls 'we came in the morning after the blitz and our home in 159 Sidwell Street, opposite the church, was destroyed. There was nothing left at all.'

Casualties

Many others neither returned to work or left the city again. Nearly three hundred died in the bombing. Pamela Taylor's family home in Marlborough Road was only damaged but the house opposite was destroyed. Then seventeen, she recalled 'I know we were very upset because we had some neighbours in for the evening and it was their house that was demolished and they were both killed. I think that made quite an impact.' Mrs E. Curtis remembers she was sixteen years old and after the blitz walked from Heavitree with her father. They came through Pinhoe Road and saw several houses destroyed. The ambulances were then removing the bodies of the casualties. The two of them walked on to the top of Sidwell Street and wept when they saw the cathedral still standing amongst the devastated city. They went home but not before coming across another body, covered over with a sheet, which had not yet been collected. On returning home she was taken to Broadclyst. She, along with a friend, spent most of the evening talking to two boys from Hele's School who were N.C.O. Royal Air Force Cadets. They returned to Exeter the following day and one of the cadets asked her and her friend to accompany him in identifying the body of his missing uncle. She later wrote 'we arrived at the mortuary gate, but the two of us were too nervous to go in and waited outside. He was gone for a very long time and eventually we went in search of him, we faced a corridor with doors with windows blown out and there we glimpsed dead bodies, we turned on our heels and fled. My friend did not eat for five days.' She later learned that the cadet, along with other schoolboys, was asked to clean the bodies. Mrs Curtis recalled her home overlooked Higher Cemetery and they watched, several days after the blitz, the mass burial from behind the curtains.[181]

Colin Hopkins was living in Stepcote Hill. He remembers he was then sixteen years old and 'I went down to the Rack Street School which was turned into a morgue. A friend's mother had to identify a woman friend of hers. I went with him and I can remember going in and seeing the bodies all stretched out. I can remember quite vividly seeing one lady with her baby on her tummy. Both were dead. In the playground, where the bicycles used to be kept, with a galvanised iron roof on it, they had stretchers in there with all bits and pieces of bodies there. Inside were whole bodies but outside were stretchers with 8 or 9 legs say on one, on another were arms, on another were torsos. Most of the bodies were covered but not all. That was the Rack Street Naval College as we used to call it.'

Nicholas Toyne recalls he was then eight years old and 'my mother and I went by car to a farm near Chagford for the next fortnight while the gas, water and electricity were repaired. My father was put in charge of a temporary morgue in Pinhoe fairly close to the railway crossing. He for two days had to try and collate the parts of human bodies being brought in. Many years later I went to many meetings and dances there. It then became a rifle range and is now demolished.'

One man remembers being told by his father that during rebuilding work in Bedford Street the workmen were told not to report bodies found in the rubble. They were instead disposed of quietly. Another man recalls that shortly after the blitz a friend of his father's visited with a great basket covered with a cloth. On being asked what was in the basket he was told 'Don't ask'. A peek revealed body parts that were found in sites throughout the city and were on their way to the morgue.

Shock

Many have memories of their disbelief and distress at the destruction.

Vivian Bussell was twenty-one years old and on duty at the Royal Devon & Exeter Hospital. He recalls 'at around 9 a.m. I was relieved and when I set forth into Southernhay I could see that our peace time offices (Southernhay West – the upper part) had been destroyed. Anyhow I made my way across the lower part of Southernhay West through the small road-way connecting with the Cathedral Green out into South Street, down Fore Street across Exe Bridge into Alphington Street. There I saw a work colleague of mine on his way to the office. I advised him to go back home again to Dawlish because the office was no longer there. Whilst talking to him we noticed a lady nearby who was shouting and crying – shocked to pieces we suspected. We asked her if we could help but she continued to rave and rant about the terrible Germans who had destroyed the cathedral. I tried to assure her that that wasn't the case – *I had just passed there and it is only one wing that appeared to be damaged* – but she wouldn't have it to be and called me a liar and likened me to the Germans. To be truthful, I just walked away and continued my journey home to Exminster.' Others remember how some were so traumatised by their losses that they became permanently withdrawn and others became alcoholic.

Animals

The city's animals also suffered. Desmond Dunn remembers walking into the city centre on the morning after the blitz and hearing the screaming of the horses in the dairy in Sidwell Street. It was not possible to get to them because of the fire. Pets are often overlooked in discussions of war and yet their safety and welfare was of great concern. Retired Inspector Stanley Cole remembers when he was a young constable and looked after stray dogs. The number of abandoned animals increased during the war, he thinks due to the difficulties of feeding them. He also thinks it was more difficult for people to attend to them with the war on. Ivy Facey remembers there were not as many pets in the city as there are now but thinks those that did keep them looked after them well. Her dog Sandy 'didn't like the bombs and when the sirens started he would look for my brother and curl up with him'. One Exeter woman remembers her mother would not go into the shelter in a particular church because it would not allow her pet dog in – instead she went to the Salvation Army who welcomed them both in. Norman Watts was fifteen years old when his family home was destroyed at Kendall's Buildings in Blackboy Road. His older brother collected their black tabby called Tim on his bicycle and brought him to their digs in King Street. Unfortunately the cat disappeared only to be found a week later back at their old address. He had to have walked through the bomb destruction of the city to get there. Likewise, Sidney Richard was twelve at the time and his family lost their cat, Peter, when their house, Gills Cottage, was heavily damaged in Cheeke Street. Three days later he was found in the rubble of the scullery, but safe, under an overturned tin bath. Likewise, the family pet of the George family in St Leonards lived through the war but there were consequences. One family member remembered Bracken. 'We of course thought that he had been killed. He turned up a couple of days later on the end of a piece of string. He ran all the way to Topsham, which is about 6 miles from Exeter, until he dropped exhausted in a garden of a railwayman who read the address on his collar and brought him back. But he was always very frightened of any loud noises. He used to shoot under the piece of furniture whenever there was a thunderstorm or something for the end of his life.' He still managed to live to a ripe old age.

Tony Westell remembers Chipper, their dog, being brought into the walking closet which operated as a shelter in their home at 8 Powderham Crescent. Joy Hawkins was fifteen years old and brought her mongrel Wendy with her when she and her mother sheltered under their Morrison. When the bombs starting falling the dog jumped from her arms, ran away through the house and disappeared. Two days later they returned to salvage what they could from their home and some workmen found Wendy while clearing rubble. She had been trapped with no food but was safe. Their home in Okehampton Street was destroyed[182] as was that of their neighbour Mrs Henrietta Baxter who owned a sweet shop. The body of John Tregale's 'Aunt Ett' was found some time after the blitz. She had left the street shelter in Okehampton Street to rescue her dog. The family searched for them only to find that the front door had blown outwards and fallen on top of Mrs Baxter. After the rescuers had been coming in and out of that doorway, her body was underneath still clutching her pet.

Phyllis McGill was living in her family home in St Thomas. She recalls 'my brother Tom had a friend, who also lived in Merrivale Road, with a beautiful dog. One day he came down with the dog and we had a small raid on the railway. This boy went in for cover and there was a direct hit. He was killed. The dog kept coming up to our gate for a few days looking for him.'

Sister Edward Mary recalls their pet cat Minnie at the Palace Gate Convent. On one occasion the sisters were sitting near their kitchen Aga and heard the unmistakable noise of a German plane but noticed that it neither got closer nor far away. They suddenly realised it was the purring of their cat under the table and from then onwards she was known as Gerry Minnie.

Rats became a feature. One woman remembers they had been on the rubble in Paris Street following the April raids. 'We were overrun with them' she said particularly of the ruins of a printer and noted how she had seen nests with baby rats. Others recall that the bombing drove rats out of their holes and they could be seen in the open on bomb sites.

Visit of King George VI and Queen Elizabeth

The king and queen visited Exeter a few days after the bombing. Douglas Newbery remembers that as a nine-year old boy he saw the Queen Mother in Buller Road and that she patted his and his brother's heads. John Langdon was then in his early teens and remembers 'I saw them in Queen Street and didn't quite know what I should do so gave them a Scout salute.' Caroline Cornish and her brother had just come back from Drewsteignton and recalls 'mother took us to Clifton Street to watch the royal car go by. This was thought to be a good vantage point and since huge swathes of Newtown had burnt to the ground, and were indeed still smoking, it was known that the progress here would be slow. Sure enough it was a great place to be, on the very edge of the pavement. An old lady standing alongside was clutching a small bunch of flowers in her hand. She asked my mother *Would your little girl please give these to her Majesty?* Well, of course my mother readily agreed and, burdened with heavy responsibility, I waited most anxiously as the motor approached. I shall be for ever grateful that my brother and his friends always expected me to wait on them in their ball games for it had taught me to be pretty adept at throwing. I tossed it directly into the air and it fell precisely between the royal couple. Deftly Her Majesty fielded it, and smiling at us all she graciously waved the modest posy for everyone to see. Attached to it was a simple note written carefully by the donor. It said *Semper Fidelis*. Afterwards my school friend Ann said *you shouldn't have done that you know. It might have been a grenade'*. It was Joyce Flack's thirteenth birthday and she recalls that she went up Polsloe Road where 'there were crowds and crowds of people. The king and queen went by in the procession. Then at the end was a small sports car and sat in it was my sister. She had been given compassionate leave and had been met at St David's Station by a friend who offered to take her home. They didn't know that they were following the royal procession.'

The King and Queen view the damage.

Rebuilding the city

It took a generation to rebuild the city. Plans were unveiled in 1945 but construction did not begin until 1949. Most of the work took place in the 1950s and 1960s.[183] There was a great effort made in demolishing buildings, some of which were damaged beyond repair and others which were merely in the way. The Reverend John Benton was fifteen years old at the time and recalls how 'I can remember once going down the old Summerland Street and cycling past the damaged buildings, and passed up along by Higher Summerlands when I heard an almighty explosion and I looked around and the facades of the houses were being all blown up. It would have been May 1942.'

The destruction of ancient buildings was then, and remains now, highly contentious. Dr Charles Marshall was an Exeter G.P. and lived in Sidwell Street. He recorded the attempt made to demolish the remains of St Sidwell Church, which had been badly bombed. He wrote 'Sidwell Street was roped off from the pillar box by Howards. It smouldered for a fortnight and troops were called in to demolish unsafe walls. When they went to finish the half destroyed tower of St Sidwell's Church the vestry under the tower with the safe and all the plate and registers was still accessible: the rector arrived to find a sapper drilling holes in the base ready for demolition an hour later. When the rector protested he said he had his orders. *Very well*, said the rector, *you carry on but I shall be sitting on the safe!* Of course when the officer came to see why the charges had not gone off, the necessary salvage arrangements were made.'

Several thousand buildings, both historic and modern, needed repair work. One notable example was the cathedral. It had one direct hit on the chapel of St James in the South Quire aisle while other bombs fell in the Close and in the Yard the Globe Hotel caught on fire through an incendiary. Herbert Read, the ecclesiastical wood and stone sculptor whose firm St Sidwell's Arts Works was based in the city, repaired damage. His daughter Joan recalls the events that led to that. 'My father was an Air Raid Warden and had to go out that night in St Leonard's. We lived opposite St Margaret's School in Magdalen Road. He kept coming back to see if my mother was all right. When the All Clear sounded my mother said *we have to see about the works*. They

The King and Queen see for themselves the damage to the cathedral.

set off and my mother said there was fire all around us, up Summerland Street where people had been killed. They got to Sidwell Street but the works was destroyed. There was nothing they could do at all. My mother always said that *I can never get it out of my mind – a cat rushed out burning without any fur on it at all. I just remember it all, and when I see a cat I think of that.* They couldn't do anything about the works because it was all burning, all gone. The next morning he went to the Cathedral and found the destruction. He said *Don't touch anything.* He had one of his workman called Pile, they got three packing cases and sorted it for days on end. He used very little in the way of other materials.'

Mr Read recalled the events shortly after they happened and said 'the bomb and blast together smashed and shattered practically every-thing in their way from one end of the great cathedral to the other. I saw nothing but chaos everywhere; stonework of the roofs, walls and windows – many lovely 15th century screens of wood and stone – broken glass from every window – lying in heaps. The choir stalls were blasted, their canopies torn off. Ancient monuments, the famous sedilia, ancient documents stored in the chapel, the choir pulpit, organ case and organ pipes, chairs, hassocks, books all piled up in a jumble and, last but not least, the mortar and the dust.

Something had to be done and done quickly too. And there and then I set to work to salvage the ancient things, and with the help of an old employee of mine, I began to sort it out. We cleared as we went along. We tried to allocate every fragment. Then we spent weeks on our knees combing through the dust with our fingers to make quite sure nothing of value be lost before the residue was taken out and dumped.

At times I discovered some specific detail was missing, such as the sword of a Purbeck stone effigy of a crusader – or the fingers of Bishop Marshall's recumbent effigy . . . although it was entirely covered in debris, was intact except that the two fingers of his right hand, raised in blessing, were missing. Ultimately I discovered them in no less than five pieces scattered in different parts of the Cathedral; one small piece had come to rest on the ledge of a monument high up on the wall, a considerable distance away.'[184] His daughter Joan recalls 'he was intent on finding the fingers. A little girl came in from the green and said *is this any good for you* and he said *its just what I was looking* for.' The King and Queen viewed the destruction that week and the king described the salvage work as 'the greatest jig-saw puzzle in the world.'[185]

Many hundreds of men were involved in rebuilding and yet there are few memories recorded of it. Graham Hessé was a teenager and working at the Post Office in Castle Street. One tea-break after the blitz he and his fellow workers watched some workmen at the ruined site of the Arcade on High Street. One 40 to 50 foot wall was only left standing. He later wrote 'a hawser was put around the top of the wall, leading back to a winch which was fixed to a still existing lamp standard, approximately 20 foot high. The winch was started and, like a slow-motion film, we saw the lamp standard, which was cast iron, gradually start to rise, completely un-noticed by the workmen who were concentrating on the wall, until it was 2 feet out of the ground. A typical Laurel and Hardy situation'.

The city's plans were for a grand modern centre but a tremendous effort was needed to secure accommodation for retailers. Nicholas Toyne recalls that 'one of my father's duties was to re-house many of the shopkeepers whose premises had been bombed-out. This had quite a few pleasant repercussions for our family. The one I remember most is that when I got married and came back down to live in Devon in the 60s, my wife had to pay by cheque for some groceries. No plastic cards then! The owner of the shop looked at the cheque and said, *Are you any relation to Wystan Toyne?* My wife said *he is my father-in-law*. He promptly tore up the cheque and said *Mr Toyne saved my business by finding me a new shop.*'

Conclusion

One resident remembered that in Exeter there was uncertainty whether the bombing had ended. There had been, after all, three attacks at night in late April before the blitz. Walter Daw recalled in 1982 that 'the big fear most people had just after the blitz was whether the bombers would come back the next night. Quite a number of people used to go out into the countryside and sleep in the hedges. I was surprised though, how quickly people began picking up the threads of life again in Exeter.'[186] There were also unusual effects of the bombing. Sue Andrewes was bombed out on two evenings after she had just washed her hair. She recalled 'an amusing, if understandable, side effect was that for weeks afterwards when ever I dared to wash my hair, a sinister little voice would say *And now, you see, there will be an air raid?* A true Pavlov syndrome. Luckily it did not last too long. I'm all right now, aged 84 years!' Angela Hancock remembers how in Crediton the fire brigade used the 'all clear' as a fire warning through to the 1960s: even then it continued to evoke feelings of fear in her.

For some children the blitz was an adventure. Some spent months afterwards scouring the city collecting shrapnel and bullet shells. Michael Godsland was one such young boy who searched Newtown looking for souvenirs through the still-smoking timbers. Another boy's great game was looking for coins from the destroyed gas meters. Sally Morgan remembers other children having fun in the ruined buildings, particularly the Lower Market. She and her friends found tea sets and ornaments which they later learned had been on display in a china and hardware shop in South Street. Owen Michael Mullarkey, then eleven years, recalls playing on the bombed sites and making dens out of the old bricks and scrap material.

Many others returned to the city to find it had been heavily destroyed. Robert Crayford was a young boy who came back in June 1942 after spending a short while in Torquay. He later wrote of High Street 'there was just nothing but shattered and burnt-out skeletons of buildings and immense mounds of acrid smelling dusty rubble. It was not only the buildings in this part of the High Street that had vanished but the actual street itself, for there was only a meandering narrow footpath not much more than 3 feet wide, and that was littered with pieces of rubble that had rolled down off the mounds if not fallen directly from the ruined buildings themselves. I looked up rather warily at that large stone statue of King Alfred which seemed to be perched somewhat precariously on top of that building principally made of columns, as I felt sure it was leaning over the pathway.' The bombing of this impressive building at 238 High Street, which had housed Commercial Union Assurance for several generations, led to its ultimate destruction. The city had it pulled down shortly afterwards.[187]

*The Commercial Union Assurance Building on High Street,
across from St Stephen's Church.*

The Building was heavily damaged during the blitz.

A view of the building after the debris had been cleared.

For Robert Crayford, and for many others, Exeter was never the same. This is one of the most commonly held views, that suddenly, overnight, the city completely altered.

Victory celebrations at Barley Mount, Redhills.

CONCLUSION

Few of the men and women who saved lives during the bombing of Exeter were honoured and only three received the George Medal. One was Victor Hutchings. He was unable to eat a proper meal for a month after the horrors he saw during the blitz. He later recalled 'it is ridiculous to say you were not frightened. I was trembling like a leaf until I actually started to do the work and then the fear seemed to go.'[13] The work of thousands of others on the Home Front was neither recognised nor remembered.

Some men and women have commented on how the war was a long struggle. One woman who lived in Tudor Street, and was born in 1914, recalls 'we hated the war. We hated the Germans. Even when we were kids it was a bad name, course we had had the first world war. We would ask ourselves *how much longer is it going to go on?* I wouldn't want another one.'

Yet for some the war is remembered as one of their favourite times in their lives and for many children it was fun. For Donald Sheppard, only seven when the war broke out, it was 'quite exciting really because you didn't know what was going to happen next.' Another former boy recalls 'it was good fun really. I know I shouldn't say it. It was probably because it didn't touch us that much, not like Plymouth. I know we had some loss of life but not as much as other places.' Kathleen Fletcher was a young girl through the war and reflects 'these were the best Christmases I had. The team spirit was absolutely incredible. Everybody pooled what they had – we all shared whatever we might have had. Jellies were quite a thing to have or a Christmas pudding –

even the icing was special. Marzipan was made with a soya flour and we appreciated that.'

Others were traumatised. Pamela Kwiatkowski was only four when war broke out and the family lived near the canal. For many years she had recurrent nightmares of hiding in ditches to avoid enemy aircraft. Many remember they had no choice but to continue working, living and trying to enjoy themselves when they could. Phyllis McGill reflected that life was not all bad. She thinks 'although the war was terrible and sad, and dreadful when you lose family, but just on some occasions there was a little bit of fun, in and out. We might have fun going to a dance – to cheer you up. There might be a notice on the time clock – this helped a bit.' Iris Rice, now 103, lived at Blackall Road during the war. She reflects 'during the blitz it was pretty horrible. But you just had to get through the war and if you put your back into it you could. You didn't let it beat you.' Even so, for some the war was too painful. Several people recall hearing of a woman who had come from London where she was bombed out. She was discovered running down the street, naked, carrying a knife.

Some think of the lucky escapes they had. Maurice Pike recalls that 'I was fourteen or fifteen at the time and it was only then that I can remember being frightened in the war. My brother and I had returned after an air raid warning. We came home to find that a bomb had exploded nearby in Okehampton Street and the window glass in our bedroom had blown in, and had shattered all over the bed. We would have bled to death.'

The war even changed some lives for the better. One woman thinks of the positive aspect of the war. She reflected afterwards 'I wasn't glad to go back to Exeter. It all seemed so empty, poor. In comparison to my sisters the war had been an education. I know it's terrible to think that way of the war, but if it wasn't for the war, I wouldn't have met my husband. I wouldn't be where I am today. The war gave me a better life. I would have married the man I was engaged to and worked in the laundry. I wouldn't have had a chance. The war gave me an education. My sisters stayed here in the munitions factory but I was able to get away. I travelled. Looking back now, I knew there was something more to be had out of life. I would read when I was younger, but I never had any chances. We had been really poor. And then I didn't really want to come back after the war. The war was an eye-opener to life – it gave us women a broader outlook and made us stronger. I think it helped give us minds of our own. Because my husband was ill when we first got married I had to do everything. He said to me *Now that we are married I don't want you to stay in the Air Force*, it wasn't what I wanted, but I loved him and did it. So he was ill when we were first married and pretty old-fashioned and said to me that a woman's place was at the sink. Well, I'm a bit of a rebel and thought *how dare he say that to me*? By then I had a mind of my own.'

Many have reflected on the community spirit. Canon Michael Walsh thinks 'some very good things came out of all that evil. That was the impression I got quite a lot.' Sister Edward Mary reflected 'I think what people need to recapture is the sense of community. In the midst of harsh tragedies, it seems it always brings out the best in people. It's a pity you have to live through moments like that to find it.' Sylvia Hart reflected of the blitz 'it really was a dreadful time, I really wouldn't want any of my family to ever experience such an event. But if good can come out of bad, people in general cared for each other. There really was a unity that you don't see today.'

Many have commented on the need for the young to know of the war and the individual sacrifices that were made to help win it. Some say that they are shocked by the young's ignorance of the course of the second world war in Exeter. Yet they have also reflected that any ignorance is the consequence of sixty years of peace – that the struggles of the 1939 to 1945 war have made it possible for those living today to lead lives without experiencing war on their doorstep. If so, then the memories are worth remembering.

NOTES

1. W. G. Hoskins, *Devon* (Newton Abbot, 1954), 527.
2. Express & Echo [E&E], 28/11/2000.
3. Imperial War Museum, 86/91/1.
4. www.bbc.co.uk/ww2.
5. Imperial War Museum, 1464, page 2.
6. D. Irene Thomas, *Fragments That Remain* (Nell Jarvis Books, 1998), 85.
7. Imperial War Museum, 86/91/1.
8. Imperial War Museum, 1464, page 78.
9. Jenny Lloyd, *People Talking* (Exeter, 1977), Volume 7, 28.
10. *DX Europe* (no date or place of publication), 39.
11. E&E, 18/12/2001.
12. www.bbc.co.uk/ww2.
13. Worrall, *Target Exeter*, 14.
14. Todd Gray, *Exeter In The 1940s* (Exeter, 2004), 47.
15. M.C.B. Hoare, *This Jewel Remains* (Exeter, no date given), 10.
16. Norman Longmate, *How We Lived Then* (2002 edn), 327.
17. Devon Record Office, Town Clerk's papers.
18. Imperial War Museum, 86/91/1.
19. Monica Felton, *Civilian Supplies in Wartime Britain* (1945), 33.
20. Felton, *Civilian Supplies in Wartime Britain*, 19–21.
21. Felicity Goodall, *Voices from the Home Front* (Newton Abbot, 2004), 137–8.
22. Danny La Rue, *From Drags To Riches* (1987), 49, 53.
23. E&E, 22/2/73.
24. Longmate, *How We Lived Then*, 308.
25. Philip M. Taylor (ed.), *Britain and the cinema in the second world war* (1988), 6.
26. E&E, 22/2/73.
27. Gardner, *Wartime*, 433; Goodall, *Voices*, 169.
28. Jenny Lloyd, *People Talking* (Exeter, 1977), Volume 7, 13.
29. Thomas, *Fragments That Remain*, 79.
30. Gray, *Exeter In The 1940s*, 18.
31. Geoff Worrall, *Target Exeter* (Exeter, 1979), 78.
32. Worrall, *Target Exeter*, 87.
33. Lloyd, *People Talking*, volume 7, 29–30.
34. Worrall, *Target Exeter*, 21.
35. Ian Maxed, *Devon Testimonies*, (Exeter, 2000), 19.

36. Worrall, *Target Exeter*, 53.
37. D.P. Davies, *The Bombing of Exeter* (Exeter, 1973), 14.
38. Gardner, *Wartime*, 193–5.
39. E&E, 22/2/1973.
40. Gardner, *Wartime*, 270–1.
41. Gardner, *Wartime*, 434–5.
42. www.bbc.co.uk/ww2, A1301680, 'Mickey Mouse Mechanics'.
43. Gardner, *Wartime*, 436–7.
44. www.bbc.co.uk/ww2, A2864270.
45. There are two versions of this account. One was recorded by Geoff Worrall in the *Express & Echo*, 22 February 2005 and the other was written by Mrs Evelyn Pearce nee Huxham and placed on the BBC website WW2.
46. Charles Grave, *Women in Green (The Story of the W.V.S.)* (1948).
47. E&E, 5/12/2000.
48. Imperial War Museum, 03/42/1.
49. University of Sheffield, Saunders, 119/A3/42, 119/A3/43i & 119/A4/28.
50. University of Sheffield, Saunders, 119/A3/44.
51. University of Sheffield, Saunders, 119/A4/28.
52. Robert Skidelsky, *Oswald Mosley* (1975), 303.
53. Nigel Jones, *Mosley* (2004), 87.
54. University of Sheffield, Saunders, 119/A3/45 & 119/A3/43i.
55. University of Sheffield, Saunders, 119/A3/44.
56. University of Sheffield, Saunders, 119/A6/147.
57. University of Sheffield, Saunders, 119/A3/40(i).
58. University of Sheffield, Saunders, 119/A3/39b(i).
59. University of Sheffield, Saunders, 119/A4/48.
60. University of Sheffield, Saunders, 119/A8/102.
61. David Renton, *Fascism, Anti-Fascism and Britain in the 1940s* (Basingstoke, 2000), 20.
62. Nigel Jones, *Mosley* (2004), 20.
63. Robert Skidelsky, *Oswald Mosley* (1975), 326–7.
64. University of Sheffield, Saunders, 119/A6/43. He may also have visited in December 1935: University of Sheffield, Saunders, 119/A5/355.
65. University of Sheffield, Saunders, 119/A6/153; Renton, *Fascism*, 20.
66. Renton, *Fascism*, 23, 28–30.
67. University of Sheffield, Saunders, 119/C15/439.
68. Gray, *Exeter In The 1940s*, 19, 47–8.
69. E&E 25/7/2000; private correspondence, letter of 14 2 2005.
70. Robert Crayford, 'Memories: things recalled to, or kept in the mind (to paraphrase the Concise Oxford Dictionary)', Contacts: the magazine for the church commissioners' pensioners, no. 52, Nov. 2004, 8–9.
71. Imperial War Museum, 85/31/1.
72. Presumably she was implying Bath.
73. Imperial War Musuem, 85/31/1. A copy of the letter by Pamela Daymond has recently been deposited at the Devon Record Office, this is a copy of the original at the Imperial War Museum.
74. Longmate, *How We Lived Then*, 72.
75. E&E, 28/11/2000.
76. Lionel Blue, *Hitchhiking to Heaven* (2004), 32–3.
77. Danny La Rue, *From Drags To Riches* (1987), 48.
78. E&E, 1/5/2001.
79. Longmate, *How We Lived Then*, 71.

80. Thomas, *Fragments That Remain*, 97.
81. Thomas, *Fragments That Remain*, 77, 83.
82. E&E, 24/4/2001.
83. E&E, 1/5/2001.
84. E&E, 20/6/1988.
85. E&E, 31/10/2000.
86. Aileen Fox, *Aileen; A Pioneering Archaeologist* (Leominster, 2000), 104.
87. Lloyd, *People Talking*, vol. 7, 32.
88. University of Sheffield, Special Collections, Saunders 11/A2/134.
89. E&E, 14/5/1998.
90. E&E, 31/10/2000.
91. Graham Smith, *When Jim Crow Met John Bull* (1987), 45–6.
92. *DX Europe* (no date or place of publication), 32–5; E&E, 11/12/2001. I am grateful to Peter Wale for loaning me his copy of the book.
93. Information kindly supplied by David Cornforth.
94. Graham Smith, *When Jim Crow Met John Bull* (1987).
95. Devon & Cornwall Constabulary Museum, Memoranda Book 7, November 1941 – December 1942, order of 4 September 1942.
96. Gray, *Exeter in the 1940s*, 93.
97. Smith, *Jim Crow*, 119.
98. Hutchinson was born in Grenada in 1900 and came to England in the late 1920s: *Dictionary of National Biography* (2004).
99. Smith, *Jim Crow*, 134–5.
100. Smith, *Jim Crow*, 195, 84.
101. Smith, *Jim Crow*, 199.
102. Smith, *Jim Crow*, 208.
103. Smith, *Jim Crow*, 206.
104. Smith, *Jim Crow*, 183.
105. Smith, *Jim Crow*, 152–86.
106. www.bbc.co.uk/ww2/, 'My Last Mission with the Dutch 320 Squadron'.
107. E&E, 4 May 1992.
108. A.H. Halsey (ed.), *British Social Trends Since 1900* (Basingstoke, 1988 edn), 104; Felicity Goodhall, *Voices from the Home Front*, 115; W. G. Hoskins, *Devon* (Newton Abbot, 1954), 527.
109. Gray, *Exeter In The 1940s*, 14.
110. E&E, 3/5/2002, 12–13.
111. Thomas, *Fragments That Remain*, 92.
112. Imperial War Museum, 92/29/1.
113. Worrall, *Target Exeter*, 2.
114. Thomas, *Fragments That Remain*, 106.
115. www.bbc.co.uk/ww2, account A2740466.
116. Longmate, *How we lived then*, 121–2, 130.
117. www.bbc.co.uk/ww2.
118. Lloyd, *People Talking*, volume 7, 31.
119. Lloyd, *People Talking*, volume 7, 28–9.
120. E&E, 9/6/1982.
121. Gray, *Exeter In The 1940s*, 56.
122. Maxted, *Devon's Testimony*, 9.
123. E&E, 31/10/2000.
124. Gray, *Exeter In The 1940s*, 75.
125. E&E, 30/10/2001.
126. Lloyd, *People Talking*, volume 7, 25–7.

127. E&E, 9 July 2002, 18.
128. Devon & Cornwall Constabulary Museum, folder on the bombing of Okehampton Street, 23 April 1942.
129. Lloyd, *People Talking* (Exeter, no date given), volume 3, 24.
130. E&E, 19/12/2000 & 16/1/2001.
131. E&E, 10/10/2000.
132. Worrall, *Target Exeter*, 89.
133. E&E, 31/10/2000.
134. E&E, 11/10/2001.
135. E&E, 11/10/2001.
136. E&E, 18/9/2001.
137. E&E, 31/10/2000.
138. E&E, 17/10/2000.
139. E&E, 31/10/2000.
140. E&E, 19/12/2000.
141. E&E, 11/10/2001.
142. E&E, 31/10/2000.
143. E&E, 31/10/2000.
144. Devon & Cornwall Constabulary Museum, folder on attack of 30 December 1942.
145. Worrall, *Target Exeter*, 49.
146. D.P. Davies, *The Bombing of Exeter* (Exeter, 1973), 9.
147. E&E, 4/5/1982, page 10.
148. Worrall, *Target Exeter*, 6.
149. BBC WW2 People's War site at www.bbc.co.uk/ww2.
150. E&E, 4/5/1982, page 10.
151. E&E, 4/5/1982, page 10.
152. Lloyd, *People Talking*, Volume 7, 8.
153. Worrall, *Target Exeter*, 49.
154. Davies, *The Bombing of Exeter*, 15.
155. Davies, *The Bombing of Exeter*, 15.
156. Worrall, *Target Exeter*, 52–3.
157. Devon Record Office, 1674m/f3.
158. Todd Gray, *Lost Exeter* (Exeter, 2002), 69.
159. Worral, *Target Exeter*, 15.
160. Ms parish history, page 19, located at the church of the Sacred Heart, South Street.
161. E&E, 4/5/1982, page 10.
162. Gray, *Exeter In The 1940s*, 76–7.
163. D. Irene Thomas, *Fragments That Remain* (Nell Jarvis Books, 1998), 100–103.
164. E&E, 26/11/1998.
165. Imperial War Museum, 92/25/1.
166. E&E, 2/1/1982, page 14.
167. Lloyd, *People Talking*, volume 7, 31.
168. Danny La Rue, *From Drags To Riches* (1987), 55.
169. E&E, 4/5/1982, page 10.
170. Michael Green, *Families at war taking the strain and Devon memories* (Wymondham, no date), no page numbers given.
171. Devon Record Office, 70/12.
172. E&E, 4/5/1982, page 10.
173. E&E, 4/5/1982, page 10.
174. E&E, 4/5/1982, page 10.
175. Hitchings, 'The Morning After', 38.

176. Imperial War Museum, 92/8/1.
177. Imperial War Museum, 97/28/1.
178. Maxted, *Devon's Testimony*, 10.
179. Ruth Hitchings, 'The Morning After', in *Today and Yesterday: An East Devon Anthology* (Exmouth, 2001), 37–8.
180. Thomas, *Fragments That Remain*, 104.
181. Maxted, *Devon's Testimony*, 20.
182. E&E, 3/5/2002, 12–13.
183. Gray, *Exeter In The 1940s*, 123–37.
184. *St Sidwell's Art Works Exeter England* (no date given, Exeter), 3–5.
185. *St Sidwell's*, 9.
186. E&E, 4/5/1982, page 10.
187. Gray, *Exeter In The 1940s*, 81–3, 86, 125, 126.

ILLUSTRATION SOURCES

Illustrations on pages 13, 15, 29, 32, 51, 58, 60, 62, 63, 65, 101, 154, 209, 216-17, 274, 310, 316 appear courtesy of the owners of several private collections; of those on pages 17, 21, 22, 26, 34, 44, 57, 72, 73, 87, 90, 91, 94, 95, 100, 103, 105, 106, 129, 136, 151, 158, 160-1, 171, 175, 176, 178, 179, 181, 185, 187, 191, 195, 198, 200, 201, 203, 225, 229, 230, 233, 236, 240, 245, 247, 251, 253, 256, 266, 292, 308 with the permission of the *Express & Echo* and those on pages 314 & 315 of Group Archive Aviva plc.

INDEX